Introduction to Media Distribution

In this second edition, author Scott Kirkpatrick draws from over a decade of personal experience in the distribution arena to provide a clear and up-to-date overview of the entire film, television, and new media distribution business.

Readers will learn what fuels the distribution process and exactly how the distribution business works from beginning to end—not merely what happens to a film or television series upon acquisition, but how distributors develop, presell and broker deals on content before it even exists. This new edition considers a much more international approach to media distribution, with case studies and analyses from across the globe. It also reflects on the ever-increasing relevance of diversity and inclusiveness in the industry, as well as the new media verticals like podcasts and the effects of social media influencers on the media landscape.

The book will be an integral guidebook for any student or professional wishing to understand both the basics and the subtleties of media distribution. The book also contains a robust appendix containing in-depth studies of legal definitions, material delivery requirements, territory-by-territory financial projections and more.

Scott Kirkpatrick is Executive Vice President of Co-Productions and Distribution for Nicely Entertainment—a Los Angeles–based production and distribution company that produces original TV movies and scripted TV series—where he brokers major content deals and has executive produced a variety of TV movies. Previously, Kirkpatrick served as Senior Vice President of North American Sales & Business Development for NENT Studios UK where he oversaw international television distribution deals on a variety of programs. Prior to this, Kirkpatrick served as Executive Director of Distribution for MarVista Entertainment, a production and distribution company that produces original TV movies and has managed international TV deals on major franchises. Before shifting to the distribution side of the industry, Kirkpatrick worked behind the scenes on major studio productions, including *Talladega Nights: The Ballad of Ricky Bobby*, and has produced and directed TV series and feature films including *Eye for an Eye* and *Roadside Massacre*. He is the author of *Writing for the Green Light: How to Make Your Script the One Hollywood Notices* and *Mastering the Pitch: How to Effectively Pitch Your Ideas to Hollywood*.

Introduction to Media Distribution

Film, Television, and New Media

Second Edition

Scott Kirkpatrick

NEW YORK AND LONDON

Designed cover image: © Getty Images

Second edition published 2024
by Routledge
605 Third Avenue, New York, NY 10158

and by Routledge
4 Park Square, Milton Park, Abingdon, Oxon, OX14 4RN

Routledge is an imprint of the Taylor & Francis Group, an informa business

First edition published by Routledge 2018

Library of Congress Cataloging-in-Publication Data
Names: Kirkpatrick, Scott, 1982– author.
Title: Introduction to media distribution : film, television and new media / Scott Kirkpatrick.
Description: Second edition. | New York, NY : Routledge, 2024. | Includes bibliographical references and index.
Identifiers: LCCN 2023032618 (print) | LCCN 2023032619 (ebook) | ISBN 9781032413983 (hbk) | ISBN 9781032413952 (pbk) | ISBN 9781003357902 (ebk)
Subjects: LCSH: Mass media—Marketing.
Classification: LCC P96.M36 K57 2024 (print) | LCC P96.M36 (ebook) | DDC 302.23068/8—dc23/eng/20230714
LC record available at https://lccn.loc.gov/2023032618
LC ebook record available at https://lccn.loc.gov/2023032619

ISBN: 978-1-032-41398-3 (hbk)
ISBN: 978-1-032-41395-2 (pbk)
ISBN: 978-1-003-35790-2 (ebk)

DOI: 10.4324/9781003357902

Typeset in Aldus Roman
by Apex CoVantage, LLC

For Zoey, Julian and Soha

Contents

Acknowledgments

I would like to thank all the following individuals: Emily McCloskey and Jason Brubaker for providing an early kick start toward the writing of this project; Simon Jacobs and John Makowski at Focal Press for their guidance and assistance throughout the evolution of its first edition; Marco Fargnoli for his insights in Chapter 9; Genni Eccles and Daniel Kershaw for championing this book's *second* edition; and eternal gratitude to my wife, Soha Saleh, for her support throughout the process of making this project a reality.

Disclaimer

The content outlined in *Introduction to Media Distribution* is for informational purposes only and should not be considered a substitute for the expertise of a professional accountant, lawyer or other accredited adviser.

This book is meant only to explain and share the distribution trends I've personally encountered during my career within the film, television, and new media distribution business in a manner that is both informative and digestible regardless of the reader's individual level of experience. All examples and inferences made herein are observations of standard business practices in the field and in no way reflect any trade secrets held confidential by any company, employer or entity with which I've been associated.

I have tried to keep all information as up to date—or as 'evergreen'—as possible and encourage readers to further investigate any concepts or industry practices they find interesting to better educate themselves on the more granular details of the media distribution business.

Preface to the Second Edition

Before diving in, I'd first like to thank all of the readers of the original *Introduction to Media Distribution*; I've received so many warm compliments from college professors, industry professionals, students just kick-starting their careers to those who don't even work in the realm of media but needed a simple source to grasp the core concepts. Their comments and feedback are what I used as my filter when writing this second edition. My driving motivation when initially setting out to write this book was to simplify the distribution process and to make the business of film, TV and new media digestible for readers of all backgrounds and experience levels; it means a lot to me personally to have delivered on that goal.

The book has been very well received; it has been enjoyed by readers from around the world and has even been adopted as a required textbook in a variety of universities. I've also had the chance to expand upon the ideas within this book during several university classroom talks, media interviews and conference panels. But, as is always the case, distribution is a constantly evolving business, and there were a few concepts I skimmed over so as not to get too granular that I'm happy to finally have the chance to explore.

In this second edition, I'll be taking a more macro approach to global film and television distribution by discussing the industry not just from the vantage point of the Hollywood and/or US market, but rather from a true global perspective. This is especially important given the rapid growth of emerging markets coupled with the maturing of Video-on-Demand (VOD) outlets throughout Europe, Asia and Africa along with the growing necessity of coproductions and other internationally minded multiparty financial models.

Since its original publication in late 2018, a great deal of social change has certainly taken place, most notably the disruption from COVID-19 resulting in altered viewing trends as well as numerous social/political awakenings witnessed around the world. However it's important to recognize that change is inevitable; 2020 was certainly a game changer, but the media industry has weathered much worse in the past and will do so again in the future. That is why in the original text—as well as in this second edition—we will focus entirely on the principles that support the foundation of the distribution business. Trends, technology and social perspectives change all the time, but principles always remain the same. Case in point, many predicted that COVID's lockdowns would kill movie theaters, forever shifting us to a VOD-first model. But the 2022 theatrical release of *Top Gun: Maverick* not only blew away box office expectations (proving that the summertime studio blockbuster was still alive and well), it also allowed a voiceless Val Kilmer an opportunity to once again take on a 'speaking' role thanks to some incredible advances of technology that offer a sneak peek into the innovations we'll likely see in the decades to come—many of which we'll explore herein.

All that said, I'd like to say thank you to all readers (new and returning) for taking the time to gain some unique insights into how the business of film/TV and new media actually operates, and a big thanks to all of those professors, instructors and educators that have adopted this book as a classroom text. I hope this second edition provides even more insight than the first.

Introduction

I never intended to be working on the distribution side of film/TV industry. When I was younger, I always envisioned myself on the production side. But now, after nearly two decades of brokering distribution deals with some of the biggest companies in the business, I couldn't dream of a more fulfilling career.

I fell in love with movies when I was a kid; by age ten I was already writing and producing my own 'films' with the family's VHS camera. Years later, after graduating film school, I packed up my car and headed to Los Angeles. I can still see myself as an overly confident know-it-all ready to take on Hollywood by storm. In my back seat was a box full of everything I thought one needed to break in as a professional writer/director: sample spec scripts, DVD screeners of my award-winning shorts and a lengthy list filled with contact details for all the major Hollywood agents, production companies and producers.

When I arrived, reality hit *hard*!

No matter how hard I tried—or in what way I presented myself (or my work)—I wasn't getting anywhere. It felt as if there was a giant invisible wall preventing me from gaining any real traction with legit Hollywood professionals. Everything I'd learned or thought I understood about the industry (from books, film school, etc.) didn't seem to apply in the real world.

I was writing what I *thought* were the right kind of scripts and putting together business plans for features I *thought* matched what Hollywood needed; but the only experience I was gaining was working as a production assistant or low-level lighting technician (finding myself serving coffee to the people I wanted to be and lighting the sets of films I wished I could have been creatively involved). It felt as if there was no clear-cut way in. And no matter how hard I looked, it seemed there were zero resources offering any practical insight on how one could position themselves for real opportunities.

Then, in my mid-20s, I accepted job that at first seemed to have nothing to do with my field of interest; it was a 'sales rep' position for a small start-up indie TV distributor (a job I only took because I was tired of sporadic paychecks from random production gigs). On my first day, I was literally instructed to "go sell some TV shows"—something I had no idea how to accomplish nor realized such a job even existed. I was given a computer, a telephone and a large file containing all the major TV acquisition contacts in the United States.

As I stumbled through my first sales calls—perplexed by the random terminology and unable to answer the most basic content questions—I began to realize there truly was

DOI: 10.4324/9781003357902-1

a reason why the Hollywood system worked the way that it did and a very strategic method behind the seeming madness. More importantly, I began to realize *why* it felt so impossible to truly break into Hollywood; I'd simply been approaching it in the wrong way.

I suddenly found myself drafting entertainment-related contracts (despite not being a lawyer), negotiating TV deals with major US companies and even acquiring content from indie producers. I was flown to all the major markets and festivals around the world and was shaking hands with some of the industry's biggest names.

I realized the distribution side of the industry provided a logical answer to just about every question I'd ever had about breaking into Hollywood—yet ironically, it remains the subject that's given way too little meaningful emphasis in film schools, media programs, blogs or texts (but I'm very happy to see that trend is starting to change). And the resources that do take a crack at the role distribution plays are either way too production focused (covering the distribution component almost as an afterthought) or way too complex for beginners (heavy with business jargon that make little to no sense for someone just trying to get a handle on the basics).

In *Introduction to Media Distribution*, I have taken my (nearly) two decades' worth of global film, television, and new media distribution experience and have broken down all of the major questions I'm constantly asked by college professors, novice producers and even industry veterans into digestible and relatable terms. And by doing so, I hope to—at minimum—offer some rational explanations for why and how the global media system operates in the manner it does (especially at the independent level, where most newcomers will be starting off). Additionally, I hope to offer future writers, producers and directors a potential career game plan for how they can better pitch their ideas to leading industry professionals and create content poised to gain traction within the business.

Whether you are working to become a content creator—or are the instructor of future content creators—having a firm grasp of how and why the distribution business operates in the manner it does is a crucial first step toward securing future success.

1

The Principles of Media Distribution

The entertainment industry deals with a recurring conflict. On one side, direct-to-consumer outlets such as TV networks, podcast streamers, movie theaters and Video-on-Demand (VOD) platforms (e.g., Netflix) need to retain high numbers of audience members in order to remain profitable—which requires an extremely high number of 'fresh' content hours (far more than they could possibly hope to produce on their own). On the other side, there are producers and production companies scattered about with the talent and capability to deliver high-quality film, television, and new media content; however, they often lack the financial resources to produce this content consistently and can only produce a limited number of content hours per year. Resting comfortably between these two extremes—and serving as the solution to this ongoing annual struggle—is where you'll find distributors. They are the linchpin holding the entire media industry together yet are often overlooked or rarely discussed in meaningful detail.

To give a sense of scale, television networks require several hundred hours of programming each year to retain their audience share, and VOD platforms require thousands of hours (sometimes *tens* of thousands). An 'hour' of content takes exactly an hour for a consumer to watch, yet that same single hour of content takes *months* to produce (and tons of up-front cash). Consequently, it requires dozens of separate production companies—all working independently and consistently—to ultimately deliver a single direct-to-consumer's annual content load. Distributors simplify this entire process; they do so by (i) assuring a direct-to-consumer outlet that they will take on a portion of their content burden—guaranteeing a minimum number of content hours—while (ii) managing the overall content workflow by engaging a variety of production companies to spread out the effort (allowing for an on-time and on-budget delivery of a large quantity of programming).

DOI: 10.4324/9781003357902-2

▶ LET'S START AT THE END

Despite the fact that media distribution is what binds the entire entertainment industry together—providing projects with funding, release strategies and profitable returns—the very notion that distribution is principally a 'business' leaves most feeling it's a subject better left handled by the professionals. But the real reason most feel out of the loop isn't because the business of distribution is somehow too complicated for outsiders to understand; it's simply that the actual process of how a film, TV series or new media property gets funded and distributed—allowing it to eventually make a profit—is usually taught in the reverse order. And because most individuals are looking at distribution from the wrong end of the viewfinder, the logic and rationale that simplify the entire distribution process is never fully explained.

When we think of producers creating movies, TV shows or new media projects, we generally follow the 'from-script-to-screen' chronology whereby a project must first be written, shot and edited before it can be released. The problem with this approach is that it leaves the topic of distribution for the very end (and is therefore consequently seen as an afterthought by most content creators—many of whom plan on tackling the distribution of their projects *after* they've completed them).

To paint a more vivid picture, most novice content creators anticipate dealing with distribution after their project gains attention (and potentially wins a few awards while on the festival circuit); by contrast, the major titles competing each year at Cannes, Berlin, Toronto or Sundance—among dozens of other major events—already have their distribution secured well in advance of the festivals (long before production commenced). The 'shoot first, sort it out later' tactic commonly boasted by DIY filmmakers is exciting for those eager to tell their stories, but leaves far too many blind assumptions regarding how a property will be formally acquired by a professional distribution company and, most importantly, how it will recoup its money—which is the precise role media distributors are there to play.

In essence, media distributors are the individuals tasked with figuring out a way to generate money from a film, television or new media property. They're the link between 'buyer' and 'seller', operating as the managing party between the factory floor (production) and the storefront (user-facing TV channels, VOD platforms or movie theaters). Regardless whether a given project is fully produced (completed and ready to sell) or simply an idea on a piece of paper (such as a script, treatment or verbal pitch), the distributor's job is to broker the deals necessary to get those projects funded and to eventually make them profitable.

But to view distributors only as a means to an end or as a financial resource misses the true value of what distributors bring to the table. What makes media distributors so critical during the development and creation process isn't that they have the capability of writing checks, offering creative feedback or brokering deals that will get projects funded, but that they serve as each media property's direct link to paying audiences.

▶ ALL ROADS LEAD TO THE 'END USER'

Let's take a step away from the 'business' side of the industry and instead consider the very sound advice offered to novice screenwriters. One of the first rules a scribe learns is that they must know their *ending* before they can begin their story. (Only by knowing how a script will conclude can a writer truly answer how its characters and plot points should be presented on page one.) The same can be said of the distribution process; just as all plot points within a script are strategically placed to drive the story toward its inevitable climax, so too are the distribution elements required to get a project funded with a clear strategy for how it will recoup its money.

The problem with this screenwriting analogy is that a script has a finite conclusion—with a literal last page. The business of media distribution, by comparison, feels much more abstract, with no obvious ending in sight. But this assumption is false; the business of media distribution *does* have a fixed end point it's working toward: it's the 'end user'.

The term 'end user' is the entertainment industry's way of describing an audience member, one who is actively engaged in the process of screening media content (meaning any individual willing to open their wallet to pay for movie tickets, a Netflix or Disney+ subscription, or anyone willing to screen an ad on TV or before watching a video on PlutoTV or YouTube). We're all end users. And as end users, each time we collectively spend money to enjoy a given media property, we're keeping the Hollywood system profitable and in full motion—which provides us future content to enjoy.

But simply stating that distribution 'comes first' isn't enough to map out the complexities as to why the Hollywood system works the way it does (nor does the vague point that Hollywood's overall objective concludes with the end user's wallet). That's because there are three crucial concepts that are rarely discussed:

1) Distribution companies (the entities actively creating, acquiring, marketing and selling media properties) don't directly serve the needs of end users; they're instead serving the needs of 'consumer-facing' platforms.

2) Consumer-facing platforms (the companies distributors sell to) are much more interested in gaining access to end users' *time* rather than just their wallets.

3) End users have a choice regarding which media content is actually worth their time and hard-earned cash; just because a consumer-facing platform—even one they regularly access—makes media content available in no way guarantees end users will pay money in exchange for access.

Let's break this down a bit:

A 'consumer-facing' platform is the vehicle that directly delivers end users their media and whom end users directly pay their money to keep that media pipeline coming.

Netflix is a consumer-facing platform that offers a 'Subscription Video-on-Demand' (or 'SVOD') service; those with a Netflix account pay a monthly subscription fee directly to Netflix in order to gain access to its library of media offerings. Free-to-air TV channels like ABC, NBC or FOX are also consumer-facing platforms, but rather than an up-front fee, they offer a 24-hour lineup of media programming that's regularly interrupted with advertisements (from which they make money). A movie theater is a consumer-facing platform; it offers a theatrical presentation of a motion picture to those select end users willing to pay the price of admission.

By contrast, major entities like Paramount Pictures, Universal Pictures, Sony Pictures or Lionsgate are *not* consumer-facing platforms; they are media distribution entities. Even though these major companies are well branded within the media content they distribute (via logos and title cards), these companies are in the business of funding and producing content that will ultimately get supplied to consumer-facing platforms (who then present those productions to their fan base of end users).

But, as stated earlier, just because a consumer-facing platform makes a prominent media property available in no way guarantees that end users will blindly fork over their money to watch it. It's also worth noting that there is no possible way that all of the world's end users are viewing the same content on the same consumer-facing platform at the same time. Just as end users have a choice regarding what content is worth their money—based upon individual taste and interest—they also have a choice regarding where (as well as how and when) they choose to engage with their media content.

Because of this marketplace reality, consumer-facing platforms must be able to clearly identify their targeted fan base of end users—specifically who they are, what they like and how to keep them engaged with their service. If end users aren't satisfied with the content offered on Netflix, they'll cancel their subscriptions (which would cause Netflix to lose money). If end users don't like what they're seeing on a Free-to-air network, they'll change the channel (which would cause ratings to dive, forcing advertisers to pull their commercials, and result in a loss of revenue for the station). And if consumers weren't interested in the weekend's lineup of movies at the local theaters, then. . . . Well, you get the idea.

For a consumer-facing platform, real estate is crucial (e.g., shelf space, server capacity, number of theatrical screens, etc.); the titles offered must not only engage end users but must also be pulling decent numbers to merit their occupation of space. If a title is not holding its weight, it gets replaced with something that will. And because each consumer-facing platform's profit margin depends on the overall performance of the entirety of their content offerings, the acquisition executives working for these consumer-facing platforms—aka, the individuals who review, select and 'buy' media content—focus exclusively on scooping up the titles that stand the best chance of satisfying their loyal fan base. As a result, the acquisition executives of these consumer-facing platforms are very particular with what content will work for them (and know very clearly how much money they're willing to spend to obtain it).

Time Is Money

While all of the earlier section makes sense on a title-by-title level—that each product must be pulling in an end user's money to maintain a consumer-facing platform's profitability—it doesn't address the one commodity that consumer-facing platforms value more than bottom-line dollars and cents: the end user's *time* engagement.

Consumer-facing platforms want end users to spend as much time watching content on their platform as possible. Television networks don't just broadcast interesting programs, they meticulously schedule their programming lineup to keep viewers watching more—hence those 'stacked' evenings on networks like ION where several continuous prime-time slots are devoted to a single series—for example, *Law & Order*, *Criminal Minds* or *Blue Bloods*—keeping viewers glued by showing teasers for the next episode while the end credits of the current one are still rolling. By keeping a well-defined audience engaged, their ratings will go up (which directly increases the value of their advertising slots). Netflix wants you to 'binge-watch'; the longer you're screening media on Netflix, the longer you're *not* screening content on a competing service. And the more content you view on Netflix, the more likely you are to inevitably reference Netflix as the source of the great movie or show you recently stumbled upon—which directly increases new subscribership. (This is exactly why Netflix, Hulu, YouTube and many other digital platforms have a 'recommended video' automatically queued after your initial program has ended; it's always tempting you to screen just 'one more'.)

This is nothing new, by the way (and it's not unique to media); this same principle is how every retail store, auto-dealership and time-share pitch operate. If they can keep a customer engaged, they can eventually get a customer to open their wallet; and if a customer is engaged with them, they're *not* engaged with their competition.

This is how Amazon found itself in the media business. When Amazon first opened its digital doors back in 1994, I highly doubt any major studio or television network could have envisioned that a dinky online bookseller would evolve into one of its biggest clients (while simultaneously existing as one of its biggest competitors). Yet, by 2014—just 20 years after its founding—Amazon had ballooned into one of Hollywood's 'Big Three' moneymaking digital outlets (with Hulu and Netflix fleshing out the full group at that time). As a revenue-driving platform, Amazon allowed vast sums of money to pour into the studio's pockets from their own underexploited film and TV libraries; but on the flip side, Amazon's own creation of Amazon Studios was clobbering established majors with original series such as *Alpha House* (2013), *Gortimer Gibbon's Life on Normal Street* (2014) and *Transparent* (2014)—the latter of which beat out the CW's *Jane the Virgin* (2014) and HBO's *Silicon Valley* (2014) and *Girls* (2012) at the 72nd Golden Globe Awards, taking home the award for 'Best Television Series, Musical or Comedy'.

But while Amazon's Prime SVOD service continues to offer some amazing programming—and its own Amazon Studios has developed and produced fresh original content—it stands out from the earlier-mentioned competition by offering something Netflix and Hulu cannot: free shipping on every purchase. Content is not Amazon's core business; media is simply a retention tool. With a single Prime subscription, end users are not only incentivized to give Amazon's library of media offerings a shot but are also encouraged to purchase even more products via Amazon than before—which is the real service Amazon is offering (and profits from). As said by Amazon's founder, Jeff Bezos, "When we win Golden Globes, it helps us sell more shoes." For Amazon, their end user's time is their most valuable commodity to the level that they have created one of the most innovative content studios in Hollywood, producing gems like *Manchester by the Sea* (2016) while also buying out grocers like Whole Foods. Just as Netflix conspired—and succeeded—in pulling end users out of physical Blockbuster Video stores in the 2000s, Amazon is hoping to get a piece of every online purchase globally—whether its related to media content or not. And for the record, Apple TV+, Samsung TV Plus and The Roku Channel are equally in the 'retention' business (investing billions into media for the purpose of audience capture in order to grow a completely different business: hardware). For Amazon, as with all consumer-facing platforms, the more time you invest, the more likely you are to remain loyally engaged and active.

From the outside, many assume that since each consumer-facing platform knows its audience so well—and knows the content best suited to perform with its fan base of end users—it would make the most sense for them to produce it directly. There is truth to this view, but it fails to recognize how expensive (and risky) producing original material can be. A handful of consumer-facing platforms do produce their own programming (e.g., PBS produces several original documentary programs each year, Netflix bet big with the massively successful *House of Cards* (2013) and *Orange is the New Black* (2013) and Amazon—as mentioned earlier—cornered a very unique audience with several of its original series, including its UK co-production *Catastrophe* (2015), but even these tent-pole titles aren't enough to keep a fan base of end users engaged. To flesh out the rest of their slates (as well as augment the major titles they've licensed from studios and networks), the acquisition executives at these consumer-facing platforms must purchase or pre-commission rights to third-party content.

This is where distribution companies enter the game. Unlike individual consumer-facing platforms (that target one core audience), distributors are brokering deals with dozens of consumer-facing platforms simultaneously. And as long as distributors focus on investing and developing projects that stand the strongest chance of satisfying a variety of consumer-facing platforms, their profit margins will be strong.

▶ WHAT ARE 'RIGHTS'?

For the rest of this chapter—and throughout this entire book—I'm going to make numerous references to intangible things called 'rights', so let's take a quick moment to define what rights are and how they drive the business.

You first need to shift your perspective a bit regarding what distributors actually distribute. Distributors, producers and studios don't sell or distribute films, TV series or new media projects as tangible objects (they're not driving around LA or other cities around the world with Blu-rays or DVDs in their trunks); they're instead selling third-party *access* to the content. If Netflix wants a new film on its service, it must pay a distributor or studio a fee in order to make that product accessible to its consumers. Netflix is essentially leasing or paying rent in exchange for the title being available for a fixed period of time. However, third parties (i.e., consumer-facing platforms) have different needs in relation to how their consumers engage with media. Some consumer-facing services stream content, others broadcast it and others still sell physical copies on store shelves. Each one of these methods of access is considered a unique or stand-alone 'right'.

Think of every film, TV series or new media property like a stand-alone office building in a city. Whomever is managing the building can rent out different offices (or entire floors) to different businesses or tenants all at the same time. The building manager can even rent out a large communal conference area for outside one-off special events. How all the different units within the building are exploited and monetized is essentially limitless, provided that the management team doesn't create conflicts by double-booking a specific office or floor (granting identical access to two separate entities). Media rights effectively follow a similar logic. Although they are not tangible (you cannot touch or hold them physically), they are dished out and managed in a very similar approach.

Exploiting these rights—or leasing/renting third-party direct-to-consumer access to them—is the business model that generates a distributor's bottom line revenue.

We'll certainly dive into more detail throughout this book, but check out Appendix I for a full breakdown of the most commonly licensed rights and how they're defined.

▶ DISTRIBUTION IS 'BUSINESS-TO-BUSINESS'

The media business can be split into two main groups: (i) entities that distribute content to other companies (known as a 'business-to-business' or 'B2B' model) and (ii) entities that distribute content directly to consumers or end users (known as a 'direct-to-consumer' or 'D2C' model). We start with this concept because most of the real-world content decisions made by executives—that directly impact what gets produced versus what doesn't—are made within the B2B category.

In many other texts, this simple split gets lost because people try to divide distributors up into jumbled buckets (e.g., film distributors versus TV distributors or new media versus traditional content). No need to get lost in the granular details. It doesn't matter what the specifics are in terms of content genres or formats; all one needs to understand at a high level is how distribution companies earn profits:

▶ **Business-to-Business (B2B)**—As stated earlier, one would imagine a Hollywood studio to be a 'direct-to-consumer' or consumer-facing entity—after all, it's the studio's logo we see at the beginning of each movie. . . . But the studios aren't directly offering media content to end users; instead, studios are brokering deals with a variety of consumer-facing platforms (e.g., theater chains, from which audiences are directly buying purchasing tickets). For a B2B entity, their client base isn't made up of individual consumers; it's made up of other like-minded *companies*.

▶ **Direct-to-Consumer (D2C)**—These are the consumer-facing platforms you directly engage with—to whom you are directly paying. Theater chains, VOD storefronts, online platforms (e.g., Netflix, Amazon, iTunes, etc.) all fall into this category. Although D2C entities broker deals with other companies, they do so only to acquire the content they need to keep their actual client base—individual consumers, like you and me (from whom they earn their profits)—engaged and paying.

There are companies that are both B2B and D2C, meaning a company can be primarily business-to-business that also earns some direct-to-consumer profit (perhaps a distribution company with a small 'digital division' that sells content directly to consumers); and there are direct-to-consumer companies that also broker a few deals directly with other companies. But the main determining factor whether a company is B2B or D2C is identifying where the *majority* of its revenue originates. For instance, a business-to-business entity with a small 'consumer-facing' website might receive modest revenue from their direct-to-consumer sales. But generally, these numbers are a mere fraction of their total annual earnings (well under 20%), therefore making the primary focus of their client base other companies (therefore defining them as B2B).

In that most decisions made within the world of entertainment are done at the business-to-business level, it can make the distribution process sometimes feel closed off to those getting their feet wet in the entertainment business—especially for those working toward a career in the creative side of the industry. The other important factor is that companies (regardless as to whether they're business-to-business or direct-to-consumer) operate in a very bottom-line approach—meaning they're viewing the content they're involved with not in terms of story, but rather the level of profits they can yield from a specific product investment.

Here's where the major disconnect comes into play: what motivates individuals who want to pursue writing, directing, acting or any other creative role in the film, television, and new media industries is to spark an emotional response from an audience. They want to create stories, express feelings and need an audience on the other side to engage. (In other words, they're thinking primarily in the direct-to-consumer space.) But the world of business-to-business is really where the magic of distribution happens. Without their investment dollars and business-minded release strategies, the very industry that allows great projects to be made—and those audience engagements to occur—wouldn't exist.

But keep in mind that for many working in the field of distribution, it was a love of the media that got them into their distribution roles in the first place. Distributors literally spend their lives surrounded by the media; they're constantly watching content, reading scripts, discussing projects and engaging in dialogues about how audiences will respond. Distributors are just as focused on audience engagement as any filmmaker or writer; they just have a completely different way of ensuring that emotional experience reaches its audience (and have an entirely different tool kit from which to work).

While content producers try to create projects that will elicit a strong emotional response from end users, distributors use data and audience metrics to first identify what a core audience wants. Once a targeted audience has been identified, distributors reverse-engineer the filmmaking process via business-to-business deals to develop and create the exact content those targeted audiences seek.

▶ DISTRIBUTION IS SYSTEMATIC, *NOT* TITLE-BY-TITLE

Distributors cannot survive with just one or two projects per year; distributors require entire slates of content to stay competitive—which means new projects are being evaluated, developed, invested in or acquired on a monthly basis.

To give some scale, a smaller indie distributor might take on 20 to 30 titles per year (some up to 50). For larger companies, especially ones with digital divisions or multiple international clients, they can easily require 75 or more each year to maintain their steady output to consumer-facing platforms.

These titles are not all picked up and released in one go; they are slowly and steadily acquired throughout the year (so that manageable packages can be staggered out and released at regular intervals). Some companies like to have two to three films released to theaters each month. Others hold for a bit so they can announce ten to 15 new projects at each major market or festival (Cannes, Berlin, MIPCOM, etc.). And others—especially in the new media space where audience churn is extremely high—might need to announce eight to 12 brand-new titles each month.

The purpose of this workflow is so that distributors always have something 'fresh' (or new) to offer their clients. For sales reps—the individuals actually selling content to consumer-facing platforms—they need to be ready to answer their client's inevitable question: *'what's new?'*. If there are only one or two new titles to pitch—and neither matches the needs of the consumer-facing platform with whom they're speaking—the meeting will end quite abruptly. Therefore, from a distributor's point of view, making sure their sales teams are armed with a steady pipeline of new content is critical.

But take a moment to understand how this adds yet another crucial component to the 'content evaluation' process: if a distributor is taking on entire slates of projects each year, then each project they're considering is being weighed against other titles they've already picked up—or plan on acquiring later. Factor in that a distributor's budget is not bottomless; they are only able to spend from pre-allocated budgets—generally calculated out during the previous year—and each of their potential acquisitions must be meticulously analyzed across multiple departments within the company (finance, business affairs, legal, etc.). That means each project is scrutinized on the basis of its variables of risk, potential for return on investment (ROI) along with how well it augments other titles within the library.

There are often occasions when a large amount of a distributor's budget is tied up in preexisting co-production deals (meaning acquisitions executives might be obligated to work with much less money while being expected to pull in the same volume). This means they're forced to make tough calls on which content is worth spending money on and which content is not. For the acquisition executives who pull in strong titles—that yield strong margins of profit—they are awarded with a higher level of budget to spend. For the acquisition executives who overspend their budget (or who pull in too many weaker-performing titles), their budgets are usually reduced—assuming they're not simply fired from their position.

Given the large volume of content that acquisitions agents must pick up (often with limited or stressed budgets due to pre-allocated investments), the best strategy they can apply to stretch their acquisition dollars is something all of us do on a regular basis: they buy in bulk. Rather than spending weeks negotiating out a contract for a single producer's project (which will require a fixed amount of money to acquire), they can instead work with a production company in a business-to-business model and spend the same duration of negotiation time while obtaining several titles rather than just one. Also, buying in bulk actually reduces the price of each individual title, allowing an acquisitions executive to be more efficient with their budget. This grocery store logic allows distributors at all levels to meet the market demand at a lower cost (which allows for stronger profit margins). And with stronger profits rolling in, they're better able to acquire more content and keep the cycle going.

▶ DISTRIBUTION IS ABOUT SELLING THE BRAND

Consider the following media distribution companies: Hallmark, Bloody Disgusting, Disney and Hustler.

Although each of these distribution companies generates large profits via acquiring and distributing media properties, the *types* of projects each company takes on couldn't be more different. Nevertheless, when each entity's target audience sees the respective company logo stamped on a project's key art, it serves as a seal of approval (assuring a paying customer they will receive what they're paying for).

Being known as a 'go-to' company that's both reliable and efficient at delivering a specific commodity generates future business (and keeps revenue streams flowing). And while the earlier-mentioned companies are very well-known entities, I can assure you that every well-established distribution company (big and small) has a clear and identifiable 'brand'. Maintaining this assurance is crucial in the world of business; when an audience loses trust in a company—whether individual end users or other business entities—their profits drop. Having a clear and identifiable brand is a major asset in any marketplace; however, maintaining that brand requires a great deal of work.

At international media markets like MIPCOM, Berlin, NATPE or AFM, walking down the aisles isn't too much different than strolling through your local shopping mall. Just as a shoe store, toy store and novelty shop can be butted up against one another—each selling a completely different type of product to a completely different demographic of consumer—media distribution companies have the same feel. Each distributor has a very clear 'brand' they're maintaining in the marketplace; some companies are known for nature and wildlife TV content, others for kids' animation films. Just as consumers 'window-shop' for everyday products, the acquisition executives serving consumer-facing platforms do the same thing.

For the acquisition executives attending these markets, in search of very specific types of content to keep their end users engaged, the brand a distribution company holds in the marketplace is a great signifier as to whether it's worth a meeting. If a deal can be closed (and the content offered matches the acquisition executives budget AND performs well with its core audience), a well-branded distributor will be able to engage in reliable and productive business with that buyer in the future—a 'win-win' scenario for both companies.

Couple this concept with the notion that acquisition executives like to buy content in bulk, and you can begin to see how commonplace and simplified business-to-business deal structures like 'output deals'—where a client agrees to buy a minimum number of programs from a distributor (sight unseen) for an agreed period of time (e.g., 'a minimum of three years')—and 'first-look' deals—where a distributor agrees to present every new project to a select client before discussing with any other—start to make sense. (We'll explore deal structures and strategies in Chapter 4). The buyer gets more content for less money, and the distributor gets a steady stream of cash for less work.

▶ THE SEVEN PRINCIPLES OF MEDIA DISTRIBUTION

Before we dive in, I want to emphasize that these are principles (not 'rules' or trends). The reason being is that rules and trends change all the time. New advances in technology, trends in storytelling techniques or innovations in marketing approaches will always be fluctuating. But the principles that explain *how* media distribution work—and why those in leadership roles make the decisions they do—are the same today as they were during the silent era.

This is not rhetoric or theory; think of these principals as a breakdown for why the entertainment industry operates in the manner it does. It's also important to note that these principles are not ordered sequentially; they can literally be plucked and pulled as needed to explain different realities of the media distribution process. Also, they are not restricted to any one segment of the business; any media distribution company (large or small, new or old) works within these parameters.

Throughout this entire book, you will see these principles applied—occasionally several at once—to explain the logic and rationale that motivate all aspects of the media distribution business.

Principle #1: Buyers Take and Sellers Keep

In the media business, whether it's a studio bigwig or an up-and-coming independent distributor, whenever someone is willing to put money on the table to acquire the rights to a film, television or new media property, they're always going to attempt to squeeze as much from the deal as possible. Since the buying party has the money to spend, they hold the leverage to ask for more and will actively work to make deals more advantageous for their needs. Perhaps that buyer is based in Los Angeles and needs to acquire rights to a feature film for the US; they might be inclined to see if they can get Canadian rights as well for the same price. Perhaps they're only interested in acquiring TV rights; however, they might see if they can add in digital rights (Video on Demand) for the same price point. Maybe the duration of the agreement is set to last for three years; a buyer might try to extend that to five years—or more—to have a bit longer to exploit the property. Regardless of the terms, buyers will always try to add in a bit extra to further stretch their investment.

For a content seller, it's the exact opposite. The seller will try to minimize the terms and isolate or restrict those terms as much as possible. Sellers will attempt to exclude those extra countries, add-on rights or extensions of term (unless, of course, the buyer is willing to pay extra in order to acquire them).

Not only will you see this concept in your everyday life regardless of what's being bought or sold, you'll also see it across all phases of the film production process (from buying and selling scripts to buying and selling production equipment). Buyers try to gain as much as possible with as little money as they can, whereas sellers try to give as little away during each sale with the hope of selling to additional buyers later.

Principle #2: A Property Is Only Worth What Someone's Willing to Pay

A house might have an assumed 'market value', and a piece of merchandise on a store shelf might have a 'suggested retail price', but at the end of the day, the real value of each will only be finalized once someone sets the bar for what they're willing to dish out. Everything is ultimately only worth what someone's willing to pay—and a media property is no different.

For the screenwriter, director or producer—who've poured everything they have (emotionally and sometimes financially) into completing a creative work—it's difficult to place a concrete value on efforts. For a distributor, on the other hand, their job depends on establishing a 'suggested' price. They do not choose these numbers blindly; distributors have a wide range of real-world market experience from which to pull. Additionally, while many on the creative side feel their individual projects are 'original', a veteran distributor has undoubtedly worked with a title very similar (either in style, tone or circumstance).

This valuation process doesn't just occur during the selling process; very often, just to acquire a property, a distributor must provide a producer or rights holder with their financial estimates (often called 'projections') for how much they believe they could sell a particular title. Although these projections are usually well within the realm of reason, they are, at best, educated guesses. And even though these numbers assume the best-case scenario, all distributors know that a title will never sell all its rights to all outlets.

And after all is said and done—after projections are scrutinized and revenues are estimated—during the sales process itself, a bird in the hand is often better than one in the bush. Distributors need to make sales to generate profits, so even if a particular title was projected to earn a certain minimum from a third-party buying client, if that client's final offer is dramatically lower than initially hoped, it's far more likely the offer reflects the project's actual real-world value. Although people love to quote or reference outliers (mentioning those unassuming projects that yielded unexpected riches), these are beyond-rare scenarios and cannot be banked upon.

Principle #3: The Audience Decides What Gets Produced

Those on the business side of Hollywood often get falsely accused of only thinking about money; truth is they're far more focused on audience (and more precisely, the meeting (or exceeding) of audience expectation).

At nearly every point during the development and production of a project, everyone involved uses the eventual audience as their primary decision-making filter. Without an end user audience to eventually watch—and transact upon—the project being produced, there'd be zero reason for the distributor to invest the cash funding the production (paying the salaries and/or invoices of those working on it). But this 'audience-first' mentality branches out into all aspects of the production process: film crews have learned which camera angles, lighting techniques and styles of set design appeal to an audience's eyes; writers and producers constantly consider audience expectation during every aspect of story development. But distributors have a much tougher job; they must select which projects will actually be appealing to audiences.

This is why distributors primarily work within the business-to-business model; rather than blindly guessing which projects have a vetted audience waiting to see them, distributors can directly ask the very consumer-facing platforms they supply. And since consumer-facing platforms are direct-to-consumer companies (with accurate metrics showcasing what best captivates their loyal fan base of end users), they're in a position to clearly articulate what works.

Principle #4: The Script Is Complete When the Project Is Complete

Most of the screenwriting books out there talk about perfecting craft, form and writer's intent; few really discuss what the script is and how it is seen by other parties within the entire filmmaking process. The script is a tool, an open-to-interpretation instruction manual guiding a project from start to finish. But unlike an instruction manual found in a box of build-it-yourself furniture, a screenplay is a constantly evolving document that will inevitably be changed and tweaked throughout the fundraising, production and completion stages.

Writing is rewriting. As new investors come on board, they often bring ideas of how the story could be 'better'. On-location mishaps take place, causing scheduling, casting and location switch-outs. Even long after a project is 'in the can', creative differences can take place in the editing room, and distributors can require reshoots to add new scenes or that voice-overs or added dialogue (via ADR) be added that greatly alter the project's story progression.

While it's easy to criticize Hollywood execs for destroying artistic merit, consider one of the great films noir: *The Big Sleep* (1946), a cinematic achievement that virtually makes no narrative sense. This is because the on-screen chemistry between Humphrey Bogart and Lauren Bacall was so strong in the dailies—and would appeal well with audiences—that studio executives scrapped the original cut and demanded extended flirtation scenes between the stars (that consequently added scenes about nothing which replaced scenes propelling the story forward). Another great example is *The Godfather* (1972); when Francis Ford Coppola screened his final cut for Robert Evans, it was a standard-issue movie (with emphasis on the action scenes within a two-hour running time); it was Evans who demanded the film be longer with more focus on the family dynamic—which is what launched this film into greatness.

Although the writing of a great script is paramount to the success of any media project, it's important to remember that a script is an ever-evolving blueprint that will be adjusted and reshaped during each phase of the process. This is also why 'cookie-cutter' genre scripts (stories that fall into very clear and audience-demanded genres) are the most likely to be green-lit.

Principle #5: Nothing Happens Until There's Skin in the Game

There's a scene in Tim Burton's biopic *Ed Wood* (1994) when a stressed-out Wood (Johnny Depp) enters a Hollywood bar and sees his filmmaking idol Orson Welles (Vincent D'Onfrio) sitting in a booth. Wood nervously approaches, striking up a conversation. To give context, when this scene occurs, Wood is in the middle of making what will ultimately become one of the worst films in history—*Plan 9 from Outer Space* (1956)—while Welles is in the middle of making one of Hollywood's best—*Touch of Evil* (1956). Nevertheless, the advice Welles offers regarding money was just as true then as it is today: "You can never tell who's a windbag and who's got the goods."

In any deal negotiation, it's all just talk until one side is willing to put their money where their mouth is. We call this putting skin in the game (or contributing risk to the endeavour). Money is what drives this business, so the party willing to pay up first is the one considered to be putting skin in the game (putting something on the table that proves their interest).

For the life of any project, this is a game-changing moment because this event officially transforms an 'idea' into a legitimate project. The moment a distributor is willing to fund a project—even if only partially—it's considered 'vetted' in the eyes of future parties (which means people take it seriously). Development is officially underway, and the odds of the project getting completed and released have greatly increased.

For that first investor to come on board, there is a certain level of risk associated. But in exchange for being the first party to put skin in the game, they often have the greatest level of influence over how the project will take shape (Principle #1). In addition to being able to make early creative decisions—such as tweaking the script (Principle #4)—the first party to put skin in the game also alters the overall direction of the end product by dictating which rights categories or countries will be exploited first (in example, a major US network will want US TV rights to be broadcast first, whereas a global digital company might want Video-on-Demand rights to lead). And depending on what the producer might have to reserve for their 'skin-in-the-game' investor can greatly influence whom they're able to work with down the line. For instance, if a skin-in-the-game distributor requires all North American rights in exchange for their investment, then the producer can only look to international distributors to fill in the remaining budget. If a skin-in-the-game distributor requires global Ad-supported VOD rights as the first method of release—resulting in the title first appearing on a platform such as Tubi TV or Roku TV before traditional forms of exploitation (e.g., theaters or TV channels, outlets that release content before Ad-supported VOD)—then the number of companies the producer can look to for the remaining budgetary gap will be greatly reduced.

From the standpoint of a distribution company, being the first investor to fund a project involves elevated risk; therefore, it only makes sense to cater the project to better match their company's brand *and* to ensure they're acquiring the rights and territories most lucrative for their bottom line.

Principle #6: All Media Devalues Over Time

Media properties generally hold their strongest level of audience appeal when they're new. A brand-new film or series—with a major marketing push behind it—will garner a strong initial audience eagerly anticipating its release. But later, after the media property has been 'available' in the marketplace for a while—and after the first wave of interested end users have already transacted upon it—consumer-facing platforms must drop their prices to maintain reasonable levels of business. And since distributors work with a variety of consumer-facing platforms ranging from theatrical companies, television channels to VOD platforms (each of which reach end users at different levels of effectiveness at different stages of a media property's lifespan), distributors must take a strategic approach regarding which companies they should assign select rights—and in which order those rights should be released.

Distributors call this process 'windowing'. Although we discuss the strategies behind windowing later on in this book (in Chapter 5), all you need to know at this stage is that every media project—from studio blockbusters to shoestring indie titles—devalues over its life, generating less and less money year on year (some more quickly than others). Distributors use windowing to stretch out a media property's shelf life as long as possible, but all titles decline in value over the long haul.

Principle #7: Relationships Fuel the Business

Within any given distribution company, only a handful of its employees are actually brokering the distribution deals that generate their company's revenue stream. Most others on staff are focused on administration, accounting, marketing, operations or legal (all required roles for the process of media distribution to function, but all of which aren't on the front lines of day-to-day industry dealmaking). The same is true for consumer-facing platforms that acquire the rights from distributors.

The reason this is fundamental is because—by default—the total number of people in the entire world who make the decisions as to what content is created, bought and sold is actually quite small. And given the other concepts discussed in this chapter (especially in relation to distributors branding themselves and developing strong output relationships with select consumer-facing platforms), one can see how difficult it can be to break into this small subset of industry decision-makers.

Factor in that all of these individuals are regular people (with family obligations and personal lives) along with simple truth that there are only so many hours in a day to read scripts and watch screeners. Globally, these people are stretched in terms of both time and attention; therefore, one thing they've learned to depend upon to help ease their workload is the 'trust' of a close business associate or colleague.

When an acquisitions executive at a consumer-facing platform needs ten titles on very short notice, they'll almost always call a close distribution friend—one whom they've worked with in the past. With this close relationship, they can talk through the terms without a lot of the games and stress. And once the ten titles are decided upon, the acquisition executive can trust all of those titles will be a match for their audience needs (and might only skim the titles rather than watch them all the way through).

The same is true for distributors; sometimes they need to get a certain title sold to win points with a producer (or for some other 'office politics' scenario); the distributor can call a close buyer from a consumer-facing platform and get them to buy the rights purely as a favor. This buyer/seller relationship is symbiotic, and these types of quid pro quo deals are what truly drive the media business behind closed doors.

The principle behind this is not the silly wisdom of 'it's not what you know, it's whom you know'. That logic can secure one with high-level meetings but won't result in a deal getting closed. By contrast, the reason for understanding Hollywood is a business of relationships is because Hollywood is quid pro quo. From the very top all the way down to the very bottom, everyone who makes it in the entertainment industry is a hustler—all of whom understand deals aren't only done on paper.

▶ THE MORE THINGS CHANGE

The old wisdom that 'the more things change, the more they stay the same' is just as prevalent in the world of media distribution as it is across many other facets of life.

One might scoff at this notion, immediately citing the explosive growth of companies like Netflix or the advents in technology that have rapidly grown streaming capabilities (and filming potential) on our smartphones—that have made it possible for YouTube or TikTok celebrities to reach mass audiences before they can legally drive a car—or even the fact that greater numbers of individuals are choosing to 'cut the cord' and shy away from traditional forms of television in favor of handpicked VOD platforms.

But many of the distribution models behind these innovations aren't much different than the deal structures that existed during other periods of rapid growth. For example, the explosion of cable TV channels in the 1980s and early '90s isn't much different than today's bundled VOD channels popping up on media streaming platforms such as a Roku or Apple TV (often referred to as 'over-the-top' or simply 'OTT' boxes); or the reactionary fads studios and theater chains introduce (e.g., massive wide-screens, 3D, etc.) to lure audiences back whenever a new competing outlet pops up—in the 1950s these fads were used to compete with TV, in the 1980s it was to compete against the VCR and in the 2000s it was to distract audiences away from SVOD platforms and Internet streaming. Even going way back to the beginning, during the 'early Edison' film experiments using the Kinetoscope; single cameras were used to shoot short-subject observational titles like *Wrestling* (1892), *Fencing* (1892), *A Handshake* (1892) and *Horse Shoeing* (1893)—none of which are too different from *Me at the zoo* (2005), the first video ever posted on YouTube—the first widely adopted user-generated platform.

Even the high-level deal structures and business workflows fueling today's modern distribution business aren't actually all that new. The principles that govern modern-day media distribution pull many of their business practices and structures from the world of book publishing. Long before the twentieth century, books needed to be developed, produced and distributed to booksellers; and just as films get adapted and translated for international markets, so too did books. 'Bundled' package deals and output structures existed back in these times as well, and the authors and content creators of yesteryear received royalties—after expenses—just as media producers receive them today.

So really, there doesn't need to be any great mystery to film, television or new media distribution—and there certainly doesn't need to be any sense that things are 'changing' so rapidly one cannot keep up—because the principles that allow the media distribution business to adequately fund, produce and release media properties are the same tried and tested methods that have served the content creation business for centuries. While there have been numerous changes to the landscape, at the end of the day the only thing that's really been replaced are the definitions and terms used in agreements.

2

Developing and Distributing Media Content *Before* It Exists

The entire entertainment industry depends upon the creation and distribution of new film, television and digital content. Fortunately, there is no shortage of great ideas or intellectual property kicking around Hollywood (with plenty of talented and established personalities creating, promoting and eager to attach themselves). But for any of these concepts to be formally developed, green-lit, produced and ultimately released into the marketplace as an exploitable moneymaking product (regardless of its genre, budget level or format), someone along the way had to be the first investor to say 'yes' to initiate its funding.

So what separates the projects that move forward versus the ones that do not? Why does one seemingly mediocre property receive a greenlight while a seemingly stronger one get shelved? And what are the real-world 'it' factors that get a production company, studio or broadcaster to finally pull the trigger and sign a check kick-starting this process?

Commonly, these questions are answered with vague phrases like 'a great story will always get noticed' or 'timing is everything'. Although there's a grain of truth to these statements, they barely scratch the surface in terms of understanding the evaluation process media distributors undertake when considering which new titles to take on. The real answer boils down to the fact that a great project—one worthy of a green light—isn't just a strong creative idea; it must be a strong creative idea that's simultaneously supported by a rock-solid business case.

▶ WHAT MAKES A PROJECT 'GREAT'?

Media projects are a dime a dozen in Hollywood; every spec script, treatment or concept scribbled on a napkin is technically a project looking for a home. But even if these

DOI: 10.4324/9781003357902-3

concepts are interesting and marketable ideas, most will never gain traction because the bulk of them fail to meet the needs of the overall Hollywood system. A 'great' project, on the other hand, arrives as a package, one that offers not just a great story or concept (which should be a given) but comes with strong on-camera and/or off-camera talent attached. These projects also have established fan bases of end users ready to transact, which builds the excitement of consumer-facing platforms. Such hype lands the producers developing such projects key meetings with major executives and agents, which creates a buzz within boardrooms.

But 'hype' and 'buzz' aren't what get projects funded. For the distributor—the one who will ultimately be that first investor agreeing to fund a major chunk of the budget (or at least fronting the cash on behalf of others)—they must brush aside the excitement and instead ask the critical questions about the merit of the project. As discussed in Chapter 1, distributors need to see evidence that the project will perform; for each dollar distributors invest, there must be a strategy for how it will be recouped with a profit margin.

So while it might seem that a solid concept coupled with strong name attachments and industry 'buzz' are all it takes for a project to gain traction in Hollywood, for distributors and acquisition executives—who are the ones capable of signing checks and getting projects funded—they need to see something more in the project before they'll move forward:

▶ Variables that *decrease* a project's risk

▶ Variables that *increase* a project's odds for success

Decreasing a Project's Risk

Not only are media properties expensive investments, they also require a great deal of time after the investment has been made before revenues can realistically be returned—even longer for a true profit margin to develop.

If a distribution company agrees to invest seed money to develop a film, it could take another year before production commences (followed by another year before that investment manifests into a sellable product). Deep pockets are required to fund an individual project. Additionally, one must remember that distribution companies develop dozens of projects each year in order to maintain a steady pipeline of new content. But distribution is a long tail business; to truly make money and build a business, a large amount of capital must be spent in order to grow a profitable library of media content. But distributors don't spend money blindly; they're actually quite conservative with their financial investments and often run detailed internal projections on potential new projects. And to ensure that each of their investment dollars has a solid strategy for how it will come back (with a profit on top), distributors lean toward projects they perceive as having lower risk.

Consider the below marketplace variables; although there are dozens more—if not hundreds—the below examples offer insight as to how distributors use 'filters' in their thinking while weighing the cost/benefit of taking on a new project from a standpoint of risk:

▶ **Audience**—When reviewing a project—even one of great interest—a distributor needs to know with confidence that an audience is out there waiting for such a film or series. For perspective, a media franchise (e.g., the *Fast & Furious* films) will undoubtedly have a larger fan base of 'ready-to-buy' end users than an indie 'coming-of-age' story with an unknown cast. Since distributors are in the business of supplying consumer-facing platforms with audience-appealing media content, projects that have a built-in audience offer a more predictable outcome. But more importantly, distributors need assurance that the audience of end users is available via a variety of consumer-facing platforms (that way a distributor has a variety of consumer-facing platforms from which to license the final product). Even if the project speaks only to a niche audience, as long as the size of that audience offers a distributor enough of a profitable margin in the marketplace, then the project is perceived to be a more stable investment.

▶ **Budget**—The cost required to produce a project matters. Screenwriting books often encourage novice writers to focus only on the story and to ignore budgets or other creative constraints; by contrast, this is *not* how distributors think. Although distributors understand investing in media property is a risky business, this risk can be greatly reduced if the expected investment is reasonable in terms of its ratio to the anticipated profit margin. In other words, if a generic but well-produced family film historically earns a specific distributor around $2 million in global sales, a new family film project—with a strong script and name talent attached—that has an anticipated budget of $600,000 would be a reasonable investment and therefore worth consideration. For that budget level, if the distributor's sales team performed at their average rate, they'd earn a healthy profit margin; even if their sales team underperformed, they'd most likely still—at worst—recoup their overall investment. However, if that same family film project had an anticipated budget of $2.4 million (costing more than their historical average earnings), the project would probably not be pursued.

▶ **Genre**—For distributors, the genre of a particular project gives a very clear indication of its exposure to risk, because some genres are simply more risky than others. Comedies, for example, can sell extremely well, provided everything fits together perfectly. But if just a few elements are out of place, they can quickly flop—especially at the independent level. Not only are major on-camera name talents required to ensure reasonable marketability of a comedy—which often carry heavy price tags—the off-camera talent required to produce a great comedy depends upon top-notch writing, directing, editing and marketing. Also, jokes and storylines rarely translate internationally, which greatly reduces a comedy's overall revenue potential. A far safer bet would be an inexpensively produced (under $2 million) action film with an aging name star; these are very successful internationally in places like Germany, Japan, Australia and the UK (all of which are some of the strongest pre-buying territories). Projects that offer a genre with a more stable expectation of return—especially one with strong opportunity for presales—expose a distributor to far less risk than a genre filled with unpredictable variables.

▶   **Company Brand**—Just as consumer-facing platforms become known for a certain style and tone of their content offerings (e.g., adult skewing vs. youth skewing, or male-skewing vs. female skewing), the distributors that supply these consumer-facing platforms also fall into similar buckets. For example, a distribution company known for hard-hitting action films would be taking a massive risk jumping blindly into the 'kids and family' space (even if their development slate was solid). Although they could probably pull off a strong product—and manage to at least break even—there would be just too many risks to jump in without a more calculated transition into the genre. From the perspective of a distributor, sticking with the content they're known for exposes them to far less risk—primarily because they're directly feeding the consumer-facing platforms they work with regularly. That's not to say distributors never expand into alternative genres or pivot from film content to TV content; it happens all the time, but it's done with a strategic game plan. The best method used by distributors when they want to dabble in a different format or genre is to grow their footprint in the space slowly with a low-risk strategy by (i) partnering with companies already branded within that bucket to produce new content and/or (ii) acquiring low-cost completed projects that are in the genre of interest (allowing them to see firsthand sales/revenues generated). After gaining a more comprehensive understanding—and slowly introducing the genre vertical in their catalog—a distributor can formally adopt the new genre or format into their company's brand.

Media investment is risky business, but for successful distributors this risk is calculated. Distributors will be held accountable for the outcome of any project they take on, so they need to see clear and measurable elements that reduce the risk before they'll invest.

Increasing a Project's Odds for Success

While reducing risk is certainly a way in which distributors can improve a project's profit margin, there are additional actions that can be taken to increase a project's potential to receive stronger revenues.

It's important to note that distributors contemplate ways they can make projects more profitable in advance of making a formal bid. This allows them to map out all of the financials they expect on the back end (which allows them to know how much they should be offering early on). What follows are a few examples of how distributors look at projects with the intention of making them more profitable:

▶   **Crossover Appeal**—Crossover appeal allows increased sales from international countries. For projects that are heavily US-centric (with characters playing American football and celebrating Thanksgiving), distributors might shift such elements to characters playing soccer and celebrating Christmas—both of which are more universally understood. Other ways to increase crossover appeal refer to including elements that open doors to more audiences. Take *The Martian* (2015) and *Arrival* (2016), two great American science fiction films that also interestingly offered plotlines that had Chinese characters coming to the rescue of the United States—a blatant move by the studios to get these films past China's strict quota system against non-Chinese films, therefore exposing the films to a massive theatrical audience (see Chapter 6).

▶   **Evergreen**—'Evergreen' is a term used to describe content that holds its value over a long period of time. Projects that are evergreen generally use timeless storytelling mechanics to express universally understood themes such as love, family, death or the fear of the unknown; because they are easily understood by a wide majority of people and focus on topics that don't age, they can be sold (and resold) multiple times over a period of several years to several decades. While the most obvious examples are works of classic literature adapted or rebooted into films or TV projects (such as works adapted from William Shakespeare, Charles Dickens or the Bible), original and/or modern content can just as easily be evergreen (consider the US film *A Christmas Story* (1983), which broadcasts multiple times each Christmas season, or the factual crime series *Forensic Files* (1996), which ran for 14 seasons via broadcast but pulls extremely strong numbers via Ad-supported VOD). When evaluating projects, distributors will often consider what value a media property might hold five, ten or even 20 years in the future. If a story or project can maintain strong audience appeal in five years or later, not only does it help reduce risk but it also increases the project's opportunities for alternative forms of exploitation. Although time-sensitive productions with a shorter shelf life—such as biopics or current event titles—can generate large numbers during their initial release, after a few months their exploitability quickly wanes (as does their profit margin); a more evergreen project allows for a longer shelf life which helps to increase a distributor's odds for a strong title-by-title return on investment.

▶   **Catering to Top Clients**—We discussed the 'buy-in-bulk' concept in Chapter 1 (where select distributors and content buyers—with a strongly established business relationship—engage in larger volume, more regular deals); although the structure of such agreements varies greatly by client, the dependability of such partnerships allows both companies to grow. Therefore, when distributors are evaluating new projects, the tastes and interests of their top-buying clients always play a major role in the decision-making process. Part of this development workflow usually involves 'tweaking' potential projects so they become more in alignment with the types of content their buying clients prefer. By no means does this infer drastic changes; these are simple adjustments that can yield a better response from a distributor's 'go-to' buyers. As an example, if a major client responds well to romantic themes, then a rewrite note might include expanding on a script's blossoming relationship or adding some kind of hinted subtlety between a few characters. Such adjustments never alter the story too intently—the property would still need to sell (and therefore work) even if a distributor's 'go-to' client(s) passed—but minor tweaks can help a distributor feel more confident investing in a project during its early stages.

▶ Where Projects Originate

This is where most books state that projects can come from anywhere (and/or be developed by anyone). Although this is technically true, I couldn't tell you the last time I came across a media property that was developed and pitched by a complete Hollywood outsider. While the common reasoning most novices use to explain this discrepancy is assuming that because media executives are 'businesspeople', they only care about money—therefore implying they lack creativity and simply don't appreciate many of the indie projects developed by industry outsiders. This view is very false (though I must admit, it's one I held for years before I started working within the system).

It's important to reiterate that producing and distributing media content is very expensive. And in order for distributors—or any potential investor—to feel confident that a given project is worthy of their investment (meaning that they'll actually see their money returned, with a profit on top) they need to feel confident the project they're evaluating will be successful. But here's the age-old problem: no one can say with absolute certainty what will be the next hit, the next award winner or the next financial disaster. But by focusing on projects that have already been vetted by trusted and experienced sources, distributors can reduce the risk of a potential investment while also increasing its potential profitability—two things distributors love most.

For a project to be considered 'vetted', it means another entity (either a person or company with industry creditability) has already evaluated the concept and sees value. Vetted projects not only indicate a specific concept is worthy of investment; they often come with measurable ratings or financial data which validate potential for profit margin.

Books are a great example; not only has a publishing company vetted the story as being one worthy of movement in the marketplace, books offer clear performance data as to what demographic responded to the material and how well it performed financially against expectations. Books also offer the added benefit of a preexisting audience; a large audience of 'ready-to-engage' consumers will always make for a great argument in favor of moving forward with one project over another.

Consider for a moment that most successful novelists are under contract with the same talent agencies representing known actors, directors and screenwriters. If an author's new novel is a success, in just a few departmental meetings, a handful of agents can transform that 'best-selling novel' into a pitch-worthy media project and even package it with their already-represented on-and-off camera talent—a process commonly called 'stacking'. For a distributor, a pre-packaged project with a built in audience is a pitch worth considering; by contrast, an original spec script from an unknown writer with no attachments simply pales in comparison.

While books are an obvious example, there are many other ways in which projects are vetted; consider the following examples:

▶ **Remakes and Reboots**—When in doubt, why not dust off a classic? Major studios (and mini-majors) often have deep libraries of older film and media content that are ripe for a modern day revamp. While it's easy to be critical of Hollywood for the practice, it's important to remember that studio projects are easily costing over $100 million a pop (and that's without the heavy marketing spend); for executives at the top, investing in a remake or reboot helps reduce the risk while offering opportunities to increase profits. But before we go pointing fingers that this is some kind of new trend (and that Hollywood has simply gotten lazy), remember that this is a process that has been occurring since the very early days of film production. Cecil B. DeMille remade his own 1923 version of *The Ten Commandments* into the classic 1956 epic starring Charlton Heston and Yul Brynner. William Friedkin's gem *Sorcerer* (1977) was a remake of Henri-Georges Clouzot's French-Italian film *The Wages of Fear* (1953).[1] Even the classic TV sitcom *I Love Lucy* was rebooted from the radio series *My Favorite Husband*. While one can make the argument that remakes and reboots lack integrity because they're simply borrowing another filmmaker's idea, I would find it hard to believe any true film lover would offer too heavy a criticism of John Carpenter's *The Thing* (1982), David Cronenberg's *The Fly* (1986) or of Sergio Leone's classic *A Fistful of Dollars* (1964) which was a nearly shot-by-shot remake of Akira Kurosawa's *Yojimbo* (1961). And with that, in the mid-2000s, large numbers of American audiences gained exposure to the quality horror content coming out of Japan—e.g., *Ju On* (2002) and *Ringu* (1998)—by first experiencing their US remakes *The Grudge* (2004) and its two sequels and *The Ring* (2002) and its sequels. Hollywood studios down to indie production companies are all equally as guilty in dusting off older titles already owned in their libraries and giving them an updated spin. How many variations of *Batman* has Warner Brothers produced? How many variations of *Superman* will there be? Or *King Kong*? New generation: new technology, new reboot. And, in a way, a reboot is a relevant creative avenue that not only plays off the original but in many ways improves upon it. As Mike Hollan noted, reboots "are built on the understanding that people liked the original and want to see more"; in other words, reboots aren't bound to the conventions of the original film or its sequels. Remakes can work beautifully, but sometimes get stuck since they must conform to key scenes and characters that might feel obsolete in today's world. Reboots, on the other hand, get to reinvent the rules and take the spirit of the original (how it made people feel) and adapt that for a new generation. For distribution executives, it's not just that this content is already owned, it's that it speaks to multiple generations, one right after the other (meaning it has a built in audience); that said, distributors are very aware their remake or reboot must respect the audience's expectations.

▶ **Adaptations**—Although books have provided Hollywood with a great number of major blockbuster studio titles over the years, they have also allowed numerous indie titles (from unknown filmmakers) a chance to gain real industry traction. Plays and other works of theater accomplish the same objective, offering stories that have already found an audience (providing verifiable metrics). But the sky is the limit: comic books, news articles, video games and even blogs have been adapted into film, television, and new media properties. Since these outlets are already 'vetted' sources—with a proven audience—it makes for a much more reasonable pitch. And while it might seem as if simply 'adapting' a book, play or video game into a movie is a cakewalk, I beg to differ. An author can write freely without any concern for budgets; plays are often confined to limited locations that work in person but feel dull on screen and alternative forms of media (e.g., video games, podcasts, etc.) have loyal fan bases, ones that approach any adaptation of their beloved content with a strong level of predisposed judgments. Film distributors are very conscious of this; even though the subject matter is vetted—and its fan base is preestablished—such projects require strategic planning. Top-notch writing talent (from writers experienced in adapting such works to cinematic or televised stories) is a must. Casting, look and overall style all play an important role—and for some adaptations, fans are choosy with which directors should be calling the shots. So the next time you hear someone cracking on a campy Nicholas Sparks adaptation or passing judgment on a tween cult book series (e.g., the *Twilight* films), remember that hundreds of boardroom conversations and careful execution was put into such projects to keep the loyal fans engaged.

▶ **Formats**—A highly rated and successful TV series produced in a foreign country is not limited to a life within its native borders or language. While the 'as is' version of this program can be dubbed (or subtitled) into other languages and licensed internationally—a process referred to as selling its 'ready-mades', 'finished program sales' or simply (and archaically) 'finished tape sales'—there is value within the abstract right to replicate and adapt that foreign-produced series into unique international versions. The process is called selling a property's 'format'. Format sales explain how the original UK-produced series *Shameless* (2004) and *The Office* (2001) got adapted into the multi-seasonal (multi-award-winning) US programs of the same names. It also explains how a New Zealand singing competition titled *Popstars* (1999) got rebranded in England as *Pop Idol* (2001) before making its way to the US as the mega-sensation *American Idol* (2002), or how an obscure singing competition from South Korea called *King of Masked Singer* (2015) evolved into the US FOX ratings hit *The Masked Singer* (2019). When a producer or distributor licenses the rights to a format, they are essentially granting permission to a third party to recreate a series for its own foreign-based territory. Often, original scripts (or a series 'bible') is handed over to the acquiring party to undergo careful scrutiny and re-versioning. Producers of the original program generally attempt wedge themselves into format deals to receive 'consultancy' fees in exchange for their advice on best practices to produce the series. In the end, the acquiring party moves to greenlight on a series with a vetted international track record (a move that helps eliminate risk), and the producer gains passive income via residual payouts included within the format deal terms. A format is different than a remake, reboot or adaptation in that it is designed to completely mimic the original program with very little room for innovation or alteration. Think of formats like the franchising of a fast-food restaurant. Regardless of what country you're in, Starbucks has the same interior look, and the coffee itself has the same taste (franchise agreements include stipulations that ensure this result). However, unlike the finished film and TV world, what makes a format sellable is its past performance in other markets. A TV series that was produced in Norway and received very strong ratings is appealing; but if that same show was to have also been produced in three or four additional countries (and still received strong ratings), then there is stronger probability that it would continue to perform regardless of where it will be produced in the future.

▶   **Original Content**—Yes, original content is developed and green-lit quite often in the media industry, but it tends to come from well-established and well-connected sources within the industry. To give more perspective, many newbie filmmakers cite 'first-time' screenwriters like Diablo Cody, who appeared to be a complete media outsider when she got her very first feature-length spec script—*Juno* (2007)—acquired, developed and produced into a major Hollywood film, kick-starting her career. From the outside, it seemed as if someone with zero connections broke through the fortified studio's walls with nothing more than a strong script (a dream come true for many). But when one actually looks at Cody's career, getting *Juno* off the ground was far from a streak of luck. She'd been a writer for a while, working as a journalist and columnist as well as a stripper (which she chronicled in a 'behind-the-curtains' online blog called 'The Pussy Ranch'). This garnered the attention of a manager, who encouraged Cody to write her debut novel *Candy Girl: A Year in the Life of an Unlikely Stripper* (2005) and helped secure its publication. After this established credibility, her manager was able to help her mold, flesh out and develop a Hollywood-ready script (that would become *Juno*) and had a generalized plan of how to leverage his agency contacts to open doors. This in no way undercuts Cody's obvious talent for writing, but it should paint a clearer picture to those working to gain professional traction that Hollywood doesn't just work on blind spec submissions (but that there are ways to get 'original content' into development). That said, most 'original' ideas are developed from within Hollywood's inner circle to help supply what's directly in demand from consumer-facing platforms. Here are some real—and more common—examples of how original content is created:

▶   **Content Made to Order**—Distributors are constantly speaking with a multitude of consumer-facing platforms (TV channels, VOD platforms, etc.) So, rather than simply guessing what content they should be developing, distributors have the direct ability to simply ask what they want. Consumer-facing platforms are thinking about their content slates months—sometimes years—in advance; any opportunity to know what content might be available down the line offers a huge advantage to strategically program their slates. And rather than producing content that *might* work, distributors and consumer-facing platforms openly talk about what will be needed in the future. Once several consumer-facing platforms touch upon the same content subjects (what we call a 'market trend'), distributors see an opportunity to produce a title that could meet that growing market need. Before going full force, distributors will actually pre-pitch (or market-test) the idea to a few platforms, explaining that they're contemplating a certain type of project to gauge that platform's level of interest. Interested consumer-facing platforms and acquisitions executives will offer sound notes (including casting suggestions, story tweaks, hook elements, etc.). In essences, this is preselling. And from this process, the majority of entertainment projects are developed and brought to life. It's not about "we're making this, will you buy it?"; instead, it's much more about distributors market-testing ideas and gaining the feedback necessary to supply what the market of consumer-facing platforms are demanding. If distributors have a reputation for delivering on their promises, a consumer-facing platform might just pre-buy the project (putting 'skin in the game') which kick-starts the formal development process.

▶ **Elevated Acquisition**—Although this phrase hasn't quite reached the level of 'industry standard', an elevated acquisition takes the concept of making content to order quite literally. With an elevated acquisition, a consumer-facing platform may seek a very specific project (a themed TV movie or a documentary series on a specific subject). The heads of the network might even have a format they'd like to emulate (a four-part documentary series to be timed with a certain event—for example, the anniversary of a major event—or a two-part miniseries adapted from a major current event). Bottom line, the heads of the network know what they want, what their budget is and usually by what date they wish to broadcast or otherwise make available the project. From here, the heads of the network will reach out to distributors or production companies who can deliver such a project (ones with a reputation of being able to deliver quality content with strict deadlines). The network will pay a sizable amount of cash to 'acquire' the project, but this amount is usually much less than if they were to commission the work directly. (What this means is that on paper, they're 'pre-buying' a project and not hiring the production company to produce a film on their behalf; what they're actually paying is much less than a normal pre-buy or commission.) The production and/or distribution company is getting a major chunk of funding in advance from a network (along with a guarantee of a US premiere); what makes this project even more interesting is that, in most cases, that same distribution company will own the rights to license or sell that project internationally. So if the production team can keep their costs down, they can effectively be at the break-even point (or even slightly into the profit zone) at the point they finish the project (making all the international sales pure profit). For instance, a channel under the A&E Networks, Fox or Paramount umbrellas might be willing to front $750,000 or more into an elevated acquisition for a TV movie—by no means a small amount of cash, but far less than it would cost to produce it out of pocket. But for an independent company—one that is very wise about cost cutting and maxing out a budget—they can easily develop, produce and deliver a film at or even under that price point (one that has a 'larger' look but might cost at or below $500,000). The network/platform gets their movie, and the independent distributor has a feature—with a US broadcast history—they can parade around the international markets. And just for clarity, it's not just TV networks that elevate their acquisitions; this process can apply to any commissioning entity (large or small).

▶ **Internal Development**—Distributors are always working unique angles to get more content deals secured (and to create more stable streams of revenue). Guaranteed revenue streams generated from 'buy-in-bulk' sales strategies—such as package deals, output deals and first-look deals—can be extremely lucrative for a distributor's bottom line, easily securing several hundred thousands (to a few million) per title. The problem is that these deals are very taxing on a distributor's library of available content—and more often than not, the only reason a major 'buying' client would agree to enter into an output deal is because their specific content needs are tough to find. For distributors, rather than having their acquisition executives waste time searching for the perfect niche product—which almost always requires rewrites and tweaks—why not just develop and produce the exact content in need internally? After all, distributors know the ins and outs of their buying clients (what they like, what they don't, what they pay, etc.); inventing the exact content in demand is a way to keep the output deals in motion and the revenue streams flowing. The added benefit is that distributors also know what works elsewhere—meaning for the territories or rights not exploited in their output deals. As a result, since they're developing properties from beginning to end, they are able to add elements that will not only satisfy their output clients but also hold value for other international territories or buyers—therefore making them stronger profit-making vehicles.

▶ HOW PROJECTS GET VETTED

Nothing grabs the attention of distributors and acquisition executives more than a project that's been vetted by a true industry insider. A project based upon solid material (such as a book) with great attachments (talent, director, writers, etc.) will certainly be taken seriously, but when a true Hollywood influencer is added to the mix—such as an established showrunner, agent or producer (the types of individuals that are on a first-name basis with leading decision-makers and have a solid track record of quality projects under their belt)—these projects become difficult to ignore.

When these individuals get behind a project they're enthusiastic about, they know how to put the right elements together—it's as if they can see it all working in their minds long before the camera roll. They know exactly which studio heads would be interested (and which ones to avoid), which talent could fill key roles (and already have preestablished relationships with their agents), they have a clear understanding of the budget required to make the project a reality and know which distributors might be willing to come on board early to pre-buy the rights. Essentially, they're able to map out a game plan from the get-go, including the names of writers or other creative individuals who might be able to add a better polish or spin to the project.

Here are the most common types of Hollywood influencers, along with a basic snapshot of how they operate:

▶ **Producer**—Producers are the individuals responsible for completely bringing a project to life (who literally 'produce' it from nothing more than determination and grit). They're generally the ones making the calls, coordinating the meetings and connecting all the other 'dots' required to get the right project—with the right attachments—into the hands of the right distributor. It's important to note that there are lots of producers on a given media project (line producers, creative producers, executive producers, etc.), but most of these are service roles—meaning they're hired or brought in to provide a specific service after a project has been green-lit (generally via an agreement known as a Production Services Agreement (or 'PSA'). What we're discussing here are the 'producer' producers, the ones with strong connections throughout the industry (friends in high places), who carry a proven track record of discovering quality projects and getting them made (on time and within budget). Essentially, these individuals are constantly reading scripts, books, treatments and meeting with writers in a never-ending search for new material. When a project clicks, a producer will option its rights (meaning they'll acquire the right to pitch and represent it), develop it for the current market (make writing suggestions, create marketing materials) and secure the right attachments (schmoozing actors and creative talents to sign on) to make it pop. And just as distributors focus on the needs and interests of their most consistent buying clients, producers play the same angle (focusing on projects they know can move with the contacts they hold close); many producers enter into multi-project deals with specific studios (meaning they're obligated to focus their talents on creating strong content for one entity—similar to a distributor's 'output' deal), whereas other producers operate as lone wolves, free to shop their projects as they please. When a well-established producer champions a project, media executives at all levels take it seriously. This isn't an easily tangible role; the job requirements differ greatly from one project to the next. But to give some insight, one of the best books I've ever read on the process of producing is *Killer Instinct: How Two Young Producers Took on Hollywood and Made the Most Controversial Film of the Decade* by Jane Hamsher, which tells the story of her and her producing partner, Don Murphy, as they found the Quentin Tarantino script of *Natural Born Killers* and developed it into the 1994 film by Oliver Stone. But for a more salacious and classic read, check out Robert Evans' autobiography *The Kid Stays in the Picture: A Notorious Life*.

▶ **Showrunner**—Showrunners are a newer idea in the world of television. Not that the role is actually new, it's just that it wasn't always seen as an actual 'job'. The showrunner serves as the leading creative filter overseeing a television series. Just as filmmakers glorify the director's role as one that holds ultimate creative control, on a TV series, it's the showrunner that holds this responsibility (their opinion actually trumps that of the director). The reason is that directors and writers come and go; when a series has the potential to be a long-running show, bringing in 'fresh' writers or other creative talent midway through can sometimes steer the 'feeling' or style of a show off course. The showrunner's real objective is to make sure each episode fits into the 'platform' of how the show is supposed to play out. They essentially act as one part creator, one part head writer and one part executive producer, overseeing the day-to-day activities of a show. It is an incredibly demanding and tough job—one that generally earns a very high salary plus back end on a show's success. But unlike a television director or writer, a showrunner wears many hats and must know a great deal about every process required to make a successful series function. Therefore, during the 'development' process of any television project, the factor that can transform an 'idea' into a fully developed and ready-to-go television series is by simply getting a vetted showrunner to take an interest. With a successful and well-connected showrunner attached, a potential television project has an unwritten 'seal of approval' (or at least a well-known or trusted leader to call the shots). A showrunner will be able to secure a strong writer—and already be close to the best ones; a show runner has direct access to key talent—both in front and behind the camera; and a showrunner understands how to be a functional creative while keeping real-world factors like schedules and budgets in check. They are the perfect jack-of-all-trades and a great project manager from the perspective of a distribution team.

▶ **Representatives**—The term 'representative' in relation to the vetting of projects encompasses two specific roles: agents and producer's representatives. The individuals—or teams—serving these roles are tasked with 'representing' the needs of specific clients (similar to a lawyer; in fact, many are entertainment lawyers or have a background dealing with law in some capacity). Although the traditional lens from which most view these roles would squarely lock an 'agent' with the needs of the talent (e.g., writers, directors, actors, etc.) and the 'producer's rep' managing the needs of a producer, rarely do projects come together in such a predictable manner. As already mentioned, writers and authors tend to be represented by the same agencies that have strong acting and directing talent signed on (meaning it's quite easy for an agency to 'stack' a strong novel, script or treatment with A-list caliber creative talent); and in addition to knowing how to develop media properties that 'move', the established producers pitching their project also tend to be very well-connected (meaning their endeavors are likely to already have strong talent attachments secured). From the standpoint of a distributor, receiving a pitch from either party is a very good signifier that a project has marketable audience and quality attachments.

▶ **Distributor**—Distributors are the final puzzle piece during the dealmaking process; but it's important to note that it's rarely just one distribution company getting behind a project; it's often several pooling their resources together. On a high level, there's generally a North American distributor coupled with an international distributor (handling all sales outside North America). In other cases, there could be a US-only distributor, a European distributor and a collection of others who have taken on the remaining international territories. For a producer, showrunner or representative working to get a project developed, getting that first distributor on board—putting skin in the game—is a major step toward accomplishing their financing goal, but generally they still need just a bit more support before they can move into the production phases. However, from the perspective of a distribution team evaluating a project, knowing that another distributor—especially one with credibility—has already come on board raises the project's profile immensely. Now there's a ticking clock; it's only a matter of time until another distributor takes what's left. Since distributors speak the same language—and generate revenues in essentially the same way, mostly from the same clients—they do need to put their money where their mouth is before their competitors do. After all, distributors need a threshold minimum number of titles to develop and release each year to stay afloat; when a competitor has identified a project that is worthy of movement in the marketplace, distributors realize it's time to take action.

▶ PUTTING THE FINANCIAL PIECES TOGETHER

We'll keep things high-level here since we do a deep dive on entertainment finance later in this book. But for now, we'll explore the three universal truths regarding the process of getting a project financed:

1) Money is almost always pieced together—slowly—from a variety of sources.

2) Few ever want to be the first to put their cash on the table.

3) Very few pay everything due all at once; instead, they stagger out small payments over time.

What makes this process even more complicated is that there is no single answer as to how to solve this 'chicken or the egg' scenario. I wish there was a simple three-step approach regarding how the financials of major projects come together, but the truth is each one works a little differently. Factors such as marketplace timing, project attachments along with the growth and recession cycles of company financials as well as international markets and interest rates all play a role. But that aside, the real reason stems back to our principles of media distribution from Chapter 1, specifically the concept of putting 'skin in the game'. For a distributor, they need to see that a given project offers them a few quick wins—meaning that they can see direct opportunities to recoup their expenses. And since the marketplace is always shifting, coupled with the fact that each project's path is unique, a distributor's opinion of what those 'quick-win' opportunities are—and how much reward those opportunities could yield—will constantly be changing as well.

But if we step back and instead focus on the earlier universal truths about money, we'll better understand the different methods used to get projects financed (and how companies see an opportunity for a revenue stream or profit). And, more importantly, we'll understand how and why certain companies come on board at different stages in the game. From here, the dots will connect on how the signature from one distributor leads to the next and onto the next until a project truly evolves from concept to greenlight.

Deficit Financing and Coproducing

On one hand, both deficit financing and coproducing describe the same financial concept: the coming together of two or more companies to finance a specific project—each of whom receive a different set of exploitable rights that are beneficial to them.

When you watch foreign films or US-produced independent titles, it's common to see the logos of multiple international entities popping up at the beginning—one right after the other. For instance, UK's Film Four might appear, followed by France's StudioCanal or Japan's Toho yet led by a US studio like Universal. When I attended the premiere of *Drive* (2010) at the Cannes Film Festival—one of the best film-going experiences I've even had incidentally—there were actually a few chuckles from the audience at the start because so many companies had their logos appearing (it felt endless); but each entity rightly deserved credit for the money they contributed.

But there are differences between the two. When a project requires deficit financing, it means the bulk of the money has been secured (well over the 50% mark; sometimes over the 85% mark), but that final chunk—which is required for the project to formally move to greenlight—still needs to be locked in. When a third-party company comes along and agrees to fill in the remainder (to 'cover the gap'), they are agreeing to finance the project's deficit. And since they are coming to the table with a strong level of leverage—essentially holding the sum that will make the project a reality—they can oftentimes negotiate for some strong recoupment or territorial terms.

On the other hand, when a project is coproduced, there is more of a formal partnership between two or more companies. Although the percentage split between the two parties is generally fifty-fifty, the parties can absolutely adjust the numbers as they see fit based upon the specific project. One entity—say a US production and distribution entity—might be willing to invest 65% of the budget, while an international company—such as a UK-based distributor—might be willing to put up the remaining 35%. Since both parties are working in tandem, they can cleanly divvy up the world in a way that merits their level of investment (e.g., the US company keeps all North American rights, whereas the UK company takes all 'rest of world' rights). The other point to consider is that a coproduction generally permits a certain level of creative consultancy (e.g., casting approvals or script revisions); a deficit finance scenario operates more as an 'as-is' opportunity.

That said, a media project can be both a 'coproduction' that also requires some deficit financing to cover the final chunk of costs. For instance, a company putting down seed money along with its coproducing partner might only be able to pool an amount that totals 90% of the budget. Depending on what rights are still exploitable—and what terms can be renegotiated in their favor—a strong number of companies would be willing to put down the remaining 10% (as a deficit financial investment) to obtain strong bargaining power on the remaining rights.

The main objective for a distributor when considering whether to coproduce or deficit finance a project boils down to what they'll get in return (which is generally buying into a film or media project that meets their specific needs).

Consider this: if two major broadcasters (such as AMC Networks in the US and the UK's BBC) were coproducing a television series—one based upon a well-known book stacked with great talent—it could be safely assumed the end product will be a strong property. But occasionally, even with two major companies backing the title, the total amount of cash being contributed between both isn't enough to green-light the project. This is a ripe opportunity for an independent distributor; such a project would be an amazing addition to their library and is therefore worth a deficit finance play (covering the outstanding gap). The catch is that even a deficit financial play would be a major investment for their indie dollars; additionally, they'd have much less leverage to negotiate favorable terms with mega-entities like AMC and BBC. So why go through the hassle? It's a marketing ploy; showcasing a project of that scale (with the logos of industry power houses) raises the image of that indie distributor in the eyes of competitors and producers alike. Although a slightly raw deal in the short term, the move could yield strong returns on other productions and opportunities in the future. By having such a program in their arsenal, an independent distributor would be able to feature an AMC/BBC copro in their catalog, on their website, in trade magazine ads and on posters at their market stands. It would be a driver title for them, one that would barely make its actual investment back—on a dollar-per-dollar return—but could greatly increase negotiating power on future deals for other content.

Presales

There's this sort of magical allure associated with the notion of 'presales'. Although the workflow really isn't all that different than coproducing or deficit financing, it feels more tangible (more doable). As a result, numerous producers have developed the false impression that preselling a film, television series or new media project is somehow easy; it's not. Putting together a marketable feature film or media project for presale purposes requires three of the following four key elements:

1) Seed money, at least enough to cover the initial first steps.

2) Marketable talent (on screen or behind the camera) that give the project an edge.

3) A great script or story with a high-concept 'hook' that matches marketable genre needs.

4) A talented distribution team capable of putting together presale deals to cover the budget coupled with a strong reputation of delivering what's promised.

I say 'three out of four' because you can cut out any one of the earlier elements and the other three will cover the gap.

If a strong distribution team has access to a great script and money, they'll have no problem securing marketable talent. By the same token, if a strong distribution company has access to strong talent and money, they'll have no problem commissioning a script made to order. And a marketable talent (a known actor or filmmaker) with a great script in hand and financial means will have zero problem honing in on a distributor.

Let's consider the following scenario: an established film producer has developed a great project—one with solid name cast attached that has been vetted by an industry veteran. A US distribution company loves the project and has decided they'd like to move forward. Of the anticipated USD $1 million total budget, this distributor has agreed to invest half (USD $500,000). While that's incredible news for our producer, it also means they still have another half million to scrap together.

This producer could attempt to find a coproduction partner (but most likely such a partner would want to pay less monies and require more territories); this producer could attempt to find a deficit finance partner (but half million on a single title is quite a stretch; deficit finance usually doesn't come into play until a project is well beyond the 50% mark); or this producer could work with an established third-party distribution company—one with a strong reputation for presales—and pull together the remaining funds by exploiting the territories our US distributor doesn't require.

Once enough presales agreements have been secured to cover the cost of production, the producer can then (i) formalize lending via a loan from a bank to officially cash-flow the project and (ii) apply for a 'completion bond'—assuming the project is big enough—to insure against any disasters which might eat away the budget prior to completion.

But let's look into this a bit more closely: not only was this project already 'vetted' by an industry veteran, it now has an established US distributor on board to cover 50% of the budget. Only with this level of industry validation does it become reasonable to approach international distribution companies with a presale opportunity. Also, the producer didn't go out into the marketplace solo; they signed with an established distributor—one with a strong reputation for delivering on presales—to get the deals closed. (And incidentally, such a well-established distributor would require select rights in exchange for their services in addition to a cut of the funds they raise; most likely, all monies secured by their presales would have to pass through their hands.) Nevertheless, only with the right sales team—and a well-positioned project (meaning one that each of these buyers sees as an opportunity to one-up their competition)—can presales actually generate enough cash to cover a project's budget.

But when a pre-buying client agrees to 'pre-buy' the rights to a media property for their territory, they don't simply write a check for the full amount and hope for the best. Instead, they stagger out their commitment over the duration of the project's production.

To use a completely hypothetical example—and to use a nice round number—let's say a German company has agreed to pre-buy our producer's movie in the amount of USD $100,000 for the territory of German-speaking Europe. Our producer—and our third-party preselling distributors—would be ecstatic. But this $100,000 will not paid up front; payments will be staggered out throughout the duration of the entire production process. To give you a sense of how this payment schedule might look, consider the following breakdown:

Total License Fee: USD $100,000

(i) Amount due upon signature: 5% (USD $5,000)

(ii) Amount due upon start of preproduction: 10% (USD $10,000)

(iii) Amount due upon start of principal photography: 45% (USD $45,000)

(iv) Amount due upon delivery of rough cut: 10% (USD $10,000)

(v) Amount due upon acceptance of delivery: 30% (USD $30,000)

Although this can be reworked in a variety of ways (e.g., the exact 'actions' can be a much longer list, and/or the exact percentages applied can vary greatly, etc.), the idea can be easily understood: no one wants to be left holding the bag.

Projects can encounter extreme difficulties during the production process. Take the tragic example of *Midnight Rider* (2014), uncompleted due to the death of crew member Sarah Jones on the first day of production; the producers were later found criminally negligent, and the project was simply abandoned. Although an extreme example, it shows accidents can happen, causing the total shutdown of a production. Even though completion bonds and a variety of contingencies can be used to aid a project through a rough patch— allowing for a completed film to still emerge once the dust settles—*Midnight Rider* reminds us that there are occasionally situations that result in a film being incapable of completion.

Generally, no matter how these payments are staggered out, the bulk of the money arrives at two key points during a project's production: (i) at the start of principal photography and (ii) at the acceptance of delivery (which allows pre-buying clients some insurance against a project that comes in radically different—or of dreadfully lower quality—than initially anticipated).

Soft Monies

Financial contributions don't always arrive in the form of liquid cash; the simple reduction—or reimbursement—of a production's monies can be as equally valuable in relation to its overall budget. Just as everyday individuals clip coupons to reduce the cost of consumer goods, or file an income tax return with the expectation of receiving a financial refund, producers of media properties have learned to allocate the predictable financial 'savings' from similar activities toward covering a meaningful portion of a production's budget. These credits, discounts and/or freebies are often classified as 'soft monies', meaning, despite not being liquid cash, they still hold a predictable and guaranteed financial value (even if the money won't be received until later on down the line).

Although one could easily venture down a rabbit hole of confusing financial terms when defining soft monies, the most common examples include tax credits and grants. Although 'soft monies' also include deferred payments, profit participation models along with discounts made available via product placement deals or wholesaler discounts, I've excluded these examples since they're rarely placed within budgets as verifiable methods of covering a predictable percentage of a production's budget.

Here is a snapshot overview of what these terms mean and how they work in a real-world setting:

▶ **Tax Credits**—A tax credit takes effect after a minimum threshold of 'qualified' monies are spent within a defined geographic area. In example, if a US state or international country offers a production tax credit of 20% and the production team behind a media project spends $1 million in 'qualified' monies within that territory's borders, then 20% (or $200,000) would be eligible for reimbursement. There are always a few catches; for instance, the money spent must be 'qualified' (generally meaning the monies must be verifiable as aiding the local economy—for example, salaries to local employees, rentals from local vendors, activities that help local businesses). After the money is spent and the appropriate forms are filed, the tax rebate is usually sent via check. The reason select state and international governments offer such subsidies is to lure those production dollars toward aiding local economies. Although there are numerous examples of increased governmental revenues from the issuance of tax credits, there are also scenarios where local, state and international governments have grossly over-reimbursed far more money than was actually spent by production companies.

▶ **Grants**—There are numerous organizations—some private, others government sponsored—that offer grants or other incentives to help fund media projects. In the US, many of these are private entities with specific agendas or key audiences (e.g., a private fund focused on promoting a specific aspect of medical technologies might invest in documentaries that show progress related to that field). Canada gives substantial funds for media projects—both scripted and factual—that reserve a large number of key cast and crew positions for Canadian citizens (especially if those projects are to be shot and completed entirely within the country); the idea here is to create Canadian jobs and increase foreign investment while also offering a bit of a showcase for the nation's media capabilities. The European Union has a large fund called Creative Europe MEDIA Sub-programme and offers producers (from all budget levels) the opportunity to receive grant money for their projects.

While it all seems easy, these funds are very difficult to obtain. And while it may appear to be 'free money'—especially in more socially focused nations—there is just as much scrutiny and 'vetting' as is found anywhere else. After all, if the nations of France or Finland choose to partially fund a media project, that decision is not intended to simply support the arts, but rather to 'invest' in its global public relations. When international media properties become global hits (winning major awards at festivals or events), the monies invested in those projects via grants ultimately trickle back home, boosting future opportunities—similar to tax credits.

But just as with commercially focused distributors, government and private entities alike want to be certain that the projects they're investing in will make it to the finish line. Consequently, funding entities—just as distributors—equally like to see 'name' talent and experienced producers on board. And contrary to popular belief, fund grantors are not likely to give a majority of the budget but will instead offer a much smaller—but still very meaningful—percentage. In order to obtain these grants—let alone apply—projects must generally be at a stage validating a likelihood of success.

▶ DEVELOPMENT HELL

Don't underestimate this phrase; developing a project is brutal! There is no finite beginning or end. It's full of ego-stroking and false leads, and most frustrating (or incredible) is that a project with years invested may go nowhere, whereas a project no one gave a second thought to can suddenly become the next 'it' property for unforeseen reasons. In many ways, this is the allure of Hollywood—that no one can ever say with absolute certainty where the next great project will come from.

Most want to know about what it takes for a project to move from concept to green light; very few ask about what it is that prevents quality projects from moving forward (yet this is the area that reveals the most about the process).

As already stated, there is no shortage of available media projects in Hollywood. But what is in great shortage are the number of distribution and production companies willing to say yes and invest monies. These entities have budgets to spend and slots to fill, but they need to be very particular with how they invest these monies. Consequently, distributors and acquisition executives must focus only on the content that has the best chance of meeting their needs (e.g., focusing on titles that mesh with their library, that have been vetted in the aforementioned ways, etc.) and this means, rather than analyzing each project with a fresh set of eyes, they are first interested in weeding out what *doesn't* work.

This is a crucial concept in entertainment because over time, distributors and acquisition executives have found it to be more productive—and more efficient—to first examine a new project with the mindset of first finding something wrong with it (so that they can more quickly 'pass' and move onto the next potential project). Successful producers and content developers know this truth and have learned to not just present their project in its best light but to instead pitch it in a manner that prevents a media buyer from being able to say no.

For example, the other day, a close contact at a major US premium-pay TV network sent me an email essentially stating:

> Hey Scott, do you have any scripted 4-to-5 episode mini-series projects that will be delivered by May of next year?

Very vague yet incredibly specific. Fortunately, I had a great project to pitch (that required this exact type of coproduction partner). It was a crime thriller about a maverick detective with a chip on his shoulder that had some solid talent attached. Here's the email I sent back (with a few required redactions since this was an actual deal with a sizable network):

Great to hear from you, (*Name of client*).

We do have a solid crime/detective series coming up. (*Major network*) commissioned it last quarter and we're willing to invest 15% if we can secure a US broadcaster—like you—which will be enough to take this series to greenlight (meaning if we get a deal closed by end of quarter, full delivery can be made by February of next year which allows you a few months of prep time/contingency).

Total episodes will be 5x60'. (*Major actor*) will be portraying the lead. The script was written by (*Known writer*) whom you know from her Emmy-winning series a few years back. I've attached the series synopsis + script to give you a better overview.

Let me know when you'd like to discuss further by phone, thanks. SK

Was the story mentioned in that email at all? Was there excessive language describing mood and feel? No. While these factors are crucial, pitching to a consumer-facing platform is not about pitching the story; it's about pitching the 'project' (and how this project will make their job easier by accomplishing their employer's goals). As a result of that partially redacted email, the client is actually evaluating the project on how well it—as a *finished* product—will fit her lineup for next year. My job as a distributor was to let her know what we have, how many episodes, who's in it and why it's worth her attention.

Although one cannot obligate their clients to invest money into one project over another, they can present their project as a clear solution to their clients' needs (making them more likely to consider rather than pass for efficiency's sake).

▶ BACK-LOT BACKSTABBING

The major advantage of getting a media project off the ground is that it's a team effort, which allows a larger group to collectively shoulder the workload and the financial risk. But this advantage is also its great curse. Projects generally best come together under the vision of a single leader (be that a producer, showrunner or other creative role), but in the long process of getting a project pitched, packaged and funded, such leaders must deal with a wide variety of egos that will insist *their* ideas and influence be applied in order to release the funding.

And while in an ideal world this process works for the better of the project—assuming everyone participating wants what's best for the project—it's a sad reality that oftentimes these outside influences can be used to stray a strong project off its intended path. Sometimes it's not the best project that succeeds in this scenario, but rather the most assertive producer, showrunner or other creative lead (willing to do whatever it takes to beat out their competition so that they'll be next in line).

This is best seen at the major studios. If you've never taken a true back-lot studio tour here in Los Angeles, I highly advise you do so if you ever have the opportunity. (And I don't mean the Universal Studios Hollywood theme park attraction; I'm talking about the actual back-lots of Sony, Paramount or Warner Bros.) These are massive properties littered with dozens of buildings, many of which you've seen in countless movies or TV shows. While all the main attention focuses on the large sound stages—where most major movies and TV shows are actually filmed—the real 'action' is taking place inside all these random little offices peppered all over the lot. The majority of these are offices of production companies, often led by a single successful producer who's gained enough of a credible reputation that he or she has secured a prominent place on the studio's back lot with the specific objective of sourcing and developing projects directly for the studio. They're effectively under contract with the studio, hired to put together specific types of projects (which allows the studio to let smaller entities do all the hard development work while they get to sit back, wait and have the best content pitched to them—all pre-packaged and pre-vetted). The production company is therefore responsible for dealing with the agents, rights holders and talent, working to patch together a concept they'll transform into a fully developed 'project' ready for studio consideration.

With so many production companies on the same lot working hard to get a project green-lit with the studio—coupled with the small number of 'green lights' the studio will grant—there's a high level of competition. If word spreads that a specific company is close to securing a major attachment—and the studio is eager for next steps—a competitor might throw a wrench in their rival company's engine by attempting to smear that project (in order to taint its image in the studio's mind). This can be done at all levels, but it is generally just bad-mouthing and rumor spreading. But the play is exactly the same; executives at major studios have worked very hard to reach their positions and need to be careful with which projects to choose to move forward with versus those they give a 'pass'. Referring back to those variables that decrease a project's risk while increasing its odds for success, if even a slight doubt or hesitancy can be placed into the mind of a decision-maker, they're likely to exercise caution and say no to a competitor's project (which is sometimes all it takes to keep a coveted green light slot available).

▶ Note

1. Clouzot's film *The Wages of Fear* was adapted from a 1950 novel by French author Georges Arnaud (which was originally titled *Le Salaire de la Peur*, which translates literally as "the Salary of Fear"). Other remakes of Clouzot's film include Howard W. Koch's *Violent Road* (aka *Hell's Highway*) (1958) and an episode of *Robert Montgomery Presents* (1950–1957) titled "The Wages of Fear" and broadcast in 1954.

3

The Acquisition of Finished Content

'Finished content' refers to films, television programs or other media properties that have been fully produced and completed yet don't have all their distribution outlets covered. While the most obvious examples would be media projects produced by novice filmmakers on spec—with the hope of securing a distributor via touring the festival circuit—major studio properties and network television productions can just as easily fall into this category. In Chapter 2 we explained how projects are financially pieced together during the development stage (before production can commence). In this chapter we'll explain the variety of ways in which content can be bought, sold, repackaged, repurposed and further exploited long after its initial release window.

▶ FILLING IN THE GAPS

Since consumer audiences are always seeking out new media content, the executives managing those direct-to-consumer (D2C) services are in a constant hunt to acquire media-fresh and/or engaging properties to keep their viewers tuned in. And for the distribution companies that feed these D2C companies to remain successful, they need to be constantly offering a steady and consistent pipeline of new content so that this business cycle can remain in motion. As consumer interests change, so will the demands of the buying clients, which directly affect which media properties distributors choose to supply. In a nutshell, this is the entertainment industry's 'supply and demand' workflow.

The role of an acquisition executive employed by a distribution company is to keep this pipeline flowing by ensuring a strong and profitable slate of media properties are acquired for a price the company can afford.

DOI: 10.4324/9781003357902-4

The problem is that audiences demand 'high-profile' or 'premium' content (which is generally extremely expensive to produce). And what might pass for high-profile or premium differs by company; for a larger company it could be a multimillion-dollar investment into a film with A-list talent, whereas for a tiny company it could be securing low-budget genre pictures with a few C-grade actors. As a result, the obstacle most acquisition teams encounter when trying to flesh out a full content slate is that these higher-profile titles consume more resources; they often require larger financial commitments—such as sizable up-front payments called minimum guarantees (aka 'MGs')—that eat away at their allocated budgets. Even a frugal company might spend 55%–65% of its annual budget in order to secure just a handful of high-profile titles. But the problem is distribution companies need more than just a 'handful' to remain relevant in the marketplace; they need dozens of projects annually to keep the pipeline at critical mass. And with more exhausted budgets, acquisition teams must get more creative about filling in the gaps of their content slates in order to provide their sales teams enough ammunition to secure deals.

Enter the notion of acquiring finished content. The advantage for acquisitions executives is that there are plenty of available titles flooding the marketplace, which allows companies to strategically pick and choose. And since these titles are already complete, they can usually be acquired at a fraction of the cost that would otherwise be expected at the development or pre-buy stage. But by no means does this make finished content a free-for-all. Finished content still costs money to acquire, which means acquisition executives must carefully balance the real-world revenue potential of each property they review. And genre styles as well as content needs differ greatly by company (not just in terms of quality level but also in style and tone); sourcing and securing the right media property is a delicate balancing act, one that takes a great deal of time, patience and market experience.

▶ A 'BUYER'S MARKET'

Every day acquisitions executives around the world screen finished productions looking for new media properties. Years ago, the exhaustive level of 'material' they reviewed was more visible; their desks were usually buried under piles of VHS and DVD screeners (along with one-sheets, scripts and other 'marketing' documents highlighting the details of a given program or film). Today, nearly all of this material has gone digital. Most trailers or full-length screeners are sent via Vimeo, Frame.io, YouTube or in some other easy-to-stream or downloadable manner, and all those marketing docs, scripts and one-sheets are now available electronically. But these innovations certainly haven't made the workload for an acquisitions executive—or their teams—any lighter. In fact, acquisitions teams probably have far *more* content to review today than ever before.

For every digital innovation that allows film and TV content to be produced more cheaply and efficiently, the more ease first-time producers have to make projects (creating a major increase in the amount of available content to screen). And whenever an overabundance of 'new available stuff' develops (whether it be houses, cars or movie rights), we shift into what's called a 'buyer's market'. A buyer's market essentially means that there's more 'supply' than 'demand' and that buyers have far more selections than they might have had previously; this means they get to be extra choosy and selective (and generally acquire at lower price points).

But by no means does that infer that acquisition executives have an unlimited expense account to work within; they too must work within very tightly monitored financial boundaries keeping their decisions at bay. Each company works in a different manner, but ultimately, a certain level of money is set aside for the sole purpose of acquiring new content (and it's the acquisition exec's job to ensure it's used in the most strategic and frugal manner possible).

If an acquisition exec spends too much on a title that doesn't sell well, it's a problem. However, if they buy quality properties that consistently generate profitable returns, they're often awarded with bigger buying budgets (which allow them to acquire higher-end content).

Some acquisition execs have a certain level of autonomy—meaning they get to decide the level of spend without too many internal or managerial approvals. Other buyers need to present a case for why each property is worth the investment (regardless of how little the price or license fee might be).

Because each acquisition has a measurable success or fail figure attached, acquisition executives have to be very mindful for how a potential title might work in the long run. Acquisition executives at a distribution company will be judged on how profitable a title is, whereas the lead buyer at a TV network is judged on an acquired property's broadcast ratings. A close friend of mine—who happens to be a major buyer at one of the major SVOD companies—confided that they are measured on how long a viewer 'invests' with a particular acquisition (a metric that is still kept quite confidential, despite the evolution of semi-visible VOD 'ratings'). As they screen and evaluate content, they will home in on the product that helps their overall company's content objectives while also satisfying their individual targets so that they can gain more flexibility, authority and autonomy in the decision-making process.

▶ THE ACQUISITION WORKFLOW

The process of acquiring finished content is much more elongated than most give due credit. After filtering out the weaker projects, acquisition teams must still present the top contenders at regularly scheduled 'new content' meetings so their sales teams can piece together 'projections' (or estimates on what they believe the marketplace will pay for such titles)—that is, assuming, of course, the sales teams see merit or potential in the content. Every company evaluates new content in a different manner. Some companies work in very formal ways such as holding 'content meetings' and screening trailers or clips for the sales and marketing teams with catered lunches, while others just forward screening links to potential titles to team members and gauge general interest by means of email response. For other companies, only the top executives are included in the decision-making process, while in other offices, everyone gets a chance to voice their opinion (including interns, juniors, etc.). Regardless of internal workflows, once teams compile financial projections, the acquisition executives make calculated decisions on which projects to bid upon—including how much capital they're willing to potentially invest. Some negotiations are successful (and the titles are acquired); others fail. Although the exact number of media properties acquired by any given distribution company varies radically dependent on its size, successful companies know their minimum threshold to maintain a reliable profit margin and do what's necessary to ensure they hit it.

The whole process really breaks down into eight steps:

- ▶ Reviewing

- ▶ Screening

- ▶ Projecting

- ▶ Acquiring (aka Procurement)

- ▶ Delivering

- ▶ Marketing

- ▶ Selling

- ▶ Reporting

Reviewing

When acquisition executives 'review' submitted content, they're not simply watching material to source whether it's good or not; they're actively looking for content that fits their company's brand or mandate.

Every distribution company has a sweet spot; a unique content offering (or 'flavor') that it reliably delivers to audiences more effectively than its competitors. Think about a few select television networks for a moment; compare HBO to Nickelodeon, Disney to A&E or, in the world of 'news', compare Fox News to MSNBC. Ratings and metrics have helped each of these networks find a hook or an angle to offer their identified target audiences, allowing each to build programming slates effective at keeping their specific viewer base entertained, engaged and loyal. A program might be spectacular, but does it fit the brand? Since a distributor's customer base (theaters, channels and VOD platforms) ask these questions, so too must the distributor.

Although the subtleties of 'on-brand' content might not be so clear-cut from the outside—and perhaps internally it's hardly spoken of and more of an 'unwritten rule'—the first litmus test of any acquisitions team is to ask whether a film or TV program they're reviewing is on-brand or not (meaning whether it meshes well with the rest of their content library). Just as an actor can get typecast, so too can distribution companies. Some distribution companies have become so focused on a particular niche or genre that they've actually made a name for themselves as being the 'go-to' company for a specific type of content (e.g., the way Asylum is known via its focus on properties like *Sharknado*).

Screening

Acquisitions execs have eagle-eyed vision when it comes to screening content. Although they might seem distracted given that they tend to 'screen' content on a background TV while they're hammering away at emails (or have two monitors on their desk, the program playing on one while they're typing away at emails or reports on the other), they have seen so many screeners that they can generally tell within seconds after pressing play the quality level and production value of the entire project. However, in addition to plot and whether or not a title fits the company mandate, acquisition executives have more granular questions that only screening a title in full can answer:

▶   **Are There 'Name' Actors On-Screen?**
Nothing makes a project easier to sell than recognizable talent; it's what gives buyers and audiences a semi-subliminal 'seal of approval'. Audiences flipping through channels will stop when they see a familiar face; therefore, distributors gravitate toward content offering those opportunities. And it's not just narrative movies or TV series that require name talent; a documentary with a solid recognizable actor serving as narrator or 'talking head' host is just as important. Although not having a recognizable name is certainly not a deal-breaker, it does make the project harder to justify taking on. Also, known talent needs to be the right talent for the project; the casting has to make sense in relation to story, but also in relation to genre—for instance, content in the faith/family genre would require wholesome name talent that's generally 'accepted' by that audience base.

▶   **Does the Running Time Make Sense?**
Running times that are way too short or way too long simply don't work. Programmers and schedulers cannot use them, or if they did, they'd be obligated to either reedit the program or fill the gap with another odd-running property to appropriately fill the remainder of the time slot. Studio content can occasionally get away with this due to their output deals—along with original network or VOD properties since they effectively own their own platforms. But for finished content being received by acquisition execs, it needs to match a time window that makes sense (see 'Running Time' in glossary for examples of acceptable running times).

▶   **Is the Program Faithful to Its Genre?**
Many first-time filmmakers—especially ones trying to make a name for themselves—are tempted or are under the false impression that they should break established genre conventions and shatter expected storytelling parameters in order to stand out. While

good in theory, this behavior doesn't translate well to distributors (primarily because audiences generally don't like these unexpected surprises). When distributors see a project pitched as a comedy, it'd better be a comedy from start to finish; or if a film is pitched as a family title, there'd better be nothing edgy or questionable thrown in to skew it off course. In no way am I suggesting there cannot be some wiggle room within here—or that distributors desire only predictable clichés (because they certainly do not)—but a project must deliver what it promises; it must 'fit in the box', otherwise it becomes problematic to sell. Consider the Emmy-winning MGM/Hulu series *The Handmaid's Tale* (2017); on one hand, it broke new ground with its futuristic dystopian storyline—told in 'present' tense with multiple flashbacks—while on the other hand, it never forgot at heart it was confined to the genre conventions of a woman-in-peril thriller. If a project is too far outside the genre boundaries, it poses a potential risk of being a difficult 'sell' (consequently being seen as a risky acquisition).

▶ Does It Feel 'Complete'?

Just because a project is said to be complete by the producer doesn't mean that it meets the industry standard of being complete (meaning that it's fully deliverable and broadcast/premiere ready). Does the sound mix feel complete or are there misbalanced audio levels, dropouts or visual sync errors? Does the look of the project feel as if it's been fully color corrected and balanced? Even if the artwork or trailer need to be spruced up to make them more 'marketable', does it feel as if there's enough elements to pull from (e.g., stills)? Just as a film editor knows when they've nailed a particular scene, an acquisition executive has an equal level of expertise in knowing if a project is truly 'completed'. (Incidentally, a project that's *almost* complete—meaning it might just need a small amount of work to reach the finish line—isn't necessary out of contention, but it does raise several legitimate questions about how much more effort (or cost) might be required for it to reach the completion mark and who will be expected to front those expenses.)

▶ Are There Any Red Flag Legal Issues?

A red flag legal issue for an acquisition executive relates to something seemingly insignificant yet, with years of experience, they recognize as a major obstacle later on down the line. A perfect red flag example would be a scripted feature film filled with commercial music tracks. While a director or editor might love the feel a particular song provides, an acquisition executive questions whether the rights have been fully cleared. Oftentimes novice filmmakers will include a few tracks with the hopes that a distributor might pay for the clearance on their behalf, but this rarely happens. Other red flag examples include major brand names or corporate logos appearing throughout the title, 'on-location' scenes with questionable releases or visible 'clips' from other sources of media. These are generally red flags of a film that lacks proper clearances and is therefore risky to acquire.

▶ Are There Opportunities for Repeat Seasons or Sequels?

With the amount of work and marketing spend required to properly release a title, the notion that additional seasons, sequels or prequels might be available later down the line is very appealing to acquisitions teams. Future versions can piggyback off the success of the original by tapping into an already-identified audience (allowing for a relatively safe investment by the distributor to evolve into an ongoing stream of reliable revenue). Although many projects claim sequels, prequels or additional seasons are well within the realm of possibility, only a handful of movies, TV shows or new media titles truly warrant additional variations; veteran acquisition executives have a strong eye for identifying the projects worthy of such traction.

▶ **Does It Fit Our Catalog?**

Content needs to fit the overall brand of the company. So when acquisition executives screen a new project, they often filter media properties via whether or not they 'blend in' with other titles in the company's existing library. A distribution company known for strong family films probably wouldn't show much interest in horror content. Equally, a company with a reputation for long-running non-scripted reality shows likely wouldn't invest money into scripted drama content. Distribution companies find their own niche strength in the marketplace; once they've identified which genres and formats generate the bulk of their revenues, they tend to stick within those guardrails.

▶ **Is It Good?**

Acquisitions execs are not watching screeners for entertainment value; they're reviewing content to measure its revenue-generating potential. They serve as the voice advocating whether a project is worth the company investing money to acquire for the sole purpose of profit (not simply because a project was emotionally engaging). It is vital that a film or program be 'good'—and it should be a given that the project is 'good'—but above and beyond a project being 'good', it needs to have marketable attributes that help make it a strong program to acquire (one that will ultimately help the company's bottom line).

Projecting

After content has been vetted out as fitting the company's 'brand' or mandate—and after the content itself is deemed worthwhile to consider—there's still a critical step that must be taken prior to acquisition executives making any type of offer or bid for the content. They must forecast revenues (or project future earnings). After all, they need a real-world understanding of how much a particular project might contribute to their company's bottom line in order to make an appropriate offer. (Spending too much and having a title sitting as a negative value to the company's books raises eyebrows about an acquisition exec's ability to make wise choices and handle a budget; they need consistent profit-generating titles to be seen as successful.)

An acquisitions executive certainly doesn't handle this process on their own; they reach out to the company's sales team for insight. Since sales executives are the ones managing the negotiations of content deals directly with potential buyers (with 'boots-on-the-ground' experience), they're the ones with the most up-to-date market values on any given genre.

During the projecting process, sales execs will review the titles of potential acquisition and note down the values they believe are realistically achievable should a deal move forward within each global territory they manage. This is where most books continue with the notion that the sales and acquisition teams come to some sort of utopian consensus of values, but that's not always the case. While in most scenarios the sales team offers clear values for each territory and the acquisitions team works with the figures presented, there are instances of internal manipulation that are important to note (that are rarely discussed outside of closed boardroom meetings):

▶ **Not All Projected Values Are Achievable**

The likelihood of a deal on a movie or program in *every* country on earth is very remote; in all my years of brokering content deals, I've never secured a deal in every country unless it was a blanket 'worldwide' deal—which is really just passing the buck to the next company. Certain countries (e.g., North Korea, Somalia, Afghanistan, etc.) simply aren't likely territories to sell. But it's not limited to war zones or failed states; some programs simply don't 'travel' in certain places. American-produced comedies with heavy dialogue have a very difficult time outside of the English-speaking world (when they're dubbed, the jokes just lose humor). Therefore, if a sales executive manages ten international territories, they might feel that a deal is realistic in only two or three; but for a rights holder to see seven or eight blank spaces when being presented an acquisition offer doesn't exactly offer much reassurance. So it's very common for sales executives to put down 'potential' numbers if a deal were to ever take place in each country (even when they know a deal is 99.999% never going to take place).

▶ **Numbers Are Inflated**

When a company really wants a project (when they know they can do some solid business on it), 'real-world' numbers sometimes aren't enough, so they inflate the values. Perhaps a sales exec screening a major film knows he or she can secure at least USD $75,000 on a deal in the UK; in order to 'secure' the title, they might offer a range instead, stating that a title could be worth between USD $75,000 up to $150,000 (looks better on paper). Even though the deal would more than likely close at $75,000, producers often see that $150,000 and ignore the rest. It's not just the sales execs that pull this stunt; occasionally the numbers all come in, and during the negotiation process, it's not adding up to a total figure large enough to make the deal make sense to a producer, so it's sometimes the acquisition executive fudging these numbers into the higher end.

▶ **People Play Favorites**

Just as sales agents tend to sell to the same clients, acquisition execs tend to buy from the same producers. Occasionally a relationship between a distributor and a producer is a strong one (whereby the producer comes to that particular acquisition executive each time they have a new project); it sometimes makes long-term sense to take on a title to maintain this relationship—even if it goes against the collective opinions of the sales team or conflicts with company mandate. Perhaps a title has a medium level of interest and the sales executives projected low figures, but if the producer churns out three or four factual titles per year (many of which are very strong), it might be worthwhile to take on the weak title to maintain the output. This can work in the opposite manner as well; distributors have been known to block titles or opportunities from specific producers or production companies (especially ones seen as competitors to or in contrast with their current base of relationships). Even if the 'new' opportunity seems promising, it could disrupt the longer-term relationships they've been reliant upon for a number of years and therefore poses too much risk.

Eventually, the acquisition exec compiles all the raw projections—creating both a real-world internal expectation they'll use for internal budgeting and forecasting along with an idealized 'high end' goal they'll use to convince the producer they're 'the best fit'—and extrapolates a likely gross value. Next, they'll reach out to the project's producer or rights holder to begin the actual negotiation process. At first, it's to gain a sense of what the producer needs to secure the title (e.g., is the producer expecting a certain level of MG, etc.). This info-gathering session coupled with the raw projection numbers are the two major variables an acquisition exec needs to begin the process of making a first offer as well as knowing when the title becomes no longer worth the effort of acquiring.

That last point is crucial; just because a sales team and acquisition team love a project doesn't mean there isn't a breaking point for when the title no longer makes sense to acquire. Perhaps a producer has unrealistic expectations, or perhaps certain required holdbacks dramatically skew the projections the sales team calculates. Bottom line, there is a middle ground where both sides win, but there is also a 'red line' whereby a distributor knows when it's time to cease their efforts on a specific title and move onto another.

(For examples of projections forms and the workflows involved, check out Appendix V.)

Acquiring (aka Procurement)

Once an acquisition executive has a general consensus of what numbers the sales team feels they can generate, they have a key piece of data they can use to put together an offer. By knowing about how much a title can realistically earn, they can work backwards to calculate how much of a distribution fee they'll need to take in order to make the project profitable along with how much of an up-front advance—if any—they're willing to spend to make their offer interesting to producers.

Although we go into great depth regarding the actual workflow of the dealmaking process in Chapter 4, there are a few unique ways an acquisitions team evaluates a finished content deal versus a sales team. For starters, if a sales deal falls apart, that's a loss in bookable revenue for the company; if an acquisition falls apart, it's technically a savings. Even though it is crucial for a distribution company to have a constantly updated slate of fresh titles to sell, there is a general understanding that if a title becomes too complicated, expensive or simply too burdensome to acquire, it's probably a blessing in disguise to simply pass. That means there is a clear red line from an acquisition team's end of the bargaining table that cannot be crossed; this puts the power primarily in their hands (and not in the hands of the producers). By no means does this imply the producers do not have several points that they can alter or shift toward their favor, but it must be understood that there are limitations at play. At this phase, the acquisitions team is working to gain a sense of what the producer might 'expect' if a deal moves forward. Are they seeking a crazy level of up-front money? Do they seem realistic about the process? How much 'hand-holding' will be involved if this title is taken on?

But let's evaluate the middle ground, where both parties are reasonable and a deal will move forward. In this zone, it's about finding points of compromise and making them a reality. Producers generally want as much money as they can receive up front; although they're likely willing to give away more years to a term or expand the range of territories a distributor takes to get there, at first they'll try to keep the years to a minimum and the range or territories quite limited.

Producers, for the most part, get paid out over a long duration of time. A deal that can put more up-front money in their pocket is very appealing because, more often than not, producers are heavily indebted to investors or unions/guilds they've had to make financial promises to in order to secure funds. When a deal is signed, investors and unions tend to request their amount due in full (so a distributor that can help in this area has a major upper hand in negotiating some strong terms).

Delivering

A title is never fully 'acquired' until all the material assets—the master files, artwork, legal paperwork, etc.—have all successfully (i) been delivered to the distributor and (ii) have all passed the rigid quality-control process (where a lab or tech team makes sure that all media files meet minimum technical requirements making them 'sellable' in the global market, and a business affairs team verifies they're in possession of the program's full chain of title). In addition, many companies do not consider a title fully delivered until it's truly ready to sell, meaning the trailer and artwork are uploaded to the distributor's website and that it's listed in the company's catalog.

We go into great detail about the types of material elements commonly required during a title delivery in Appendix IV, but for purposes of workflow, I will assure you that this process is much smoother than most are led to believe.

There are absolutely certain minimums required to make a title sellable, but when a producer is unable to deliver everything according to the technical specs, operations teams working on behalf of the distribution company are generally quite open to finding solutions. If there is an advance, minimum guarantee (MG) or other up-front payment the distribution company is willing to pay for the rights to the title, it is customary for them to hold these funds (at least a portion of them) until a full delivery is made. It's important to note that these up-front payments are being shelled out for the right to distribute the film (which means it's understood the film must be in sellable shape for the monies to be owed); producers hoping to get these funds in advance to then spend in order to create the necessary materials are usually a bit frustrated when they learn otherwise. That said, as long as a title meets certain minimum necessities to be sellable—and the other required materials can be created from what exists—there is a way to reach a completed delivery.

Marketing

One of the key components required during the delivery process are copies of performance agreements and talent releases; this is by no means just to ensure no unexpected claims from talent in the future, but also because for many 'name talents', there is very specific language included with regard to how their name, image and likeness can be used in marketing campaigns.

Years ago, I was selling a great thriller called *Dolan's Cadillac* (2009), starring Christian Slater and based on a short story by Stephen King. We only had select international rights (meaning a lot of the world, including the US, was already spoken for by other companies; we were picking up smaller territories that we happened to be very strong in). We wanted to redesign the poster so that it'd be impactful to our buyers and show off Christian Slater's star power. The first thing our marketing team did was comb through the performance releases to find out what restrictions were imposed. Were there minimum or maximum sizes we could print his name? How big could his face be in relation to other cast members (including costar Wes Bentley of *American Beauty* (1999) fame)? Were we required to show a minimum number of other cast numbers if we put Slater on the poster, or could he be front and center? These are the real-world questions marketing teams must ask.

I brought up *Dolan's Cadillac* because it's not always just cast members with strict parameters we're allowed to work within when pushing and marketing; this movie was based on a short story by Stephen King. King's contract literally had a giant block of text (nearly two full single-spaced small-print pages) about how his name could be used in relation to marketing the project. At first I couldn't believe how overly particular his lawyers were, but after a few readings I realized it was just a very specific way that his name would be given proper credit for the work and not exploited or misrepresented. Go check out all the films that have been adapted from his novels or short stories; you'll notice they all have the same wording (and that none of those films or programs leech off his name as a cheap marketing ploy).

Distribution companies do incur costs during the marketing phase of acquiring a title. It costs time and money to design and print one-sheets and catalogs. On higher-profile titles, special ads might be purchased for market circulation. At markets and festivals, there are dozens of trade magazines available to buyers and sellers; these are often filled with full-page ads and editorials pitching and promoting new content offered by distributors (all of that costs money). On the low end, a full-page ad in an internal trade magazine can go for $1,500 or more; that's for one ad in one magazine. Higher-profile trades can charge $25,000 or more. And buying out the landing page of high-traffic websites (e.g., IMDB, etc.) can easily surpass six figures.

As a result, there are often permitted marketing expenses included into acquisition deals (that allow the distribution company reasonable flexibility in pushing and promoting titles). These commonplace allowances are often 'capped' based upon the level of the title (for instance, a small indie film with a micro budget might cap its marketing expenses around $1,000 to $2,000, but for high-end titles with name talent, these can easily extend into high five-figure numbers (or more)). On higher-end titles, there are sometimes minimum spends associated (meaning a distributor is required to spend money on marketing and even purchase full billboards, banner ads or on-air promos); these can easily rise into the seven-figure zone on larger projects.

These costs can also be used to recreate trailers if the present version isn't 'salesy' enough.

Selling

Although acquisition execs are rarely involved in the sales process of the distribution game, they do take a keen interest in how titles they've acquired are performing. They do this for two reasons: (i) they need to be able to speak intelligently to the producer as to how their project is performing (either with positive news, or to prepare reasons as to why sales might be lagging), and (ii) they need to be able to justify their decision in having moved forward with a specific project.

But another key role acquisitions execs perform during the sales process is serving as a sort of mediator. More often than not, offers on specific titles don't come in at the level anticipated by (or projected to) producers—or they can sometimes include unexpected terms that require discussion. There are times when films or programs simply aren't gaining any traction, and the few deals that are in play are far below projected license fees or have unexpected terms or conditions. Since acquisitions execs were the ones holding hands with the producers through the acquisitions process, they often serve as the go-between in such situations. They might call the producer to reassure them of the sales team's efforts. They might request permission to move forward with a deal that's below the projected value. They might act to better position a seemingly 'mediocre' deal that's actually a strong opportunity even though it seems weak on paper. There are often occasions when deals come in that slightly cross the rights line (meaning a deal might arrive that requires 'rights' not expressly assigned to the distributor). An example of this might be a distributor picking up 'international' rights to a media property (meaning without US and Canada). However, a sales agent receives an offer for South American rights that include Puerto Rico (a US territory) and US Spanish-speaking rights (meaning the production can broadcast in the US, but only in the Spanish language). Based upon the level of the deal—a polite way of inferring how much profit margin can be gained—the acquisitions exec might reach out to the content producer to inquire how those specific rights might be acquired.

Reporting

After a distributor has commenced exploiting a title within its territories—and has started closing deals—it is customary to 'report' to the producer the sales activity. This is done by sending a statement of financial data related to the media property summarizing how much money the project has cost to distribute, how much it has earned and, therefore, how much is due to the producer (based upon their negotiated terms).

During the negotiation phase, the level of reporting (and payments if monies are due) is agreed and often listed in the actual contract. Although each company works in a different manner, the general industry standard is that the producer should be issued a statement every quarter. Some companies only issue annual statements; others have an open database where the producer can log in for up-to-date results, but quarterly is the most common.

Although we go into more detail in Chapter 8 (Accounting Practices, Monetization and Business Practices), it's important to note that these are generally automated statements. Distribution companies have dozens of titles—the bigger ones have thousands—so these are often filled with random internal codes and potentially confusing language. (Think of these like automated insurance or government documents that sporadically arrive in your hands; they can leave one feeling a bit perplexed.) Producers have similar reactions (and it is often here where they experience what all those contractual terms they agreed to come into play).

Novice producers are often miffed when they see their first report or two with major negative numbers associated with their titles. Remember, it costs a great deal of money for a distributor to take on a new title and get it out into the market—and it's expensive to attend those big markets where the business is done. Having a negative balance on a few reports is actually pretty common. However, if the negative numbers persist beyond the second report, it's perfectly reasonable for a producer to inquire when real monies are to be expected. Although some distribution companies do play creative accounting games to hold on to more cash, more often than not they are following the financial waterfall the producer agreed to during the negotiation phase.

▶ AUDITIONING NEW CONTENT VERTICALS

Just as sales teams work to improve revenues on a quarterly and annual basis (not just focusing on immediate targets), acquisition teams also have longer-term objectives. Examples can include scaling up the level of productions as well as delving into new content verticals. Focusing on 'finished' content is a great strategy to slowly step into this new realm.

Let's say a distribution company wants to shift its content mandate slightly; instead of low-budget horror films, it now wants to move into the realm of mid-level family-friendly titles (something completely out of its normal 'brand' and workflow). Rather than blindly going in early on a few projects (which requires a heavy financial commitment), they can allocate a much smaller portion of money to begin acquiring rights to several already-finished family-friendly properties. And since they're new to the genre, acquisition teams might screen and evaluate a much wider range of 'family' content to see what sticks with their slew of buyers (as well as ensure they have enough 'back catalog' to be seen as a real family-friendly provider in the marketplace).

With minimal investment, companies can use completed content to step into a new space and glean critical details about price points, marketplace realities and client relations to make informed decisions on whether or not to publicly step into a new genre vertical.

▶ WHERE DO ACQUISITION EXECS FIND NEW CONTENT?

Although company requirements and mandates might seem quite rigid, acquisition executives themselves are very open to reviewing new content and will always give a project a fair shot. Truth be told, one never knows the quality of a title—and how much revenue potential it might hold—until it is screened and thoroughly evaluated through the review process. That said, there's still the open-ended question of how and where acquisition teams find new content to screen.

Although there is no finite list, here are the most common places acquisition executives find new content to take on and how they approach each:

▶ Film and Media Festivals

These events would certainly include the high-profile events such as the Toronto, Cannes, Sundance and Berlin film festivals (among dozens of others), but also include numerous smaller-tier festivals—although there are way too many to list, I'll just express here that niche festivals are just as likely to have serious acquisition teams seeking quality pickups. Contrary to popular belief, most of the titles at the major festivals are already spoken for and are being showcased for marketing purposes or award opportunities; it's quite the opposite at the mid-level to small-level festival range. Therefore, acquisition executives are able to meet with—or gain quick access to—rights holders and find out information up front. Important to note is that most of the major film and television festivals of the world are accompanied with a business-focused market as well.

▶ Film and Media Markets

Unlike the commonly glamorized 'festival' circuit where film and media properties are lauded and celebrated, the business-focused 'markets' are heavily trafficked by acquisition teams. MIPTV and MIPCOM are TV-focused 'markets' taking place in Cannes, France; both are majorly important regarding the business of media distribution yet hardly receive the attention as the major film festival. These are heavily professional events and offer few screenings. Primarily, clients have very packed schedules (arranged well in advance) where they meet key clients in a speed dating fashion. Small talk is minimal; pitches are from the angle of numbers and ratings rather than pizazz. And while the industry marvels at the red carpets of the Cannes Film Festival, few outside the industry discuss the hustle of the Marche du Film (film market) taking place concurrently. Same holds true for Berlinale along with its European Film Market (EFM).

▶ **Private Screenings/Premieres**

Many indie producers, production companies and producers' representatives bypass the targeted submission process and instead hold a private screening (sometimes called an 'industry' premiere) where key buyers from several distribution companies are invited to a single event. The assumption would be that such screenings take place in the evenings (with drinks and hors d'oeuvres), but oftentimes the more savvy teams will schedule these screenings for the morning or early afternoon hours. This allows busy acquisition teams the opportunity to plan in advance to either personally attend or ensure a member of their team is present during normal business hours rather than pulling anyone away from evening activities. There's very little of the intro speeches or 'thank yous' that you see at festivals; instead, there's usually just a very quick thank-you and intro to the business elements of the title (what territories are available, some of the key talent, along with budget information—all providing subtle clues to the 'range' a rights holder might require before signing the film over to anyone). Usually the film starts within three to five minutes of the anticipated start time. Also, unlike a festival screening, it's not really considered rude for people to be skimming emails on their phones or even stepping out of the screening early.

▶ **Agency Submissions**

Agents and top agencies rep more than just talent; they too have a hand in the distribution game. Occasionally they acquire the rights to titles at a very early stage in the hopes of bidding them out or securing strong projects for their own talent. Other times they hold onto rights of certain titles with up-and-coming talent they're repping (just to make sure it's signed over to a certain level of buyer). There are a variety of reasons, but it really boils down to the same thing as everyone else's reason for involvement: money. Agents will rep, broker and wedge themselves into any transaction taking place in Hollywood to get a cut of the action. The properties they possess are generally very high quality and require a minimum of six-figure buy-ins (or higher).

▶ **Producer's Representatives**

These are very well-connected individuals who serve as a great way for unsolicited projects to be placed in front of potential buyers in a professional manner. The win-win is that the producer's rep generally has a strong relationship with a wide range of buyers and can easily reach out. A great number of acquisition execs will have regular meetings or calls with producer's reps that they mesh with to get a general 'update' on what they have available. Although I wouldn't necessarily consider this a negative, it's important to understand that a strong relationship between an acquisition executive and a producer's rep might also have a precedent deal structure—meaning, since they've done a large number of deals, they more or less have terms they prefer sticking too. In some cases, these cookie-cutter terms might work out great for a producer; other times it might be a bit of a raw deal.

▶ **Blind Submissions**

Blind submissions of completed films and media properties do get evaluated, though it's important to note there's generally not as much priority placed onto these submissions (especially if no one recognizes where it came from or they don't arrive with obvious sellable attributes (e.g., name cast)). That said, companies with which I've been associated have acquired numerous properties by means of blind producer submissions, some of which have been quite successful given the low costs associated with their acquisition.

▶ **Recommendations**

Although acquisition execs certainly keep an open mind with regards to content, just like everyone else working in Hollywood, these are busy people and are always open to finding ways to sift through content more quickly. Content that is 'recommended' or presented from a trustworthy source is almost always screened more quickly (and with a more open mind) than blindly submitted or stumbled-upon content. These recommendations can come from anywhere: colleagues within the same company, acquisition executives working for competing companies, friends, family, etc. But remember that acquisition executives often develop close relationships to a handful of producer's representatives and agents they've worked with over the years, whose opinions and tastes match their own; a recommendation from these individuals would carry meaningful weight.

▶ NEGOTIATING THE DISTRIBUTION FEE

The distribution fee is the percentage of monies the distributor gets to pocket from every dollar generated throughout the distribution term. Keep in mind that not all dollars are equal; when distributors pay up front MGs or advances to secure the rights to a media property, they first get to recoup those monies (meaning they get to pay themselves up to that figure *before* the distribution fee structure takes effect). After recoupment, the distribution fee starts carving out its percentage, while other expenses—such as costs incurred to distribute the title (e.g., marketing expenses, materials expenses, etc.)—might eat up the remainder of each dollar. Again, we dive much deeper into all these accounting practices in Chapter 8, but it's worth discussing the general concepts here since these factors help acquisition teams decide what distribution fee a particular title is worth applying toward a specific film or media property.

There are really three ways a distribution fee is determined:

▶ **Is It 'High-Profile'?**—The more high-profile a film or media property, generally the *lower* the distribution fee. The reasoning here is that bigger projects have more market value (meaning the distributor has a stronger chance of major sales which gives the rights holder more leverage in determining the splits). A marketable film with a strong cast will yield big interest; in addition to simply putting up a large advance for the 'privilege' of distributing the property—which again is recoupable—a lower distribution fee (perhaps in the 20% or even 10% range) might be presented just to make the offer more appealing. But earning a low distribution fee on a high-caliber film can still yield strong benefits; a low percentage of a strong earner is probably worth more than a high percentage of a dud—besides, a high-caliber title generally gains more market attention, elevating the profile of a distribution company which can bring in stronger buyers and allow the sales team to negotiate stronger deals on other titles.

▶   **Will It Cost Money?**—Regardless of the 'level' of a particular media property, if there's the chance it might require above-and-beyond out-of-pocket expenses to acquire (in addition to MGs or advances), chances are a higher distribution fee will be required. If there's finishing work required (to mix audio or color correct), if there's incomplete marketing elements (meaning it requires a new trailer or revamped key art), or if there's legal matters (such as music clearances). The more up-front money a distributor must dish out to legally secure the title, the more they'll increase the distribution fee.

▶   **How Limited Are the Opportunities?**—Will this title sell? Are there clear and identifiable markets or platforms we could easily place this media property? Distributors weigh the efforts required to move a property against the likely levels of financial return. If a title is being picked up for a very limited rights (such as digital only or in limited territories), its distribution fee will be increased. If a title is not easily sellable—without name cast, complicated genre, etc.—then a much greater amount of effort comes in securing potential deals. And most of the deals that come into play will be package deals (meaning the complicated title will be included into a 'package' of other titles and sold at an overall reduced title-by-title price). During such a package offering, it's generally driven by a strong title (one that required more up-front cash to obtain coupled with a smaller distribution fee)—sadly, it's the lower titles that are sometimes used to pick up more of the financial weight.

▶ THE PRODUCER'S ROLE

I contemplated placing all content related to 'producer's role' into a separate chapter, but truth be told, acquiring a finished piece of content is a two-way street (and the producer's willingness to play ball is just as critical in getting an acquisition deal over the finish line as the acquisition executives). It's a great deal of effort for acquisition executives to find and bid on finished media content, but it's also a taxing experience for the producer. Distribution companies are generally evaluating dozens of titles each week, whereas a producer has several months—if not years—of invested time and money in one project. Not only do they need to work a deal they feel comfortable with, they oftentimes need to convince third-party investors it's the right move. Given that level of stress, even veteran producers sometimes have a difficult time dealing with the standardized workflows and delays of the acquisition process.

But eventually, in order to get a media property distributed in the marketplace, the rights holder or producer must put ink to paper and sign the rights over to a distribution team.

A major fear producers have is that they'll sign their title over to a distributor and that that'll be the end. That the communication they'd had with the distributor will cease, and they'll lose all visibility to how their project is performing (and what royalties/ payments they might be owed). There are certainly crooked distribution companies out there—but in truth they're few and far between. After all, it's a small industry; at the end of the day people talk. Word spreads quickly about a company with a bad reputation. But most producers will never sign their titles over to such companies, because they'd be able to read the 'crook' flags a mile away. Instead, the problems most producers encounter when signing over their finished title is really of their own doing (simple lessons they should have avoided but simply didn't know to watch out for).

Here are the most common ways producers negotiate against themselves:

▶ **Producer Approval**—I have witnessed countless deals fall apart due to having Producer Approval requirements built into a rights holder's contract. Although I am completely understanding of the desire a producer has to accept or reject a potential deal, I've also seen the damage it can cause. More often than not, producers have assumptions about how the distribution process works and fail to see how their single film fits into the big picture. So when a deal arrives and the sales agents negotiate out the terms, it is presented to the producer for approval—but generally they start critiquing a variety of terms within the overall deal rather than simply approving the deal and allowing it to move forward. From their perspective, they're protecting their title from a deal where they feel it's being undervalued, but in reality they are wedging themselves into a conversation at the end stages. Sales agents tend to get stuck in a catch 22 at this point. If they go to the producer too early, they often get their hopes up (very few deals truly pan out), but if they go too late, the producer might pull the plug last second and not approve a deal that the sales agent worked very hard to make possible.

▶ **Desperation**—When major film festivals or markets loom near, producers sometimes panic, fearing that if they don't sign immediately, they'll miss a huge opportunity (and that they'll have to wait for a full year before sales will start). Truth is there's a major market or festival nearly every other month; some even stack on top of each other—Sundance is in January, Berlin in February, with Hong Kong's Filmart and Austin's SXSW in March; you get the idea. But when a producer has their eyes on a big one, like the Cannes Film Festival, the notion of missing it can sometimes cause them to agree to terms that aren't in their favor or that might cause problems down the line (i.e., saying they have E&O insurance when they don't or not capping expenses (see later)). Although being reasonable, compromising and adaptable is always a must during any negotiation, being too aggressive to close a deal can sometimes backfire. And this is all assuming the deal closes; some producers get so desperate calling (and recalling) asking about the status of a contract that they push their hopeful distributors away.

▶ **Not Capping Expenses**—Distributors invest a lot of cash and resources when acquiring a title (even for films with no minimum guarantees); marketing and deliverable materials (media assets) are legitimate and significant line items. It might cost $4,000 or $6,000 to produce a flashy trailer, another $5,000 to design a poster art. And that's just to get the title out there. Later, during the sales process, a deal might close that requires closed caption files—a standard delivery requirement that many producers never provide when delivering their project—these will have to be created (and sometimes rush ordered for the deal to take place). All of the earlier-mentioned costs are legitimate out-of-pocket business expenses, but if these aren't capped at a reasonable allowable amount (say at $10,000 to $15,000 total on a low-budget indie film), then distributors will continue to bill back legit out-of-pocket expenses toward the producer. If a Latin American channel requires neutral-speaking Spanish dubs to be produced, then that cost would be placed back against the producer's revenues unless they cap the total allowable expenses. In the indie space, $10,000 to $25,000 would all classify as 'reasonable', but the lower the figure, the more advantageous to the producer. Although the figures vary widely depending on the type of media project, for an indie feature film, the out-of-pocket marketing expenses should be capped somewhere between 2.5% to 7.5% of the project's actual out-of-pocket budget.

▶   **Not Including Performance Benchmarks**—A fear many producers have when signing over their film to a distributor is that they'll hand it over for a five-year term but that it will just get shelved and forgotten about after only a few months. While this kind of activity rarely occurs intentionally, distribution teams do tend to focus more heavily on newer titles (meaning older ones can occasionally get overlooked). It is also common for distributors to pick up 'all rights' to a title but intend to primarily use it for VOD platforms only—which can have a significant impact on the producer's anticipated returns. Because of these real-world scenarios, it would be advisable for producers to have some kind of performance-related 'exit clause', ideally one related to performance benchmarks (whereby the producer can cancel the agreement should the distributor not deliver a certain minimum level of sales or revenue within a given time period).

▶   **Not Limiting Materials Requests**—A distributor deals with a wide range of direct-to-consumer clients, each requiring a unique material delivery. Some clients can work with a general mezzanine digital file of a media project; others need extremely complex conversions; some clients still require physical tape delivery. Therefore, when contracting with a producer or rights holder, it's to the distributors better interests to request the widest possible range of deliverable 'flavors' in an effort to cover all those potential requests later down the line that might cost a little excess cash. A producer should take time to understand what is being asked of them within a materials delivery list—and should check with someone familiar with the requests—otherwise they could incur a major 'negative' balance in their account through no fault of their own.

▶   **Playing Multiple Offers Simultaneously**—The notion of a 'bidding war' is attractive to some producers or investors, the idea that two massive companies love a project so much they're increasing up-front payments and reducing their takes just to get it in their hands. I've never really seen a true 'bidding war' take place. Most distribution companies know their limits, and most acquisition agents must work within budgets and approval workflows. And there's so many titles floating around at varying levels of completion that it would be very unlikely that a strong and marketable title worthy of a true bidding war would actually be completely available across the board. But in those rare circumstances where a title does meet these standards, a war of bids is not really what takes place. It's more that several companies will put their best terms together and make an offer. But once a better offer comes into play, there might be a little back-and-forth (or tweaking of terms), but after one or two rounds, most companies simply hold their position or back off rather than 'go to war'. And let's hypothetically say two companies truly did start battling it out in an attempt to outbid one another; the distribution business is very small (and people talk). Once it's clear that one of the companies is backing off, the 'winner' doesn't necessarily have to sign. They might waffle a bit, asking themselves if they've gone too far with their offer. They might even lower it a bit or pull some other move since they're now the only kid in the sandbox. And if that producer were to go back to the other offers, I would expect that they would have dropped a bit (no company likes to feel they're the 'plan B'). Also, each distribution company has their own dealmaking style (and distributors get to know their competition pretty easily). So when a producer tries to pull a stunt like saying, "well, a competitor is offering me XYZ terms", an acquisition agent will be able to see through the vagueness and know with whom that producer is likely speaking.

▶ **Dragging Their Feet**—There is a real phenomenon content creators feel as they near the end stages of their project. It's an almost 'fear' of being done, a mild panic about having a finished spec film or project. Once it's completed, they cannot change anything (it is what it is at that point). It's not uncommon for producers of finished content to reach out to distributors at the very final stages to initiate conversations and build interest. But I've noticed many films that are anticipated to being completed within a week or two start to drag out. It's as if the producer or content creator is finding little things to tweak in order to put off the inevitable. Needless to say, it's counterproductive, but it can backfire on producers because they might turn off the distributors to whom they reached out too early.

▶ **Focusing on the Wrong Things**—Anything in a contract is worthy of discussion, and it is expected that producers (or their representatives) will ask detailed questions about contractual language. But after a few rounds of redlines and other revisions between both parties, some producers start to nag on insignificant terms—dragging out the entire acquisition process—while ignoring vital clauses. Keep in mind that I'm generalizing here (and that no two deals are the same), but on one occasion, a producer I was dealing with kept skimming over important details—such as revenue share splits and marketing costs—to instead fight over the point that the acquiring distributor (meaning our company) should seek their approvals on price points posted by direct-to-consumer companies. The deal eventually fell apart because the producer was arguing a point that was essentially out of our domain. Whenever a contract is drafted, the receiving party should make any corrections and tweaks they feel necessary—specifically to put the terms of the deal more in their favor—but eventually, as both sides start cleaning up what can be worked with versus what is a nonstarter point (a term or condition that cannot be altered), smart producers start to focus on the things that will benefit them versus holding onto points that hinder the deal or change nothing.

▶ Spec Project Purgatory

Generally speaking, a film or media property only has market value if it's finished. A great number of 'spec' projects ('spec' meaning projects speculatively produced before a distributor or direct-to-consumer platform is secured) get close to completion and simply run out of funds, or they reach completion but have empty pockets and cannot effectively market or promote the project in a meaningful effort to get a deal closed. Unless an independent media project has a veteran producer on board who knows how to properly budget out for the end stages, most projects simply run out of steam.

So what happens to all those projects that are technically finished but not 'completed' enough to be considered 'finished content'?

More often than not, many of these projects sit on the producer's desk collecting dust. The belief far too many producers have is that a distributor will see the merit of a project and willingly invest the necessary capital required to both acquire as well as successfully distribute it. Many novice filmmakers cite micro-budget examples like *Paranormal Activity* (2007), *The Blair Witch Project* (1999), the *Terrifier* (2016) or the most famous example, Robert Rodriguez's *El Mariachi* (1992)—which cost $7,000 to produce, funded by Rodriguez himself being a human guinea pig for medial drug experiments—as if these were common scenarios. They're not. The problem is that most don't realize it cost hundreds of thousands of dollars for each of these titles to be cleaned up and made professionally 'complete' for release, and it is dangerous thinking for a novice producer to assume a distribution company will simply pick up their unfinished project and willingly cover the necessary expenses to complete it.

However, if a project is commercial enough and it ticks enough of the right boxes for the independent distribution space, then a distributor might move forward with a 'deficit finance deal' deal (where they 'acquire' a presently indebted or incomplete film, fund the 'gap' required to complete the title in lieu of an MG, then distribute the title). Although distributors generally reserve gap or deficit financing for titles in advance of their productions, this is a great way to scoop up lower-budget indie projects to beef up a library or quarterly slate.

The problem for the producer with a deficit finance deal of this style is that they hold absolutely no leverage. As our principles of distribution state, he who owns the gold makes the rules and buyers always buy more than what they need; both of these are almost always ironclad guarantees that a producer will be waiting quite a long while before they see a dime in returns.

▶ Internal Politicking

The distribution process only works if deals are getting closed. For distributors and producers alike, the workflow is pretty straightforward: distributors must broker and close deals that allow money to be generated, and producers must create and deliver commercial content that meets marketplace demands; both sides depend on the other's efforts equally to ensure success.

Yet behind closed doors, the efforts of lawyers, agents, technical teams, marketing teams, among many others, are absolutely vital to keep the entire system in full motion. One would assume these individuals or divisions would be fully supportive and collaborative during the distribution process—especially since it's their job to do so—yet ironically, their actions occasionally add roadblocks and obstacles to the process. By looking at distribution companies purely from the producer/distributor dynamic, it's easy to forget that each of these individuals or teams has their own company workflows, mandates and objectives. And additionally, the roadblocks they're putting up might be to the company's overall better interests (in terms of protecting the company against potential legal matters, problematic material setbacks or marketing conflicts).

Therefore, when working to acquire a finished media property, one major component to a distributors day job is not just brokering deals with outside parties but also brokering deals with internal ones. Balancing the risk aversion of one division while catering to the risk aversion of another isn't easy. Therefore, the seemingly simple process of acquiring the very content required to keep the system in motion is yet another layer distribution executives must deal with to get media properties they're passionate about through the acquisition process.

For anyone in a position of authority within each of these divisions, it's far easier to simply say no and pass on a particular project than to take a risk by saying yes. Saying yes and acquiring a project creates added workloads, costs money and opens the door for risk. If sales are slow, it's the acquisition executive who must relay the bad news to an upset producer; if legal matters arise, it's the business affairs team who must deal with third-party lawyers and claims; and if the producer is unable to deliver materials properly, the operations department can go through a lengthy process attempting to fix the title (which eats at their allowable budget). Teams are forgiving of these extra workloads when the title in question is successful; but if a title is a weak performer, all this effort feels as if it's simply gone to waste.

So on the surface, while it might seem that all these internal teams are cogging up the process—slowing down or even preventing the acquisition of commercial properties— they're really looking out for everyone's best interest from a macro perspective. Therefore, if an acquisition or distribution executive goes silent during the negotiation of a deal, chances are they're busy making the rounds to reassure those playing devil's advocate and gain internal support.

▶ FINAL COMMENT

We're often bombarded with a culture that stresses fighting for one's individual vision (that seems to encourage a 'take-no-prisoners' attitude toward deal negotiation); while it's very important to be assertive—standing up for yourself and your work—it's something else to jeopardize an opportunity by refusing to compromise with those who have the ability (and are willing) to work with you. Although good content will always gain the attention of the entertainment industry's decision-makers, it's generally the producers who learn how to play ball and compromise where and when appropriate who gain long-term traction in this business. As stated in our principles, entertainment is a business of relationships; one can be a team player without sacrificing their integrity.

4

Negotiating and Brokering Content Distribution Deals

▶ RIGHTS IN, RIGHTS OUT

For a content distribution deal to exist, you need three key elements: a buyer, a seller and a media property (meaning a film, TV program or other piece of media content). Assuming the media property is worthy of movement within the marketplace (that it's commercial in nature, of good production quality, etc.), the distribution deal is nothing more than an everyday back-and-forth negotiation between buyer and seller. Only this exchange has nothing to do with the buying and selling of the media property itself, but rather the transfer of its intangible rights from one party to the other.

Intangible media rights aren't just limited to a media property's means of transmission (e.g., theatrical, television or home entertainment rights), they also include a property's remake, clip and non-theatric rights (meaning airline, cruise ship or other specialty screenings) and extend to define the geographical boundaries of the rights (limiting the acquiring party to which country(ies) or regions it has the right to exploit the title within (aka its 'territory')), the permitted window of time the rights can be exploited (aka the 'term') and even what languages or formats a property can be distributed (e.g., defining the United States as either 'English-speaking US' or 'Spanish-speaking US').

When brokering these deals, the buyer's objective is to secure the widest scope of these rights for the least amount of cash. On the flip side, the seller's goal is the complete opposite (attempting to grant the narrowest margin of rights in exchange for the largest amount of revenue). But if buyers weren't closing acquisition deals, then we'd have no media to watch, and there'd be no ticket sales or ad revenues for buyers or producers to benefit from; and if sellers weren't brokering content agreements, there'd be no return on investment for themselves or the content's producers and, therefore, little incentive

DOI: 10.4324/9781003357902-5

for future content to get created. It's a food chain; since both parties *need* deals to close in order to independently stay afloat, there's always common ground upon which both sides can settle. This rhythmic rights-in, rights-out workflow is the heartbeat that keeps the film, television, and new media industries in motion.

(Sidebar: The concept of buying and selling a media property's rights rarely has anything to do with the transfer of its copyright. If a producer—or a producer's production company—owns the copyright, that ownership will not change when the producer enters into a deal with a distributor. The producer has instead leased out the property's rights to the distributor for the sole purpose of exploiting them for financial reward (similar to how a landlord leases a vacant apartment)).

But this leaves out many of the realities both buyers and sellers actually face in their day-to-day business activities that have a drastic effect on how they approach the deal-making process. In an ideal scenario, the negotiation works itself out naturally; both parties collaborate to get their minimum needs met and walk away with a balanced deal in hand. There is no ticking clock in an ideal world. And not surprisingly, this scenario is rarely how negotiations go down in the *real* world.

In the everyday real-world game of distribution deadlines are critical; and external factors such as marketplace trends, interest rates and/or broadcast deadlines have a major influence during the decision-making process. Content sellers are often held accountable to monthly, quarterly as well as annual sales numbers; when pressured, they're very likely to fold on a select few terms in order to get a deal closed before month's end (especially if they have a commission looming over their heads). For buyers, they have schedules, marketplace time frames and limited budgets to work with; buyers have their own key terms they're willing to fold on when a deadline is approaching.

Although the intentions of both sides are in the right place, it's these external pressures that play a starring role in how the bulk of distribution deals evolve from an initial prospect into a fully brokered deal—and ultimately affect how we as consumers experience our everyday media.

▶ QUID PRO QUO

One common—and shortsighted—view far too many distributors hold is that because they possess the content all other parties rely upon for success, they should exploit their leverage by pushing their buying clients to the financial edge (metaphorically holding them upside down and shaking every penny loose). Harsher demands, stringent payment terms, a 'fuck you, pay me' approach. Although this sounds great in boardroom presentations, in reality this behavior often results in very short-term and inefficient business.

Although film, television, and new media distribution is very much about brokering quality content, at its core, *relationships* fuel everything. The buyer is a distributor's lifeline in terms of staying in business; sellers live and breathe based upon the quality and level of the buyers they're in contact with. Even if a distributor secures the strongest catalog of content, without strong relationships with buyers (and the ability to work with them in a collaborative and efficient manner), few deals would get closed. A strong buyer/seller relationship is crucial for a distribution company to maintain steady and consistent dealmaking. If either side starts playing games or misrepresenting details, trust can be broken, causing those reliable revenue-driving deals to evaporate. And both buyers and sellers talk; it doesn't take long for a shady individual to gain a poor reputation (or a trustworthy one to be recommended).

Smart distribution companies know this; they're willing to fold and allow a little more leeway toward their trusted buyers to maintain these relationships. (And the same goes for buyers; they're willing to be flexible in order to maintain a close relationship with a trustworthy seller.)

This is in no way to suggest that either side is simply bending over backwards to accommodate the other. Buyers and sellers both must uphold their own integrity (as well as the better interests of the companies they represent). After all, no one respects a pushover. It's healthy in the buyer/seller relationship to give a little pushback on terms as each new deal opportunity surfaces—it's even acceptable for either party to pass on a deal to instead close with a competing client. It's about *how* it's done. That's the delicate dance distributors and their third-party buying clients play year after year.

▶ THE DEALMAKER'S MOTIVES

On paper, the vast majority of distribution deals are between two parties: (i) the party owning or managing the rights to a media property (formally called the "licensor" or the seller) and (ii) the party purchasing, acquiring or being granted select permissions to exploit that media property (the "licensee" or the buyer).

There are occasions when a third party might enter the scenario, for example an agent, producer's representative or any other 'brokering entity' that might have formally put the licensor and licensee into business together (similar to a real estate broker overseeing the sale between home seller and home buyer). Their presence within the agreement— and possible signature alongside the licensor and licensee's—is generally to have a clear paper trail for purposes of credit and/or to obtain a finder's fee or brokerage commission.

Although licensors and licensees are generally two separate companies (e.g., a distribution company as licensor and a television station or 'all-rights' movie buyer as licensee), the parties could just as easily be agencies, individuals (e.g., producers) or even personal estates (wherein rights to a media property are lumped alongside other assets). Regardless, every distribution deal clearly defines the licensor (or media seller) and licensee (as media buyer) by means of identifying the company name, location of their business address and the name(s) of select individuals representing each party.

But that's a very surface-level view. It's easy to read a contract and see two affixed signatures at the bottom and assume those were the two individuals brokering the whole agreement, but it usually requires a collection of individuals (working as employees, each with their own responsibilities) working as a team to get that signature on paper. Factor in that every company has its own unique corporate culture—which inevitably bleeds into its dealmaking style—and we gain a sense that social politics and timing play as important a role as the quality of the media property (and the prices being discussed). To truly understand the dynamics of the buyer/seller relationship, we need to uncover the common employee responsibilities of each party (and explain what these individuals need to keep the pipeline in full swing):

Licensors (aka 'the sellers')

Sellers are the ones with rights in hand or access to content with the obligation of 'moving it' in exchange for profit. Although this covers sales of 'finished' content, it can also include representation of optioned projects in development, 'paper' proposals or other forms of intellectual property (IP) that could warrant value in the marketplace (as outlined in Chapter 2). Responsibilities within the licensor's end of the agreement range from business development executives (overseeing a company's overall long-term goals) to sales executives (fixated on hitting monthly revenue targets). Here are the more common job descriptions filling this role and how they approach the dealmaking process:

▶ **Business Development/Distribution Executives**—Developing, producing and releasing a single film, television or new media property takes a great deal of time and money to successfully complete. And since distribution companies need a pipeline of consistently rejuvenated content to release for purposes of creating and maintaining cash flow, they generally have an individual (sometimes a few) on staff thinking long term. They ask the high-level questions, such as "What are the larger goals of our company and how can we get there"? (They contemplate a variety of distribution scenarios in order to mathematically see how different content volumes or alternative genres could potentially affect them years in the future). Not only are these 'big-idea' people with a clear vision of where they want the company to be in a few years down the line, they're also putting multiyear strategies in place (nudging their visions forward one day at a time). At smaller companies, these are often the CEOs or upper-level executives overseeing production slates and sales teams; at larger companies, these can be strategists called upon to map out game plans for new opportunities (reporting to the CEOs and upper-level execs). In general, these are well-paid individuals who are often sent to the film markets and festivals, wining and dining with big clients, and inventing large-scale opportunities. They're not focused on today or even this year, they're thinking five to ten years down the line. This level and above generally represents the executive tier of thinking—the top brass. Although business development (commonly referred to as 'biz dev' or simply 'BD') is sometimes the legitimate title of an employee's role, you can find these individuals leading the business affairs (or legal) teams, overseeing the entire sales team (as head of sales or EVP), heads of content acquisitions and development or serving at a senior level role that acts to 'filter' company decisions to ensure the CEO's vision is on course to be met. The content being acquired and later exploited by a distribution company would all need to first be vetted by this individual (as would the marketing strategies and the general approach for *how* top titles would be managed and presented to the marketplace).

▶ **Sales Representatives/Sales Agents**—Sales reps are the ones actually answering calls and meeting with global clients face-to-face in an effort to close finished content deals. On occasion they can dabble in the realm of 'presales', but for the most part, sales reps handle the very straightforward deal structures involved in brokering a media property's rights in exchange for money. They can perform a variety of roles (e.g., international sales representatives, whose primary focus is selling North American content to the rest of the world, or domestic sales reps, who manage foreign-produced content and sell it within their own borders). They know their product well enough, but their main target is meeting monthly or quarterly sales goals (and are likely to push their clients for 'add-ons' and 'upsells' by transforming a one-to-two title deal into a package of five or more programs). While the executives at a distribution company create company mandates of what content they'll represent (and what revenues must be brought in), these are the individuals making those visions a reality. When they succeed, they are highly rewarded through perks (such as bonuses and commissions), but failure can result in missed income opportunities—since a major compensation component is their commission structure—to outright termination. But this role is not without its influence within a company. Sales representatives possess valuable marketplace understanding that's crucial for a company's success. Since they're 'on the ground' working with their clients, they have the most up-to-date information regarding what content is trending, what real-world revenue exists for new content, not to mention a strong sense of marketplace timing. Executives tend to create strategies based upon the information and advice sales reps provide, internal acquisitions teams screen titles under consideration for their sales reps to gain a sense of what programs are worth their pursuit versus which to avoid and marketing teams generally consult with sellers since they know what their clients need to see in catalogs and trailers in order to 'buy'.

▶ **Indie Producers**—A great number of projects are produced completely on spec (meaning out of the pockets of an individual eager to make the film in advance of a traditional distribution deal); these can range from first-time filmmakers to very well established producers. As a result, once the film or media project is complete, producers can either represent the film or media project on their own or assign a producer's rep, agent or distribution company to represent the sale of rights on their behalf. Oftentimes, producers are so involved with their project (having spent years making it a reality) that they have difficulty signing over the rights to other parties. Nevertheless, for a film or media project to start generating money, an indie spec producer must serve as 'licensor' at least once to kick-start the process. There are often scenarios when producers attempt to manage the sales of their title independently; even well-connected producers generally fail at this approach since they often lack a full library of additional media properties distributors use to balance out their individual title (nor are they willing to fold to the external marketplace demands that commonly take place during the distribution process, to which distribution companies are more accustomed).

All three licensor 'types' work in smooth unison. Sales representatives have a clear understanding of what works in the marketplace (and how much revenue a particular title might be worth); the executives or business development execs have the authority to allocate monies towards producing and/or acquiring the content identified by the sales reps as worthy of movement; and the producers have the creative integrity to produce (either on spec or for hire) the very content being sought out by the executives and their sales teams. If any one of these three veer off course, the system gets off balance.

Licensees (aka 'the buyers')

Buyers, or more appropriately 'acquisitions executives', represent the party with cash in their pockets, intent on finding and purchasing profit-generating content. Not to add any confusion here, but buyers exist on both sides of the distribution workflow. While distribution companies (and their sales reps) sell media rights to their buying clients, that distributor must first acquire rights to those titles (and therefore have an acquisitions team on staff alongside their sales teams).

Finished films, TV pilots or any other project (at nearly any stage of development and/or completion), are all passed through the acquisition team's filter within a company. They might vary in size, but all acquisitions departments all have the same general workflows:

1) Content is formally submitted.

2) Content is 'logged' (meaning all details including genre, cast, budget, synopsis, etc. are clearly noted).

3) Content is evaluated (meaning content is screened by members of the acquisitions team, usually by someone quite junior who sifts the good from the bad, later by a top executive who makes the decision on which project(s) to move forward with; also during this phase, a more formal discussion is initiated between the acquisitions party and the licensor to understand 'expectations' on license fee, MGs, etc.).

4) Content is projected upon by the sales teams and marketing teams (the company needs to get a real-world sense of how much they expect to earn from a project along with the level of expenses they foresee).

5) Content is 'approved' and formally negotiated upon with the intention of an eventual acquisition of the media property's rights.

Acquisition executives generally follow a company mandate which they use as a filter while screening content (similar to the 'vision' created by the distribution executives)—for instance, an individual tasked with acquiring properties for a 'faith-and-family'-focused distribution company would have little interest in screening shoot-'em-up action films. Although the individual filling the role of acquisitions executive certainly has their own integrities and standards from which they view potential projects, they're able to place their personal tastes to the side in search of media properties that meet the needs of the company. Most acquisitions executives are given a budget to manage during each fiscal year; although they can allocate however much they choose on any particular title, they want to buy low as often as possible (and focus on titles with the strongest potential of returning a strong profit margin). The lower the cost against the stronger profit margin is considered being 'efficient' with money. Expensive titles might return a large profit on paper but generally not a massive profit margin above its initial expense (making a title 'less efficient'). The more efficient an acquisition executive is with the company's money, the larger budget they are provided to allocate during the next year. After a particular title is secured, their objective during the contracting phase is to take on as many rights across the widest possible territorial reach for the longest possible duration of time all for the lowest cost and least amount of revenue sharing—that way they can arm their internal sales executives with more opportunities to bring in higher levels of revenue (increasing the title's efficiency).

▶   **Programmers**—From the outside, this role may seem low-key—from the name, it'd be easy to assume a programmer to be nothing more than a button-pusher, simply plugging in a few shows where instructed by a superior. Although not as sexy as 'acquisitions executive', the programmer at a major broadcast network (or digital platform) holds a great deal of responsibility in executing an overall vision for the channel. They must sense where the audience will be months ahead of time (and have the right schedule of programs in place to captivate them into a continuous viewing experience). When they attend markets, they have tunnel vision for their content interests. They generally have minimum running time numbers, a minimum number of episodes required for a series, specific content formats and specific themes in mind (and rarely do they deviate from their needs). In addition to requiring very select types of content, programmers are straightforward with what rights they want and are fine dropping the rights they don't. Buyers by nature try to secure more with less, yet programmers are generally quick to shave off the rights they don't need (for instance, many channels try to 'future-proof' themselves by including VOD rights for any potential shifts later on, but if a programmer doesn't require VOD for their immediate TV needs, they're usually fine dropping these and moving forward without). Incidentally, programmers are just as necessary for streaming services—including ad-supported and Free Ad-Supported Streaming TV (FAST)—as they are for traditional broadcast networks.

▶   **All-Rights International Distributors**—Due to similarities in business workflows and content interests, most international countries or territories (e.g., Canada, the UK, Scandinavia, Australia, or Germany + German-speaking European countries, just to name a few) are relatively open to direct distribution deals with US-based companies. However, there are other regions in the world where attempting to broker deals directly is much more complicated. One might assume these regions are predominantly 'emerging markets' (a polite way of referring to the third world), but that's far from the truth; although territories such as the Middle East, Africa and Latin America would be included in the more 'challenging' list, so would several Westernized nations (including Spain, Italy and Japan). Again, it's not solely the quality of the content and the level of price that make it complicated to get business done in these more challenging territories; it all falls back to the point that the business of media distribution is largely fueled by relationships (and cultivating and maintaining relationships within certain territories is the heart of the problem). For example, not only is 'Latin America' comprised of over a dozen countries, each of which uses a different dialect of Spanish (or in the case of Brazil, Portuguese), each has a completely different economic status along with radically different levels of technological infrastructure. Add in the fact that there are only a small handful of powerhouse media entities (that act as monopolies, owned by powerful (and richly influential) families that follow their own rules and interests) coupled with heavy layers of bureaucratic red tape, and one can see that doing business in this part of the world can get quite complex. To solve this problem, global distribution companies will seek out the talents of 'regional distributors' to serve their interests within these complicated corners of the world. A regional distributor is generally a company acting as a 'middleman', one that's established and has existed within a complicated region throughout their careers and can serve as a fixer or 'expert' on getting business brokered. They know all the players and know the tricks of the trade to see return business. US-based distributors will often seek out and enter into exclusive deals with regional distributors to represent either a single title or their entire library. Once the deal is secured, that regional distributor will effectively manage all rights to all title(s) granted with the expectation of delivering results. It's common for regional distributors to dub and/or subtitle the media properties (and accompanying marketing materials), and in certain parts of the world, it's understood that these regional distributors must 'grease the wheels' of the big media buyers in order to ensure business (by means of bribes, kickbacks, etc.). Regional distributors also leverage their entire libraries to broker package deals with the local players (meaning a regional player could easily use a major studio title in their catalog to lump in a package of films pulled from several other of their indie 'clients'). There is always a bit of a vetting process when entering into a deal with a regional distributor, but more often than not it's the only way to truly gain traction across the board. For studio-level content, regional distributors must fork over a large amount of capital for the exclusive right to represent all rights to top-tier content, but indies' regional distributors can pick up entire libraries for nothing more than a revenue share.

▶ PHASE 1: THE INITIAL OFFER

There are plenty of scenes depicted in movies and TV shows about Hollywood that present the acquisition and sales process as some high-intensity battle (e.g., screaming phone calls, face-to-face boardroom bidding wars, etc.). Although I will certainly agree that there are extremely high-stress situations throughout the dealmaking workflow (and a few larger-than-life eccentrics to be dealt with at all levels), on the whole, the actual dealmaking workflow is relatively straightforward—more akin to a slow-moving chess game rather than an episode of *Entourage*.

Usually when an offer is made, it's done via a simple email laying out the broad-stroke terms. There are certainly times when these matters are discussed by phone or in person (especially at markets or film festivals, when the competition is high and time is of the essence), but eventually it's got to be put in writing for things to progress.

For smaller companies, deal terms might be casually sent in the body of an email; for larger companies, their legal teams generally draft formal 'term sheets' with precise legalese and additional language stating deadlines for response (explaining that the offer still requires internal approvals and is not legally binding, etc.)

Here are the general deal points thrown out at this initial stage:

▶   **Title:** usually restated, just so there's no confusion later in the process; also important to list out all titles for larger 'package deals'

▶   **Territory:** listing the country or geographical area the acquiring company wishes to exploit the property within. For example, are we talking about the single country of France or all 'French-speaking *world*', which includes Africa, Polynesia, Switzerland and Belgium?

▶   **Rights:** the exact rights (e.g., television, VOD, airline, DVD, or even simply 'all rights' etc.) the buying company wishes to exploit. They can also state whether these rights are required to be exclusive to them or nonexclusive—meaning 'shareable' with other entities

▶   **Term:** the amount of time the buying company wishes to manage the property. Usually listed in number of years (e.g., 'two (2) years') but could also be listed in months (e.g., 'twenty-four (24) months')

▶   **Start Date:** an exploitation 'window' is a defined period of time whereby the licensee may exploit the media property. Usually there is a clear 'start date', which defines the official date a licensee's term commences. Generally this is a date set several months in the future to allow time for the licensee to properly pay the license fee and for the licensor to properly deliver the material elements required for the licensee to broadcast or otherwise exploit the property. In the case of presales or coproductions (which require action by third parties such as levels of outside financing, select cast members being secured, etc.), start dates can be established years in the future and might even be contingent on certain 'events' taking place (for example, a minimum level of capital being raised, etc.). For second-window deals (meaning deals closed later in the life of a property), these 'start dates' might be ruled by an event such as a minimum period after the title's initial premier date

▶   **Holdbacks/Restrictions:** a buyer acquiring Pay TV rights might insist they have the rights for a minimum period of time (e.g., six months) *prior to* the seller licensing an alternate—and potentially competing—right such as SVOD rights; this would mean the first six months of a two-year term would restrict or 'hold back' the SVOD window, whereas the remaining eighteen months allow it

▶ **Language:** most countries (or territories) have overlaps of multiple languages being spoken (e.g., Canada has both English and French, the US has English and Spanish) the exact use of language is clearly stated to avoid unintentional conflict). This can also be defined in how the languages can be used (e.g., for the US, a title might be restricted to native English but allow subtitles of Spanish while restricting dubbed audio Spanish tracks

▶ **Runs:** a limitation is always applied defining the number of times the acquiring party can 'broadcast' or exhibit the media property. In the case of a theatrical run, it could be limited to a number of weeks, for a TV program it could be limited to a number of transmissions (also called 'telecasts' or 'playdates'), and in the case of a VOD deal, the word 'unlimited' might be stated since no restriction actually applies

▶ **License Fee:** this is the amount of money the buying company is willing to put down for the acquisition of the rights. If this is a structured 'flat' payment, it's referred to as a license fee; if there are royalties or additional contingent revenues added on top, this down payment is called a 'minimum guarantee' (MG) or advance followed by language detailing the revenue share model that will be used for future payments.

Setting Precedents

Either party can submit the first offer, but getting the offer in first is all a part of distribution strategy. Generally it is the buying party who submits the initial offer (listing out the most advantageous parameters they can, along with a price point and duration of term). But a seller can just as easily put together an initial deal proposal spelling out the same points. Once a formal offer is put forward and the basic terms (price, rights, territory and duration of term) have been established, a line has been drawn in the sand. Certainly all of the previously offered terms are open for negotiation (and will most likely change from where they were initially proposed), but once a price is established, a counteroffer can only tether so far from the proposed number before it seems out of reach. Same holds true with duration of term, reach of territory or scope of rights.

Whenever a buyer makes a financial offer on a title, they know the sales rep will come back with a counteroffer (one usually much higher than what was initially offered). For example, if a buyer were willing to spend $50,000 on a program's rights, they would never start with that figure (they'd probably start more in the zone of $25,000). If a seller was to make the first offer (again, assuming they'd be willing to close that deal in that same $50,000 zone), their 'asking price' might be closer to $100,000.

Both parties are obligated to negotiate what's best for their side (meaning the buyer needs to push the number as low as possible, and the seller needs to inflate to as high as possible). But there is a tipping point: if the buyer offers too low, the seller might not come back with a counter; if the seller asks for a figure way too high, the buyer might just assume that company isn't in the same realm and therefore isn't even worth engaging in potential business. And the above 50% margin is by no means a 'rule'. Some buyers might offer $25,000 and might only be able to stretch to $30,000; and some sellers may counter at $75,000 and be obligated by producer's approval to not accept less than $60,000. Point is, whomever throws out the first offer sets the general scope of the deal terms (this is sometimes referred to as 'anchoring' the terms).

But even if the pricing is spot-on, there will generally be some level of pushback elsewhere in the relationship. Whenever a first offer is made, especially between new clients who haven't yet worked together, it's extremely important to negotiate the most reasonably achievable favorable terms. Reason being, it's very common that when deal #2 comes along (or #3 or #4), the other party will be primarily interested in simply copy/pasting the gist of the first deal rather than negotiating from scratch. This is especially true for independent producers selling content to major studios or platforms; the first offer made essentially sets the stage for the entire relationship.

That said, it's important for buyers and sellers to never grow too comfortable with their established terms just because 'that's the way it's always been done'. Not all productions are the same and external factors (inflation as well as marketplace changes) do take place. Whenever an offer is received, there needs to be some level of pushback (even at a higher level) to help make the deal slightly more favorable—even between buyers and sellers who've been working together for years.

▶ PHASE 2: ESTABLISHING THE TERMS

Once the general numbers and broad stroke terms get discussed, the real odds and ends start getting picked apart. Perhaps the agreed number was higher than the buyer wanted, they might compensate by insisting on a longer duration of term to make the deal 'more efficient'. Consequently, the seller might be okay with an extended duration of term, but insist that certain rights (e.g., VOD or other 'home entertainment' rights) become nonexclusive at some point during that period (meaning more than one party can exploit the exact same right, even at the same time).

The art of negotiating a successful distribution deal requires delicately balancing four elements:

1) Limiting the scope of rights to only those *required* to make the deal work

2) Granting the *shortest* window of time to allow the licensee to make a fair (albeit limited) profit

3) A guaranteed monetary figure in alignment with fair market value against the rights being signed away (and to be paid in a reasonable manner (e.g., 50% upon signature

of the deal followed by 50% upon delivery of all material elements related to the property)

4) Establishing a framework for any potential future extensions of the deal (e.g., renewals or the first right to negotiate on prequels or sequels) or, simply, future deals between the parties

As with everything in life, there are several asterisks I would apply to each of these. I wish there was a simple formula to plug in here (believe me, I tried to come up with a gimmicky A + B = C, but Hollywood—nor any industry—truly works that way). So let's break apart each of the steps one by one to gain a real understanding of all the variables at play during a typical distribution deal:

Limiting the Scope of Rights

Scope of rights doesn't just refer to 'theatrical rights', 'TV rights' or 'VOD'; it encompasses the how, where, when these rights are permitted for exploitation.

When granting 'TV rights', designations must be defined to answer whether these rights are for Pay TV channels, basic cable channels or Free TV channels (and even define the means of transmission for these TV rights, including 'terrestrial,' 'satellite' or digitally via Internet Protocol Television (IPTV). But the negotiation process delves much deeper into how the content can be used within that space of rights.

Distributors must map out how many times a specific media property can be broadcast on television. Older content (reruns of an old series or telecasts of an older film) might permit dozens (if not 'unlimited') of runs during a term; newer content is going to be a bit more strict, limiting the exposure to the minimum possible for the deal to move forward. (As an example, I once sold a TV movie to a Canadian broadcaster where I granted 'four telecasts' but was required by the film's producer to guarantee a minimum window of six weeks between each transmission.)

Languages must be defined. As already stated, most countries have some level of language overlap that must be stipulated (e.g., Switzerland can be included into French-speaking Europe, German-speaking Europe and Italian-speaking Europe). When selling content into the US, for example, it's important to designate that the rights only cover English-speaking US (and therefore exclude all the Spanish-language channels available throughout the country); however, there could be situations when the deal calls for the Spanish language only and restricts English or perhaps grants both.

Granting the Shortest Window

The longer a licensee has permission to exploit a media property, the higher the overall profit margin they're likely to earn. But for the licensor, the longer the rights are off the market (licensed away to a client), the larger the overall loss in projected revenues from that same media property.

The balancing act when it comes to term length is for the licensor to give a long-enough window to keep the licensee happy (allowing them to make their fair share of profit from a film or television program) but to ensure those rights conclude just at the point of that profit margin getting a bit too cushy—in the hopes they'll come back for more.

To paint the clearest picture on this, consider a Christmas-themed TV movie or television special. There is really only one broadcast or retail season for such a property: the Christmas season (which runs from mid-November until New Year's Eve). In order for a TV channel, VOD platform or DVD company to properly acquire and schedule and release (or broadcast) a Christmas property on time, they need to be concluding their deals in summer (early autumn at the latest—which would be far too late for a physical DVD release). The licensee might request a term of 18 months (so that the deal could extend across the upcoming Christmas season *and* next year's Christmas season (effectively securing a strong title for two market seasons). The licensor would push back, insisting on a maximum of a one-year deal—but potentially even just a six-month term (in an attempt to avoid any gimmicky 'Christmas in July' stunts that channels or platforms occasionally push).

The licensee tries to secure a longer term for additional exposure, but the licensor calculates the minimum amount of time required to make the deal work (one Christmas season) and establishes the term accordingly. Please understand that this is only an example; there are many occasions where deals last for multiple years—occasionally decades—if the price is right. In the event that the licensee offers additional monies for a longer term, then the duration of term can be extended, but only because the overall licensee fee has been increased, making up for the lost revenue. But if the licensor doesn't push back (and grants the initial eighteen-month term, next year's Christmas season has one less title generating income.

Guaranteed 'Fair Market' Monetary Figure

'Fair market value' is a relative term. Media properties (just like houses and commodities) fluctuate with the market. Global market recessions impact the disposable income in people's pockets, which inversely affects their ability to buy movie tickets or pay monthly SVOD subscriptions. And during recessions, banks aren't as likely to dish out lines of credit or approve loans (which can stall productions and freeze the budgets of acquisitions executives). The problem is, most of these events are unforeseeable. And even if the writing is on the wall that a major shift might be in the works, there's no real way to tell when it might occur (or if it will even have the impact that analysts fear). Sometimes these shifts happen in select regions (such as Brazil, which was a major buying nation in 2012–2015 during a commodities boom, then suddenly tanked in 2016, causing a massive drop in buying power), or the entire world in 2008 after the US housing market took a dump (I recall at the MIPCOM television market in Cannes that year, nearly every meeting was with clients trying to back out of contracts we'd already closed or renegotiate payment terms on legacy deals).

Unsuccessful distribution companies turn a blind eye to these marketplace realities. They hold onto what content was worth in the past and refuse to adapt. Smart distribution companies recognize these shifts and adapt their pricing accordingly. The company willing to work with a buyer's budgets—through good economic times and bad—is the company that will see more deals close.

Establishing a Framework for Future Deals

Once two companies have engaged in business, there is a high probability that they will do more deals in the future. Distribution companies tend to focus on similar types of content (which ultimately attracts the same circle of buyers seeking out that specific programming). And for buyers, it's easiest to go back to familiar companies (where they know the content is solid, previous deals have played out smoothly and that the elements were all delivered in a timely manner) rather than start from scratch with a new company.

This is why for the selling party it's extremely important to take any negotiation with a new client slowly. When cash is being tossed around up front, it's easy to agree to terms that can play out poorly in the long run. If all goes smoothly, the seller will have a new contact to reach out to when new content arrives (with a high probability of an easy sell). That new deal can quickly stall out if a fresh negotiation has to commence rather than a quick and easy repeat of the most recent deal structure. Although slight adjustments can be made (a small extension or decrease to the license fee, the term length or even limited rights holdbacks), the precedent has already been stated as to how the companies will engage in future business based upon the deal terms of the initial agreement—making it very difficult for the seller to steer too far from the first deal structure.

When moving an offer from the initial discussion phase all the way through to a fully executed agreement, both parties tend to negotiate with long-term thinking (under the mindset of how they'd like this present deal and all future deals to work).

▶ Phase 3: Moving to Long Form

After exchanging emails back and forth (either with terms spelled out directly in the body of the email, or via term sheet attachment), eventually the licensor and licensee agree to the basic parameters of rights, term and price. When this transition takes place, the parties officially move their deal 'to long form'.

Despite numerous acronyms applied to this stage (e.g. 'LFA' for Long Form Agreement, or 'DM' for Deal Memo, etc.), they all refer to the negotiation transitioning from shoptalk and into a more formal stage. This is the point—especially for companies that have never engaged in business together—where both sides show their true colors. Deal points typed out clumsily in an email or the generic language of a one- or two-page Term Sheet rarely provide much context for how certain rights or details will be defined.

The first draft of a long-form agreement paints a vivid picture for how the deal will truly play out.

Licensors or licensees can both issue long forms. One might assume it would be welcomed for the 'other party' to take on this legal burden, but in truth most companies would prefer using their own agreements. (Reason: If it's their own agreement, drafted by their own lawyers, all the fine print is to their better interests; additionally, all internal departments are used to the format/workflow and therefore know how to interpret and input the deal within internal systems.)

▶ MAKING IT 'BLEED'

Whenever a long-form agreement arrives, there are always a few details that need some additional ironing out. Even if all the general terms were previously agreed, the long form offers expansive definitions and add-on text covering every conceivable scenario and how both parties need to remedy potential conflicts. Since the vast majority of this language is brand-new to the party receiving this text, they generally have quite a few comments and/or questions to ask.

Decades ago, notes and changes were handwritten onto a hard copy, but in today's world, companies will exchange word docs of an agreement (not PDFs or other fixed file formats), specifically so that the other party can type their notes, adjustments and/or comments directly into the document. With 'track changes' enabled on most files, each edit or adjustment turns the altered text bright red by default. This process of revision is often called redlining (coined from the old publishing days of marking up manuscripts with red ink). The company sending the long-form agreement will usually include a note akin to 'please send us your redlines for further discussion', thereby opening the floor to continued negotiations.

Sometimes deals require very few redlines (or none at all; instead only a few comments for clarity on definitions); other times, legal departments go cowboy and revise every other word (causing the text of almost every page to turn predominantly bright red). This abuse of the redlining invitation is known casually as making a long-form 'bleed'.

Although at first glance, the 'make-it-bleed' agreements would seem like the problematic ones, but in truth it all goes back to common ground. Redlines, questions and alterations are expected during this process, but the ease or burden of getting the deal closed all boils down to how rational the revisions are. A bleeding contract with dozens of rational tweaks is no issue at all, whereas an agreement with one single but massive correction could stall the whole opportunity. (I once shuddered with nerves as I clicked 'send' on an email with an agreement attached covered with redlines; as I waited for the phone to ring assuming my client would be furious at the volume of redlines, I was surprised to receive an email reply accepting all the adjustments; whereas another time I submitted an agreement with only one sentence removed that stalled the deal for nine months—we only got the deal closed after I convinced our lawyers to put the sentence back in.)

▶ OBSTACLES AND SETBACKS

Even when the buyer and seller are moving forward with a deal in a smooth manner, roadblocks and obstacles can still stall or even end constructive distribution opportunities. Although these can come in a multitude of forms, the most common culprits for breaking the momentum of an otherwise positive dialogue are usually found in one of the following:

Licenses and Clearances

Although generally a standard line item in a materials delivery schedule, some producers conveniently 'forget' that certain elements within a title have not been properly cleared and elect not to bring that information up with their distributor. Licenses and clearances—especially in relation to music or on-screen clips/imagery from other copyrighted works—are absolutely vital when attempting to distribute content. Whenever a media property is being negotiated, especially one heavy with music or focused on the life of a famous person (e.g., a narrative biopic or one-off factual television program), an experienced buyer will always triple-check the supporting licenses and clearances paperwork. This is the zone where the bulk of claims and legal threats stem from (that a company is profiting from a title that contains uncleared works belonging to someone else). When studios and major broadcast networks are producing content that could be seen as 'similar' in nature to another property (or contain elements, even if only coincidentally, that could be misconstrued as misuse), they will go so far as to 'acquire' rights to names, likenesses and clearances as a form of insurance (just to be extra safe they've covered all their bases)—this is also the reasoning behind why Errors and Omissions (E&O) insurance becomes a required deliverable. But studios and major networks have deeper pockets than independent producers, and it's usually the independent producers who are more likely to let a piece of music or a background clip 'slip' by hoping it will be unnoticed.

Often the problem is discovered during the material delivery process (most distribution companies are quite rigid during the delivery process, specifically to prevent any such backlash), but sometimes deadlines get the better of sales managers and the decision is made to commence sales on a brand-new title *before* all the checks have been made. When deals are negotiated and agreements get signed, it can be a real problem for the distributor if they're unable to provide all the clearances to their buying clients—potentially a breach of agreed contract or a misrepresentation, but ultimately one that wastes valuable time and exposes both parties to unanticipated expenses.

Materials Issues

Quite often, the buying party and the selling party are both guilty of simply 'assuming' the materials are up to standard (meaning that a master version of the film or

TV program exists in a format the buying party can work with, along with the necessary audio tracks, clearances, paperwork and art elements). Savvy buyers are generally quite clear very early in the discussion about what materials they'll need for the deal to close—especially if their required materials are outside the normal parameters of deliverable elements. It's a big problem when either the seller simply agrees that the materials exist (without actually checking), or discovers later on that the materials don't exist and comes back with a 'materials charge' to be applied to deliver in the requested format.

The latter is at least a solvable issue (that the required spec can be delivered, but that a price needs to be negotiated); but the first scenario can greatly tarnish the relationship (and cause major headaches down the line). If a deal is closed under the expectation that a specific format can be delivered but it's later discovered those materials don't exist, the buyer can be in big trouble. Theatrical and television premieres can be jeopardized and physical release dates can be missed, all of which are expensive errors.

Disorganization

Distributors can shoot themselves in the foot if their media library, assets and rights are not well maintained, documented and organized. When sales executives enter into discussions with potential buyers, they rely on their internal rights management systems to see if a particular title is available to sell (or if any holdbacks, restrictions or clearances might prevent a deal from moving forward). Although there are several servicing companies that have developed rights management software tools to help simplify this process for distributors—which are very costly to purchase and remain as major annual line items in terms of maintenance and support—some companies simply maintain their rights records via excel sheets. But all of these systems are only as reliable as the data entered into them. If the data is accurate, no conflicts or errors occur; however, if a previous sales contract was not properly entered, it can cause a major backlash down the line (both in terms of the costs associated with cancelling a deal or even legal ramifications from breach of contract). Distribution companies have scores of employees working to prevent such errors from getting made, but accidents happen.

Producer Approvals

To recap a bit from earlier in this book, one of the more common holdups comes in the form of 'producer's approvals'; there are occasions when a distribution company finds a strong film or media property that they wish to acquire, but the catch comes in the form that the producer needs to 'approve' any deals the distributor wishes to move forward with. After the producer signs on the dotted line and the distributor's sales team commences on pushing the title, the initial offers will start coming in. From the onset, all seems fine; the distributor's sales reps negotiate terms and get the deal into the best shape possible. But then they must go back to the producer to receive 'written' approval to move forward with the deal. Occasionally, the producer is happy with the offer and gives approval right away. But more often than not, the producer feels the offer isn't strong enough and insists on pushing harder on select terms. The sales agent is then forced to go back to the buyer and push for better terms.

The most stressful scenario with 'Producer Approval' clauses is that they can end a strong deal before it closes. This is especially complicated during film and TV markets (especially when they're taking place abroad (e.g., Cannes Film Festival in France or the European Film Market in Germany). A distribution deal can be discussed at local times in Europe, but the producer is nine time zones behind in Los Angeles (and won't even see his or her emails until early evening European time if everyone's lucky).

Some producers can be so difficult to work with in order to gain an approval from that I've seen many sales agents simply refuse to discuss their titles. They'd rather tell a client 'it's not available' rather than go through the whole song and dance of a negotiation only to lose the deal because of a stubborn producer. In no way am I suggesting a producer shouldn't have insight or visibility into how their title is being promoted and sold (the distributor/producer relationship should be transparent), but it's vital for a producer to understand that the marketplace works in mysterious ways and it's the distributors who are on the front lines in a constantly changing marketplace inventing real opportunities. Although the distribution company a producer moves forward with should be one they trust to do an effective job with their title, they still must understand that a distribution company needs a certain level of flexibility to bundle, package and cross-collateralize a variety of titles.

▶ CLOSING THE DEAL

When all terms in the long-form agreement are accepted and approved, it moves to the signature (or closing) stage. Since the vast majority of agreements are traded back and forth by electronic means, one of the parties must sign then scan and send to the other (usually by email). Although traditionally the 'buyer' signs first, it's just as accepted for the 'deller' to lead with their signed version. This single-signature version is called the 'partially executed' copy (often shorthanded as the 'PE'd' agreement). The partially executed agreement is either docu-signed or scanned and emailed to the other party, who then 'executes' the agreement by affixing their signature alongside the previous party—transitioning the agreement into the 'fully executed' version. Some countries still require 'original' copies of their agreements, in which cases they'd sign and send two original hard copies of a partially executed agreement (with original 'wet-ink' signatures) to the other party; once the other party fully executes both, they'd keep one for their own records and send back the other so that both sides have an original copy of the deal. (This is especially common at film and TV markets, where two copies are signed in unison so that each party walks away with an original version in hand.) In addition to a single signature of each party on the signature page, it's also quite common to see the initials of each signatory on every page of the agreement. This custom offers both sides confidence that no pages or terms will be altered later on (and the signature page conveniently attached to a tweaked agreement).

Once the fully executed agreement is in the hands of each party, the internal workflows kick-start within both companies. For the buying company, this pings their marketing teams to start requesting artwork from the licensor, their accounting teams to prep monies and their materials team to prepare element requests. For the selling team, this prompts their rights management teams to adjust the available rights of the titles involved, their accounting teams to invoice for the monies due, and their materials teams to make necessary order requests to facilitate the deal.

▶ CATEGORIES OF DISTRIBUTION DEALS

Although there are dozens of distribution deal structures, eventually they all fall into only one of two categories: (i) an 'all-rights' deal or (ii) a 'select-rights' deal.

The 'All-Rights' Distribution Deal

These are the bread and butter of the presale business (and of the international film distribution business). When an indie film distributor is presenting new titles for 'pre-sale' opportunities, they are generally working with regional distributors (who manage or oversee specific foreign territories, such as the UK, Pan-Latin America or Japan). If a Japanese client wants to pre-buy a movie, they're putting a large amount of risk on the table and therefore expect to own all rights to the film within their entire territory. On that same token, even for finished content (already-produced movies or series), more complex territories which generally require local agents to truly close deals (e.g., Spain, Middle East, South Eastern Asia or Latin America) might simply acquire 'all rights' to a title so that its ownership within the territory is clean—preventing them from potentially having to share rights with a competitor.

In both of these instances, the acquisition of 'all rights' is more of an insurance policy for the licensee—that they won't have to compete with any other players in their home country and can map out a distribution strategy that makes the most sense for them.

'All rights' by no means implies any form of ownership of the IP, only permission to exploit all direct media rights in a particular media property.

The 'Select-Rights' Distribution Deal

Whereas an 'all-rights' deal is quite straightforward in its approach (it covers everything), a 'select-rights' deal is slightly more open-ended. Please note that 'select rights' is not a commonly used industry term; I'm stating this purely to relay that these are deals focused on a select set of limited rights. Although a select-rights deal can cover a single right (e.g., theatrical rights), it can also cover a collection of rights categories (e.g., DVD, VOD, Non-Theatric, Mobile Phone and Clip rights). The point is that even if a large quantity of a property's rights are included in the deal, there's still remaining rights available for other select-rights buyers to acquire).

For sellers, 'select-rights' deals allow acquisitions teams to acquire only those exact rights they're interested in exploiting (meaning they do not need to worry about—or pay for—the other rights only to see them go unused).

Broadcast channels, for example, are really only seeking the exact television rights required (e.g., a Pay TV channel would only want to negotiate and pay for Pay TV rights—carving out free-to-air television, pay-per-view, etc.); however, as technology has advanced and the majority of major US networks have shifted their views—opportunistically or fearfully—toward the digital playing field, many broadcasters are attempting to future-proof themselves against the rise of VOD outlets (such as Hulu or Netflix) from preempting their broadcast (and potentially weakening a programs ratings performance). To combat this scenario, many buyers of Pay TV rights are requesting either additional rights on top of their normal Pay TV request (such as including SVOD into their rights package) or simply requesting a holdback against the competing rights (transforming those original 'Pay TV Only' rights into Pay TV deals with holdbacks (e.g., Pay TV rights with a holdback against all other forms of television and SVOD for (fill-in-the-blank number of) months after its premiere date on the channel). There's also the more commonplace trend where a major broadcast entity simply creates their own internal self-managed direct-to-consumer SVOD or AVOD platform, thereby limiting the exploitation of their content to their own outlet—as has been seen recently with the rise of Disney+, Paramount+ and Warner Bros. Discovery's Discovery+.

Some companies are not interested (at least at face value) in acquiring *all* rights—yet once the paperwork is finalized, there are so many holdbacks and restrictions included they seemingly become 'all-rights' deals by default. For a distributor, such situations are not always a bad scenario; as long as a reasonable monetary figure is applied, the deal is worth at least considering.

Multi-Territory Deals

As the media business becomes more globalized, so too are many of its biggest players. Most major broadcast networks (e.g., Paramount, AMCNetworks, BBC, etc.) have their native territory-based presence along with streaming and/or broadcast feeds beaming their content to key countries throughout the world. For programmers representing such channels, when screening strong content worthy of an acquisition, they're generally considering which of the other countries under their channels umbrella could be a good add-on. Digital platforms are following the trend as well; Amazon has steadily grown its global presence by building infrastructure and audience in one key country after another. Roku, Pluto and Tubi have followed the same strategy, launching first in the US before rolling out a slow and steady strategy of international flag planting. Netflix remains the only major entity to have flipped the proverbial switch, launching itself from a handful of international countries to worldwide exposure (requiring worldwide rights in the process).

Selling several countries all at the same time (often to one buyer) is becoming a new norm in the distribution business. Although there is still the option to 'carve out' (or geo-block) select countries, selling a property into multi-territory deal is a solid way for a distributor to gain a large pull of up-front cash while allowing a buyer a solid deal when compared to the geographical reach they now own.

Barter and Revenue Share Deals

Not all deals involve acquisitions executives paying up-front cash (e.g., advances, license fees or MGs); there are a wide variety of distribution deals that have *no* up-front payments due (that are quite commonplace across all facets of the business). Instead, they split or share the revenues generated by advertising inserts.

Companies that manage VOD platforms generally operate on a revenue share basis (where zero money is placed up front but a clear split on back end revenues makes the deal lucrative—generated from advertisements and/or subscription fees). YouTube is a classic example on the user-generated side, but mainstream distributors and even mini-majors often license large packages of strong titles to modern AVOD giants under the same deal structures.

Even for independent producers signing away their media property to a distributor for global representation, not all of these deals have a monetary advance associated (especially on more risky titles, or films without high-level selling points (e.g., a lack of known talent)).

For these deals to work, a large amount of vetting and due diligence is always advised. It's of vital importance for the licensing party to fully understand the exact waterfall of a deal's financial structure (how and when money will arrive and eventually get paid out) as well as knowing what 'expenses' or additional 'costs' could be applied against their cut of the receipts. It's also important for the licensee (the party receiving the rights without paying any up-front advances) to share in on the risk in some meaningful way; after all, if they're not putting money down as collateral, what are they giving up to help shoulder the risk?

▶ STRATEGIC DEAL STRUCTURES

When a selling and buying company find themselves continually engaged in recurring business, mutual ease can be created for both parties by entering into a more formalized 'precedent' on how future deals can more easily be structured. This can come in the form of a standardized term sheet or by means of a larger ongoing business relationship. Once two companies find their common ground, they like to keep the easy flow of content in full motion. Often, they enter into one of the following strategic deal structures:

Output Deal

An output deal is a great win-win deal for the distributor and licensee. For the distributor, they are able to guarantee a minimum number of titles sold for a fixed amount of money (even if the content doesn't yet exist—as outlined in Chapter 2). For the licensee, they are guaranteed a minimum number of titles they have access to for a cheaper price than if they would have had to negotiate for each title individually.

With an output deal, a distributor can forecast monies to develop a slate of projects for their client base. They could also use the deal to gain a line of credit from a bank to have cash flow they can use to acquire new product.

The key component of an 'output' deal is that the distributor gets to call the shots on what the licensee takes. The risk for the licensee is that they could be forced to buy one awful film after the next. But a savvy distributor would be smart enough to ensure quality titles for the licensee (with the hope of keeping the deal alive from one year to the next).

Occasionally, a provision is included for the licensee to pick and choose the titles. For instance, a US distributor might have a five-title output deal with a UK broadcaster, but that UK broadcaster is allowed a certain number of 'passes' before they commit to the five they'll buy. It's still an output, but with a contingency that takes a bit of leverage away from the distributor (still a solid win, but a bit more difficult to presell titles).

First-Look Deal

Unlike the output deal, where titles *must* be acquired, the first-look deal simply requires a distributor to approach a select licensee prior to reaching out to competitors (effectively giving that licensee the 'first look' and the first opportunity to make a bid on any new business opportunity). There is usually clear language dictating a time frame the licensee has to officially 'pass' on a title—usually a period of several 'business days' up to a few months (depending on the level of the deal and the current stage of the project).

Licensees will pay for this first look right (generally an annual or quarterly minimum guarantee that can later be applied towards a project should it choose to move forward with something).

Representation/Agency Deal

As outlined earlier, exclusive sales agents or sales representatives can be very influential in more complicated parts of the world (e.g., the Middle East, Africa, Russia, Spain, etc.) where they can bypass red tape in ways that are difficult for US-based companies to manage. They'll take on 'all rights' for a select territory and oversee all deal negotiations within—either for a 'one-off' deal focused on a single title, or by means of a much larger relationship (where an agent or representative is hired to oversee all of the distributor's business interests in that territory).

There are also situations that warrant exclusive agents or representatives for select-rights groups or content types. For instance, a US-based television channel might have enough audience reach to merit producing its own film and television content for network broadcast but might not have the infrastructure (or time) to oversee the digital or ancillary rights to its own properties. That network could enter into a deal with a digital rights agent who manages and represents content specifically for the digital space.

That same US-based television channel might also be managing its content just fine in English but is missing the US-Hispanic audience by not focusing on brokering deals with the Spanish-speaking stations; the channel may enter into a deal with an agent to specifically represent its US-Hispanic rights.

These deals can cover any variable of specifics (language, format type, rights category, etc.) and can also include 'consultancy' scenarios, when a third party is brought in to advise a company on best practices to help give it a leg up in future negotiations.

▶ Life of Series Clauses

As outlined in Chapter 2 (regarding methods of 'preselling' content), Distributors will occasionally include a 'Life of Series' clause in deals associated with television series. The intention is to obligate the buyer (e.g., the broadcast channel) to acquire the present series along with all future episodes should they ever exist (meaning they are acquiring rights to the episodes currently finished and any future seasons). This same concept applies to films and books, including sequels, prequels and/or derivative spin-offs. The terms and fees associated with those future episodes would generally mimic those for the existing content (or rise at a pre-agreed rate to account for fluctuations stemming from inflation and/or talent costs).

This strategy serves two purposes: (i) it effectively presells future episodes (thereby having tangible presales on the table with a clear license fee) and (ii) guarantees future streams of revenue for the distribution company.

Although these seem like solid ideas and easy to include, they are generally a major point of contention during the dealmaking process. From the perspective of the acquiring party (the licensee), they are opening the door to a large volume of risk if the series is a flop. And who's to guarantee that future episodes would meet the technical or marketing standards of the original? Most companies I've worked with, who've insisted on including such language, generally end up with these clauses removed before the point of deal execution.

That's not to say that acquiring parties (broadcast channels, platforms or home entertainment outlets) aren't interested in having first access to future episodes; however, they tend to include this language as an option and not a requirement. As an example, let's say an established TV channel is acquiring first-run global rights to a brand-new television series; they're putting a great deal of money on the table for the rights (as well as putting a great deal of money on the table internally to cover marketing and promotions). It would be a real slap in the face if they've invested all this time, effort and risk into making a program's first season a big hit only to see the show's second season getting licensed off to a competitor (who can simply ride of the coattails of the other company's marketing campaign). So, to mitigate this risk, they'll place a variation of the 'Life of Series' clause into the contract, which essentially states they have the right of first negotiation and last refusal to acquire future seasons (or future episodes) on 'no less favorable terms' (meaning, at minimum, the same money and same duration of agreement).

There might be some back and forth on this, mostly in that the distributor would want to right to 'shop' the title around should it become a smash hit—at which point the licensee would have to match—but in the end, the principle of this clause remains the same.

▶ CHERRY-PICKING

Since buying clients generally have strict content quotas—with limited budgets to spend—they tend to be very meticulous with their acquisitions. Experienced buyers rarely fall for flashy promos or gimmicks; they'll always insist on having access to all available episodes (either by means of screening completed episodes, rough cuts or reading shooting scripts) from which to base their decisions.

Occasionally, especially in the world of factual or documentary television series, a buyer might be very intrigued by a few select episodes from a series but have reservations about the series as a whole. In other words, from a series of ten episodes, the buyer might only have confidence that two or three of the episodes will work for their specific territory or channel. This is a classic example of a buyer 'cherry-picking' content—and it happens in all facets of the business.

The dilemma for the distributing party is whether to accept the opportunity or pass. Outside simplified logic states that a distributor should hold true to the series as a whole and insist that all episodes get acquired (and broadcast/exploited) as one unified 'project'. But in the real world of film, television, and new media distribution, there are numerous strategic or contractually required situations where it makes valid sense to get creative with 'cherry-picking' buyers.

For many producers, having a small selection of episodes plucked from a full series to be acquired by a foreign-based client is seen as 'better than nothing'. This exposure can make producing future projects simpler. This can also be the same on the 'talent' side, where agents or managers might agree to select episodes of their series being 'cherry-picked' in the hope that a leading talent might gain wider international appeal.

There are numerous financing scenarios where an investing party might require a producer to assure a deal will be closed in select international territories. In example, a Canadian entity might issue a grant towards a program's budget, but in exchange, that entity might require the program be visible in fellow commonwealth nations (e.g., the UK and/or Australia). Contractual obligations can also result from merchandising deals, where a kids' TV series is required to be 'visible' in specific countries to widen exposure of toys or associated retail items. There are also instances when a series has holiday-themed episodes (e.g., a 'Christmas' or 'Halloween' episode); many broadcast-ers around the world will run holiday 'stunts' and are always in a scramble to find the content, but they only have the budget for one single episode (not the whole series). The reasons can be all over the map.

Although this practice is by no means uncommon, distributors will always do their best to keep a series, trilogy, anthology or other package of programming as a bundle. In most instances, if a buyer only wants two episodes from a ten-episode program, the distribut-ing party will simply take the license fee for the two episodes and spread it across all ten episodes (and include language in the agreement stating the network is not obligated to broadcast all ten episodes). That's a win-win where the channel gets their two episodes and the distributor has a full series licensed as a single package.

▶ PACKAGE DEALS AND INTERNAL ALLOCATIONS

Although 'packaging' is a much more common trend for indie feature film companies, who have more to gain by packaging several titles versus pushing for one-off deals on a title-by-title basis, the strategy is used across the board in the film, TV and new media distribution business.

The idea is simple: when an acquiring client has interest in a specific title, a savvy sales agent will hook them in with other content (that's very similar in terms of cast, genre, style or tone)—if asked about the price, the sales agent will generally toss out a large number for the solo title but increase the total by only a small margin if both films (or a small package of films) were to be picked up instead. Perhaps the client was interested in purchasing the rights to a single film for $10,000. A sales agent might offer a second film for an additional $5,000 (or at a 50% reduced price for a $15,000 deal). The negotiation might continue; perhaps the deal lands at five films for $25,000. The buyer walks away with several movies for only $5,000 a pop (or at half the original cost)—leaving behind residual monies in their pocket that they didn't have to spend elsewhere—and the sales agent has a larger total license fee from which to earn a commission AND has the product successfully out of their inventory.

At face value, one might assume the buyer's assessment earlier is correct (that they walked away with the rights to five films at $5,000 each (or half the cost of a sin-gle title). Splitting $25,000 across five films evenly would result in a $5,000 per title allocation, but that's not how most distribution companies account for media properties.

But don't all films or media properties have different values? Yes, but the way a distri-bution company values a title might not be the same way a buyer, producer, agent or individual producer might. Where producers, buyers and agents use signifiers such as budget, cast level, production value and ratings to 'value' content, a distribution com-pany uses the bottom line figure of how indebted they became to acquire the title. After all, in order to sell content, a distribution company must acquire new product—and not all investments pan out. When a packaging opportunity arises, a smart sales agent will be sure to include a 'problematic' title within a volume deal—as many as possible. The overall deal value increases, the buyer walks away having scored a jackpot and meanwhile the distribution company has a lump sum of cash they can now allocate towards their problematic title(s).

With this lump sum of cash, the distributor now has an opportunity to spread these funds across the five films in any manner they feel is most beneficial to their bottom line. Perhaps one—that's currently behind on recoupment—receives an allocation of $9,000, leaving $16,000 to be evenly spread across the remaining four titles. Although an extreme example, a distribution company could internally allocate $23,000 from the earlier five-title example toward a problematic title, leaving only $500 to be split evenly across each of the remaining four films.

We explore these topics more in depth elsewhere in the book (especially within Chapter 8) but the key takeaway is that distribution companies are primarily in the business of moving product and increasing revenue wherever and however possible.

▶ FLIPPING TITLES AND 'PASS-THROUGH' DEALS

By no means is it a rare occurrence for a distributor to reach out to a competing company in the event of a mutually beneficial opportunity. After all, business is business, and both distributors have a bottom line to meet.

On the surface level, a company might need additional titles to get a specific deal off the ground—and rather than going into the open marketplace of indie producer negotiations, that distributor could simply tap into a competing company's library. For example, Company A might have a package opportunity but needs additional titles to secure the deal (and Company B might have excess titles it's been unable to move and is willing to sell them at a cheap rate). Company B could then license those tough-to-move titles to Company A so that Company A can 'flip' them or 'pass them through' to a third-party client. Everyone wins.

But there can be far more complex reasons why a distributor would agree to position itself as a 'pass-through' entity. For instance, a major, well-established player (e.g., HBO, Netflix, etc.) might have keen interest in a niche movie or TV series but isn't interested in applying too many resources to the game of picking it up—or doesn't want to get caught in the situation of overpaying simply because it's assumed they have deep pockets. These major entities might contact another distributor they're already in business with—a mid-level or smallish company, one they have a comfortable relationship with—and ask that they 'aggregate' the titles on their behalf (meaning that the third-party company serve as a wall between both sides). Again, the benefits of such a scenario serve all parties favorably.

When well-established companies reach out to independent rights holders (producers of indie films or TV shows), more often than not, those rights holders see the dollar signs start spinning and tend to ask for way too much, ultimately botching their own opportunity. For the mid-level 'in-between' company, this can serve as a great opportunity to build clout with a major client while growing its own library. And the little guy (the niche rights holder) gets its property acquired by an established company.

▶ AGGREGATION

As buying companies grow in size and scale, they often reach a tipping point of how many selling companies they can reasonably acquire content from before overseeing all the deals becomes too much of a time suck. Even if relationships are strong (and workflows run like clockwork), there comes a point when there are far too many clients to manage and not enough employees to oversee them.

Apple encountered this exact situation several years ago when digital-savvy audiences started seeking out content on their iTunes platform. They had been entering into direct deals with each content vender, coordinating the entire delivery process client by client. But Apple's delivery requirements for iTunes were (and still are) strenuous, and many sellers had difficulty meeting the demands. As one iTunes acquisitions exec told me, they were spending more time attempting to get content QCd—quality control checked—for placement than finding new quality programming to make available on the platform. So they streamlined. They selected a few reliable and trusted key content providers to serve as official iTunes 'preferred vendors'—or what are commonly referred to as 'aggregators'. From that point forward, if a distributor wanted to broker a deal on a title for iTunes placement, it had to be done through one of its vetted aggregating partners. This same exact concept is currently in play with all the usual suspects in the VOD space today.

And it's not just digital players pulling this move; it sometimes simply makes more sense to have a few trusted entities filtering and dealing with the small details so top buyers and executives can allocate their focus/attention to revenue-driving initiatives. As mentioned early on, once a strong buyer/seller relationship is established, it just becomes easier to 'copy/paste' the terms into the next deal (making the brokering process much simpler). Aggregation takes this to the next level, where the buyer/seller relationships between a few key companies become the only entities they'll do business with.

For some distribution companies, this move can be seen as a major obstacle. Not being 'direct' with a major client can be seen as a massive loss in revenue (or forever hindering the reach their content might gain if sent through an aggregating party); for others— especially smaller based distributors—the notion of 'aggregation' can be a solid opportunity for growth. As a distributor, having that close of a relationship to a major player (whereby they request you to be the 'go-to' source to represent their content deals) would open the doors to found money on titles you'd never have previously had access to.

5

Windowing Rights and Strategizing Releases

Author's note: portions of this chapter rely on industry acronyms to describe variations of media rights and the means by which end users engage with content; please reference Appendix I as needed, which offers a breakdown of commonplace 'exploitable' rights with digestible definitions.

▶ CONCEPT OF 'WINDOWING'

One of the principles discussed in Chapter 1 referred to the concept that the value of any given media property decreases over time. In other words, every media property—from the major studio releases to the micro-budgeted independent titles—has a limited window of time wherein an active audience is willing to spend money to see it. And as time goes on, the amount of money each active end user is willing to pay decreases until consumer demand fully fades.

There are obviously the rare exceptions (i.e., projects that suddenly blossom years after their initial release, ones that are given a 'second wind' due to unforeseen circumstances or those rare projects that, for whatever reason, reach a plateau in revenue and hold onto it for an extended period of time), but these are outliers; their success is not forecastable no replicable across a wide slate of content. While hopeful filmmakers and novice producers love to quote these scenarios in business plans, it's important to note that distributors don't value media with this logic; they know all too well that revenue streams from even the greatest of media properties will eventually dry up. This overarching time scale applied to a media property's financial capability is often referred to as its 'shelf life'.

DOI: 10.4324/9781003357902-6

That said, every media property is different; therefore the shelf life of every title is unique. And even those media projects that seem very similar—and can easily be lumped into the same buckets in terms of genre, cast, clichés, plot points, etc.—will inevitably be released into the marketplace at different times (in which new platforms are constantly popping up, audience expectations are always fluctuating and new competing trends are skewing everyone's attention). Because of these constantly evolving factors, distributors must go back to the drawing board for each new title's release strategy.

But despite all of these shifting variables, distributors are not in a reactive position. The one constant principle—that all media properties devalue over time—provides enough of a foundation to guide distributors toward the correct title-by-title release strategies to ensure the strongest margin of profit.

> As a general rule of thumb, a project's initial release is it's best opportunity to gain wide audience engagement—making this the most profitable point in just about any media property's life. This is why there's generally so much hype and build up toward a major theatrical release or broadcast premiere. Regardless of what changes have affected the marketplace in terms of where or how consumers choose to transact upon their content, distributors know that initial release is the best chance for a big return.

After this first wave has started to die down, distributors will exploit other available rights by placing that same media property into a new location—at a slightly reduced price point—for a wider audience to discover. This process repeats itself over and over until one of two things happen:

1) The property drops so low in price that it is forever made available as 'free', earning money on a revenue share basis from ads (e.g., Free TV commercials, ad-supported streaming on platforms like Crackle, YouTube, etc.).

2) The title is earning so little money that the cost of maintaining the property for marketplace exploitation no longer makes financial sense—meaning the property is essentially pulled from the market and abandoned.

We call this process 'windowing'. And each exploitation phase in a property's life is considered a different window.

For a movie, its first window might be a major theatrical release followed by a Pay TV window, a home entertainment or Video-on-Demand (VOD) window and eventually conclude with a Free TV or Ad-supported VOD (aka AVOD) window where it garners rev share receipts indefinitely from embedded ads. For a major series, the first window might be an exclusive deal on a single Subscription VOD (aka SVOD) platform (i.e., Netflix, Hulu, etc.), followed by a wider SVOD window (across all SVOD platforms non-exclusively) to be followed by less lucrative windows (e.g., Free TV and ad-supported plays).

How any given title is windowed—and the duration of each window—is completely unique based upon marketplace demand, current social/cultural trends, external international events or innovations in technology; but the workflow and logic behind a windowed release strategy has always been the best response to tackle the inevitable fact that no individual media property will be raking in the cash forever.

For a visual representation, consider the following:

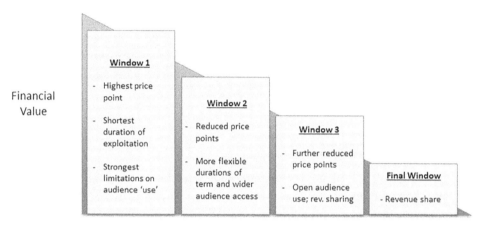

Value over Time

Figure 5.1   The vertical line (Y) on the left represents money (or value), whereas the bottom line (X) represents time. Note that as a title moves forward in time (from left to right), the 'value' of each window decreases.

Although the pricing associated with each window varies greatly title by title (e.g., a major Hollywood blockbuster being released in IMAX 3D will have a much different ticket price than a local art house playing a foreign gem), but the value of that property is generally at its highest 'per-unit' level during that initial window and drops as it transitions from one window to the next.

But the heavy marketing and buildup to the initial release of a media property isn't just to recoup monies at a premium price point; the 'buzz' impact associated with a successful initial release can stretch out the duration of each successive window (and make them more lucrative). This is why 'winning' the weekend box office is such a point of pride; it's another form of promotion. In the mind of an average moviegoer, sometimes that number one spot is enough for them to select that property over another the next time they're deciding what content to watch. This audience behavior can keep a title in theaters for a few additional weeks, which allows it to be priced a bit higher when it shifts to its home entertainment/VOD window and gives the distributor leverage to request higher license fees for future windows in the Free TV and AVOD space. You'll see the concept applied in a variety of ways. A great example is Amazon highlighting a certain product as an "Amazon Best Seller" in a chosen category; that tag alone yields a dramatically higher volume of clicks with more confident 'buys' from consumers (most of whom don't even check alternatives on the same page). For distributors, 'winning' their initial window of release sets the stage for the valuation of all future windows in a media property's life.

This same process of price devaluation is not limited only to media properties. From mom-and-pop convenience stores to Fortune 500 corporations, all businesses operate with a similar logic: price high when a product is new, and discount appropriately with age. For a broader view of how this business strategy can be applied within other industries, check out Chris Anderson's 2004 book *The Long Tail: Why the Future of Business is Selling Less of More.*

▶ VALUING RIGHTS

Not all projects will be exploited across every single available potential rights category—and the ordering of rights in relation to whether they're exploited first, second or simply all at the same time—varies from deal to deal. While one movie might get released to thousands of theaters across several countries on the same date, another might premiere on TV first (or even on a VOD platform like TubiTV or RokuTV). And as technology continues making content accessible in ways never before conceived, the volume of exploitable rights (and the potential combinations in which they can be sequentially ordered or patch-worked together) will only increase.

But that said, there is a logical indicator distributors use in order to decide which route provides the best opportunity for a strong first window: money.

As discussed in Chapters 2 and 3 in relation to how projects are funded, distributors do not take blind guesses with regards to investing in the media content they develop and distribute. They spend a great deal of time analyzing what their consumer-facing platforms are in need of and then supply the content that's in demand.

If a major consumer-facing SVOD platform (e.g., Netflix) is ecstatic about a new project in development with a distributor, that's because they know their audience will likely respond favorably. In order to maintain their audiences' engagement—and keep them actively subscribed to their platform (and not shifting toward any competitors)—it would be worth a strong investment to acquire this new project's first window on an exclusive basis. And in order to secure this first window—along with preventing other rights from being sold that could interfere with its 'audience-first' objective—this consumer-facing platform understands it will need to place a premium level of cash on the table.

For the distributor, this large up-front sum of cash could be enough to completely fund the project—and potentially allow a small level of profit—all before a single frame has been shot. And with this type of scenario, it's actually not the distributor selecting which rights category should be windowed first; the decision is effectively being made for them. And in time, after the exclusive period with this first client comes to a close, the distributor would be able to begin exploiting different rights across future windows—with every dollar coming in as pure profit.

But there is one critical variable distributors must consider: not all-rights categories hold the same financial value. Just as each window decreases in value over time, the specific rights that are being exploited must logically fall into the appropriate order based upon the associated price point at which they can reasonably sell. To put this concept into real-world terms, would you pay $20 to 'buy' a movie on Amazon Prime—on top of your monthly Prime subscription—if you could stream the same film on Netflix at no extra charge? By using the earlier example—of an SVOD platform paying a large-enough license fee to effectively 'buy' the first window—the future rights windows that a distributor enters into must be at the same or below value level of the SVOD rights. Therefore, a distributor cannot work backward and suddenly charge a premium rate to new clients; they'd have to work only with those rights categories at or below the market value of SVOD.

This concept gets a bit tough because the valuation of rights is all over the map as they relate to each specific media property. Some genres perform very well in one rights category, while others rarely gain traction. So rather than try to order rights based upon their value, let's instead keep this concept high-level.

Every distribution deal—and consequently every release strategy—follows the same financial workflow:

1) Premium Pay rights followed by

2) Discounted Pay rights followed by

3) Revenue Share rights.

What's important to note here is that a single set of rights can actually exist within each of these three pay scales (as can some companies!). Consider this in relation to Video-on-Demand rights: Transactional VOD (TVOD), Subscription VOD (SVOD) and Ad-supported VOD (AVOD) are all VOD rights (all part of the same rights category), but each has a different rights *value*. In example, a brand-new title with strong audience demand could be placed onto a TVOD platform (e.g., Apple iTunes, Vudu or Amazon's transactional model) at a 'premium' price point and garner strong returns. After maximizing the exploitation of the premium price point, distributors can shift the title into a less-revenue-generating-but-still-lucrative 'discounted' category such as non-exclusive SVOD (Netflix, Hulu and Amazon Prime). And after maximizing the exploitation where discounted license fees can be obtained, distributors will place the title onto AVOD platforms (Roku, Tubi, Amazon's Freevee along with ad-supported tiers of Hulu, Netflix and others)—that offer revenue shares of embedded ads in lieu of license fees. If this were to be changed so that the mid-tiered non-exclusive SVOD rights category were to be exploited first (meaning the right with the medium value of the three), a distributor could only shift the title downward to AVOD. Once a title has been placed in the market at a specific price point, that price can only move in a downward direction over time (which directly affects which rights categories distributors are able to work within).

Let's explore examples of rights categorized by value:

▶ **Premium Pay**—Rights exploited in these early windows will be those considered behind 'pay walls' (meaning the only way they're legally exploitable in the marketplace is if a consumer must transact upon them). Examples of a premium pay rights phase include theatrical rights, premium TV rights (pay-per-view or premium networks like HBO, FX, Starz or Showtime that require direct payment for access) and TVOD or electronic sell-through (purchasing download-to-own or download-to-rent versions via platforms like Amazon, Apple iTunes or Vudu). When a project is being developed as an 'elevated acquisition' or is being created as an 'original', it can be made available to end users without a pay wall. A major Netflix original would appear to a consumer alongside all other available SVOD content, but the license fee Netflix pays to the distributor would be of a 'premium' level (making the deal worth closing despite losing out on other traditional first-window premium rights). Same can be said of AVOD platforms such as Tubi or free-to-air TV channels like public service broadcasters (CBC, BBC, ABC, etc.). Even though consumers have 'free' access, for the distributor, the license fee in discussion might be premium enough to bypass all other rights windows.

▶ **Discounted Pay**—The next phase is slightly more abstract since, typically, end users are 'paying' to access media properties, but not always for the specific content they're screening. When a consumer subscribes to an SVOD platform, they pay a monthly fee with the freedom to watch anything available within that platform's library. Regardless whether one person consumes hundreds of hours of media content per week versus another who only catches two films per month, they both pay the same subscription fee. Although SVOD platforms can occasionally pay distributors premium prices for exclusive access, most of the time these deals are non-exclusive (which, for a distributor, means placing a film onto one platform for a heavily discounted (cheap) license fee, but because the rights are non-exclusive, the same film can be placed onto a multitude of SVOD platforms at the same time—allowing those 'discounted' license fees to add up). Basic cable television is another example of a 'discounted' rights category; a basic cable package from a traditional entity like DirecTV or DISH—and nowadays a streaming entity like Roku or Sling—offers consumers a 'bundled' set of cable channels (e.g., Lifetime, AMC, CNN, Nickelodeon, etc.). Primarily, basic cable still has advertisements embedded within the programs—which generates additional cash for the broadcasters—but the channels get extra kickbacks from the cable companies themselves from your monthly subscription. For a consumer, basic cable bundles are a discounted television alternative to their premium pay competitors; for a distributor, since the price points passed on to the consumer are lower, the license fees they're capable of paying are smaller. (If a premium pay channel is willing to spend $100,000 on a single hour of content, a basic cable channel might only have the budget to pay $40,000—potentially much less.) Another factor here is the decreasing of price points on already-exploited VOD content; even if a title was placed onto a TVOD/EST/PPV platform at a premium rate, after a few weeks, the distributor can request a decrease in asking price (similar to how retailers shift slower-selling products to the discount shelf).

▶   **Revenue Share**—While end users might not pay a cent out of pocket to watch content on a free-to-air network or AVOD platform, others spend a great deal to make that possible (namely advertisers). People tend to forget that the content they're watching in the 'free' category is really just filler. All of the greatest media content—classic films, new series, sporting events, news programs—are really just entertaining interstitials to keep us around for the next batch of ads. Generally, when ad monies are in play, networks and platforms attempt to 'barter' (or share) the revenue. Although major Free TV channels can pay distributors strong license fees for revenue, it's generally not as lucrative as basic cable channels—not to mention these deals are much more complicated to obtain since Free TV content must be suitable for a much wider audience demographic. For distributors, this tends to be the last window they enter into (unless there is an overwhelming reason—generally an up-front license fee paid by the platform—to bypass the premium and discounted cycles to dive straight into the rev share space). The idea for a distributor is that all other pay wall models have been played out; therefore, any money—even if only from a rev share model—is considered a bonus.

▶   DURATION OF WINDOWS

There is no finite rule for how long one media property should remain within a particular rights window before shifting to the next. In that every media property is different—and is released against a different set of marketplace variables—the duration of each exploitation window varies drastically. But that's not to say there aren't generalized averages. Please note, we'll dive into alternative release strategies a bit later in this chapter (specifically windowing shake-ups like Disney's 2010 *Alice in Wonderland*), but for now let's keep things in broad brushstroke terms to cement the core ideas.

For ease—and to ensure we're covering a wide variety of potential windows—let's use the example of a sizable feature film (one commencing with a major theatrical release and stretching across several other rights windows). And to keep things clean, we'll assume that each of these windows is for exclusive rights.

What follows is a generalized workflow of a 'traditional' windowing strategy:

▶   **Theatrical Window**—Theatrical windows work on weeks, not months. This window will generally require a few weeks (e.g. four weeks or 28 days) as an exclusive window. For smaller, very limited theatrical windows, these can be even less. For larger films, they can extend six weeks and beyond (and be stretched as long as enough tickets are being sold). But as of today's writing, for a reasonably sized movie in a few hundred theaters, 28 days is the average minimum exclusive period for a theatrical run.

▶ **TVOD/EST and Pay-Per-View Window**—In the digital sphere—after or while a film is still in theaters—most of the sales in the home entertainment transactional space will take place within the first week (often within the first few days of release); so although the idea is also a four-week exclusive run, I've found most TVOD/EST platforms are perfectly comfortable with a two-week exclusive run. This is assuming TVOD/EST is the first home entertainment window or a presale period in advance of theatrical. If the TVOD/EST window is being exploited the same day as theaters, then these are generally non-exclusive with no 'windows' required—unless a platform like Apple iTunes, Vudu or Amazon is intending to do specialty promotion.

▶ **Premium Television**—After theaters have had a movie for several weeks and the TVOD/EST sales have waned, the premium TV window is usually next to kick in. Premium television channels (like Showtime, HBO and Starz), are willing to pay top dollar to have content soon after its theatrical run, yet long before a consumer can see it on Netflix, Hulu or Amazon. . . . Generally, there is mild exploitation on the transactional side during this window (e.g., iTunes, Vudu or pay-per-view platforms), but these don't infringe on the premium channels. The reason for this window is because a monthly fee for a premium channel isn't too much more than purchasing a digital copy of a movie via TVOD. Therefore, if consumers are keen to see a few different titles that channel is offering (and it's going to be a long while before they can see it on SVOD), it makes more sense to just subscribe to the channel and have access to a wide selection of premium content. To ensure this, premium channels place strict holdbacks and blackout periods against SVOD exploitation. If a consumer can simply access the title on other platforms, then there's little incentive for them to make the switch and become a subscriber to the channel itself. A 90-day period is generally the minimum these channels will accept before granting a distributor permission to begin an SVOD or basic cable window; however, six months or longer is not uncommon.

▶ **Ancillary Rights**—Soon after a premium TV window has commenced, distributors are able to exploit their titles to more niche markets, namely airlines, hotels and cruise ships. In these venues, the content can still be placed behind a pay wall (in a pay-per-view or TVOD/EST format) but is exposed to a very limited audience that doesn't encroach the rights generally defined by premium TV channels. Within six months after a theatrical premiere, 'free' modes of ancillary will also be exploited; these can cover passenger airplanes, military bases and also include educational facilities, libraries or even prisons. (Please note: in North America, ancillary rights refer to airlines, hotels and cruise ships, while in the rest of the world, ancillary rights refer to remakes, reboots and sequels/prequels; internationally, licensing to airlines, hotels or cruise ships would be considered 'non-theatrical rights'.)

▶ **SVOD and Basic Cable**—A full year after the initial theatrical release date is generally the start of most SVOD windows. However, this right has the most flex in terms of when it starts due to the explosive growth of Netflix. Although SVOD is a completely separate 'right', the way consumers perceive its presence (and how consumers acquire access) is very similar to premium pay TV channels. Only for access to more content with less money, SVOD platforms become an easy sell. Again, four weeks is generally the minimum after a theatrical run (assuming a traditional release), but the start of an SVOD window can be all over the map these days. The general rule of thumb I've encountered when brokering deals with SVOD platforms is that they'll pay top dollar for exclusive rights at the earliest possible start dates. If they can 'premiere' the title, even better. The way Netflix, Hulu and other SVOD platforms have started branding acquired content as 'originals' has had a very positive effect on new subscribership. Each SVOD platform has now started to form its own content identity (just as HBO, Showtime and Starz have all worked to remain premium yet cater to different consumer groups). By offering exclusive content that cannot be seen elsewhere, SVOD platforms have given the 'cord-cutting' generation an option traditional premium channels had never anticipated. Of course, the traditional players are catching up and offering their content via SVOD channels as well (e.g., Disney+).

▶ **Free Television and AVOD**—At the tail end of the windowing game come the 'free' windows. Although by the time these entities gain access to content it has been made available several times within the territory, it still holds channel-surfing value via targeted advertisements. Exclusive windows here primarily prevent a distributor from selling the rights to two Free TV channels at the same time (that's really where the value of the license fee comes into play). But at the Free TV level, non-exclusive deals certainly exist. On the AVOD front, license fees are very rare (but it's important to note that some AVOD players do pay license fees for strong content and that well-established players in other arenas (e.g., Hulu and Netflix in the SVOD world as well as RedBox from the TVOD realm) have started making a much larger shift toward exploiting within the AVOD marketplace.

If one had to sum it up into bullet points, a 'traditional' windowing strategy would play out as follows:

(i) Theatrical run (exclusive period lasts four weeks to 12 weeks)

(ii) Premium television run (commences three to 12 months after theatrical premiere)

(iii) Ancillary exploitation (commences three to 12 months after theatrical premiere)

(iv) SVOD and basic cable (commences three to 24 months after theatrical premiere)

(v) Free TV and AVOD (commences 12 to 24 months after theatrical premiere)

The exact starts of when and how each window commences boils down to the deal structures the buying party is willing to make with the distributor. If a Free TV channel is willing to pay dramatically more than a premium TV channel, then the premium window can be skipped. If an AVOD platform sees strategic value in a property and is willing to pay premium money, then it could make it worthwhile to skip the SVOD window. So although there's no single pathway for a project, there is a fixed ordering to which rights must be exploited prior to others.

▶ ALTERNATIVE WINDOWING STRATEGIES

Although the 'traditional' windowing strategy is what most texts use to illustrate how a media property is commonly exploited, it is certainly not the only workflow distributors follow (and rules are meant to be broken). There's a significant amount of media content produced that has little to no merit ever screening in a theatrical setting (e.g., TV movies and series, straight to home entertainment content and new media).

Here are some examples:

▶ **TV Movies**—Movies of the week (MOWs or TV movies) grew in popularity in the 1970s and held a firm audience well into the '90s. Once premium channels like HBO and Showtime started producing strong original films, the Free TV channels pretty much dropped TV movies outright. However, basic cable channels with a largely middle-aged female audience (e.g., Lifetime, Hallmark) found strong numbers from TV movies and continue to broadcast them to this day. Much like other alternative release strategies, TV movies were a way to bypass the traditional studio level content (that was expensive and could take two to three years until it was made available for Free TV audiences); TV movies could be produced cheaply, discuss current events in a timely manner and could essentially be made to order (which allowed the network to invent a perfect title to boost its own ratings scheme). The added benefit was that usually the single commission by the network covered the cost to produce the title (or at least most of it), which allowed stable business for independent distributors taking on low-risk investments while building valuable internationally exploitable libraries. After a TV movie completed its initial premiere on a television network, it could be licensed to home entertainment companies for physical DVD sales as well as VOD platforms and ancillary rights. Additionally, TV movies can be sold off to competing networks as second-run content, making them a very lucrative asset.

▶ **Series**—Just as with TV movies, any form of televised series—either network produced, independently produced—will experience its initial window on the small screen. But in today's world, the small screen can range from premium channels, basic cable channels down to Free TV channels and streaming platforms. There's also the growing advent of VOD platforms commissioning and producing original media content for themselves (which can comparably range from TVOD, SVOD down to AVOD as the initial launch pad). Strong original series can gain a premium TV channel or an SVOD platform new subscribership, or increase the unique viewer counts on Free TV channels or AVOD platforms (which increase their respective ad sales). And for successful series content, home entertainment deals can be brokered. Take the classic HBO series *Sex and the City* (1998)—a premium release that was later licensed to home entertainment, VOD, basic cable, ancillary and Free TV. Aside from the two feature films and spin-off series (an outcome very few TV series ever experience), *Sex and the City*—among many great TV shows—exemplifies the ability for a TV series to be licensed and relicensed across multiple rights categories all within the realm of the small screen.

▶ **Straight-to-Video**—There's no rule saying a feature must start in theaters; for many independent titles, a theatrical run might be way too expensive to consider (since the marketing budget required can easily match or exceed the production budget). Just as the 1960s and '70s started producing lower-budget movies for direct-to-TV sales, the advent of VHS opened up the straight-to-video titles of the 1980s. Films that never stood a chance of getting produced in the theatrical space were suddenly in high demand because they could go right up alongside Hollywood blockbusters on the same shelves at video stores. Family films, low-budget action titles, indie horror films—all of them could be shot with minimal cash. Adding in a former TV star for legitimacy could make the cover art pop alongside its competition. And the mainstream video distributors were paying big money to have the content. Major studios jumped on board and started stretching out franchises they already owned (for instance, only the original version the animated dinosaur film *The Land Before Time* (1988) appeared in theaters, while its thirteen sequels were all released via direct to video; *Bring It On* (2000) was a major success in theaters, yet its four sequels were all straight-to-video). For studios, a major theatrical release is a great way to launch a title with franchise potential to the masses while making that film's straight-to-video sequels—with cheaper casts and reduced budgets—massive vehicles for profit. However, a title certainly isn't required to have a theatrical run prior to its straight-to-VOD release. The 2014 film *Camp Takota*—produced and featuring then-YouTube influencers—drew considerable attention for its financial success as a self-promoted TVOD release via iTunes and Amazon. Numerous narrative features—as well as a strong margin of documentaries—have opted to bypass traditional theatrical releases (or even limited releases) to simply premiere behind a direct-to-consumer transactional paywall. After these films have garnered strong attention in the straight-to-home entertainment space, they can often find later exploitation windows on SVOD platforms, basic cable channels, ancillary rights and later on Free TV and AVOD platforms.

▶ **New Media**—Alternative forms of new media (web series, podcasts, vlogs, e-sports gaming, etc.) can bypass traditional forms of exploitative rights windows altogether to instead be released purely as AVOD streaming content (via YouTube, social platforms or user-generated platforms) or as focused subscriber fare and/or live events (made available via platforms ranging from Facebook, Amazon or Twitch). The 'value' here is feeding a targeted audience a constant pipeline of content catered especially for them—which in turn keeps revenue derived from ads and product placement rolling in. The unique thing about content in the new media space is that because it does not require traditional exploitation windows, it does not need to adhere to traditional media specs (e.g., those related to running times, formats, story arcs, etc.). And although new media generally holds a very limited shelf life, it can exist on a platform's channel indefinitely. Additionally, content can be repurposed—meaning it can be reedited into compilations, mash-ups, countdown specials or other interstitials. In many ways, the new media content of today is as experimental as early silent films of the 1890s–1910s; the form and language of storytelling—regardless whether the content is narrative, parody or factually based—is still being written. But regardless of what emerges from the new media space, the fundamental concept that rights windows can only progress from premium windows toward 'free' windows will keep them forever limited to the 'free' or 'revenue share' space. That is why new media has little to do with the content and much more to do with the 'influencer' or brand associated with the content. Major YouTubers, Instagrammers or TikTokers are what keep the audience engaged to their channels; despite what video is shared or livestreamed, the influencer brands it as their own. Later, that influencer can be pulled into conventional forms of media that can be windowed more traditionally—as evidenced by YouTube Red's *Escape the Night* (2015) series or TikTok's Ariel Martin (professionally known as Baby Ariel) who landed a role in Disney Channel's *Z-O-M-B-I-E-S 2*, *Z-O-M-B-I-E-S 3* and *Zombies: Addison's Monster Party*. Companies have tried to manage and/or 'brand' the distribution of the shared-video and new media universe, but most are beholden to the latest influencers of the moment— making them unpredictable in terms of revenue generation—or simply incapable of retaining managerial control, as evidenced by the collapse of Defy Media that once managed YouTube channels like Smosh, Screen Junkies and Clevver Media.

▶ **Day and Date**—On the opposite end of the windowing spectrum, a day-and-date release essentially places a title across several (sometimes all) exploitable rights windows on the same date at the same time. That means a title will be available for purchase via iTunes, Vudu and the other TVOD platforms along with the cable pay-per-view channels on the same day it premieres in a movie theater or first broadcasts on television. While at first counterintuitive—why would anyone outside of die-hard cinephiles go to the theater if it's available on TV already?—there is real merit for this approach from an out-of-the-box financial perspective. Placement is crucial for success in the digital space, and titles placed into 'most popular' or 'most watched' categories tend to perform substantially stronger than their competition. Several cable VOD platforms noticed this trend and created a column for the newest of the new content: 'in theaters now' (designed for successful movies that had a theatrical run still in motion while the TVOD/EST/PPV window initiated). In the pay-per-view (PPV) world of consumers, end users would commonly gravitate towards the 'in theatres now' option and bypass all the other new releases in order to see Hollywood's latest. For indie distributors, this presented a very unique idea for how to get smaller indie titles more 'buys'; they could make them 'theatrical' runs, but in very limited ways. The question then became what constituted a title to be a 'theatrically released' film? The first answer was having the film playing on at least one or two screens across the top ten major US markets (e.g., New York, Los Angeles and Chicago representing positions 1, 2 and 3). If a film was being shown in all ten markets on the same day, it would be considered a 'theatrically released' title. There was obviously a cost to doing all this (theaters would have to be rented, digital prints would have to be delivered and ads would need to be taken out for purposes of legitimacy), but the investment of $30,000 or $40,000 could yield a return of an additional $100,000 to $250,000 on top of the profits that would have already been generated. A critical point here is that the title had to be in theaters while the title was simultaneously available via TVOD. With this strategy, it really didn't matter if audiences came to watch the title in theaters; ticket sales were not on the agenda. And because these smaller films were 'theatrical' with strong first-window performance, they could garner stronger license fees at later—lower-valued—exploitation windows. Equally, international sales increased in value since the film had been 'theatrically released' in the States. Keep in mind, the definition of a theatrical release is a constantly changing thing, but the principle of releasing additional rights into an initial release window to increase a title's performance will always be a consideration for distributors. Also, in a post-COVID world, theatrical rights have shifted slightly toward a 'franchise'-building right (one of many marketing or branding tools utilized to grow a potential franchise's audience awareness).

▶ EXTERNAL INFLUENCES

Global economic market trends—including economic events that seemingly have zero relation to the entertainment industry—can occasionally play a major role in how executives view where/when/how to place media content and in what order to window a media property's rights.

In 2010, Disney made a seemingly bold move by shortening its theatrical window of *Alice in Wonderland* from the then-traditional four months down to just three months prior to the film's home entertainment release. Not only were theater owners frustrated by the pivot, some Disney executives questioned the move—especially in that so much additional money was invested to make the film a 3D theatrical experience.

No question about it, reducing a theatrical window so dramatically was a bold shift in windowing strategy. And there are several who love to cite *Alice in Wonderland* as verification of a radical shift in how media content is released (claiming that things are permanently changing). But it's vital to filter this example—and other similar outlier examples—through a macroeconomic lens.

To keep things simple, macroeconomics essentially is a fancy way of describing the global economy as a whole. While *micro*economics defines the revenue ins and outs of a single subject (e.g., a specific company), *macro*economics explores or defines *all* companies globally, all at once at the same time. Although things like international oil prices, commodity fluctuations, interest rates or real estate trends seem completely unrelated to how films, TV shows or new media programs are financed and/or windowed, they're actually closely intertwined because revenues funnel through the same banking institutions.

What was the economic climate during *Alice in Wonderland*'s release? Pretty stark, actually. In 2010, the global markets were struggling in the wake of the 2008 financial crisis. Although 2008 was related to a real estate bubble—that really started faltering in 2007—the ripple effects wreaked havoc on banks, which had a direct impact on how major corporations borrowed and spent money in 2009 into 2010 (and arguably to this day). Consequently, individual everyday consumers suddenly found themselves living in a deep recession causing the dollars in their pocket to shrink in both volume and buying power. To simplify, consumers had less money to spend, and companies were way more conservative with the limited cash they had to invest.

Disney is a fantastic company to evaluate in terms of its distribution decisions, especially for its distribution strategies during times of economic turmoil. What makes Disney so unique is that its massive in size, generates billions of dollars annually, is a true global player (through good economic times and bad) and owns not only the production process but also has direct ownership over direct-to-consumer distribution outlets (e.g., Disney+, Disney Channel, Disney Jr., etc.). In addition to this, Disney's revenue also stems from theme parks and merchandise—both of which are heavily influenced by global market trends. It's not that Disney doesn't have to play by the same rules—which is how many view Disney's business decisions—it's that Disney holds the capability to window content distribution on a title-by-title basis since it directly owns/manages every step in the process, whereas others are beholden to precedent deal structures or larger windowing strategies that sometimes obligate them to hold a title in a select window for a longer period or shorter period even if all parties preferred a different time duration due to external macroeconomic trends (e.g., Netflix's five-day theatrical release of *Glass Onion* when many analysts argued the film left tens of millions in revenue by cutting its theatrical window short for a preestablished shift to its owned-and-operated platform).

In 2010, during a period of recession and high unemployment, Disney wanted to squeeze windows to meet as many consumers' needs as possible—as a result, they shrank theatrical windows on *Alice in Wonderland*, making the film more widely accessible. Disney pulled the same move during the COVID-19 pandemic when they bypassed theatrical runs for *Mulan* and *Soul*, but theatrical will continue to play a strong role in Disney's future releasing strategies, as will its future windowing shifts during future economic recessions (or in relation to whatever future direct-to-consumer initiative Disney thinks up next).

These shifts in windowing are very important to track, but one must always filter these decisions through a macroeconomic lens. Sticking with our principles, executives will always window from most lucrative to least (following the transactional, subscription to ad-supported model as best they can). Executives will tweak and adjust windowing durations as time goes by—some companies directly in real time, others during their next contract renewal process with third-party vendors—but this is the model they'll always follow.

▶ DETERMINING RELEASE STRATEGIES

Let's now focus on specific factors and variables that lead a distributor to choose which path is most appropriate for a given media property's release:

▶ **First Monies In**—When producers are piecing together a project, the parties initially investing into the property play a massive role in deciding how it will eventually be released. If it's a network (e.g. Showtime or Starz), they'll want to own the worldwide premiere. For some of the major multi-territory networks (e.g., BBC, HBO or Disney, ones available in multiple countries), oftentimes they'll want the program to play on all their worldwide channels simultaneously—(meaning a program premiering on Disney Channel in the US will also premiere on the same day on Disney Channel Australia, Disney Channel France, etc.). If a digital SVOD platform puts down heavy money for a program, they can also dictate domestic, international or worldwide premiere (in the case of Hulu it'd be US only, but for Netflix they can literally acquire for the world and make a property available across all countries at the same time).

▶ **Genre**—Major franchises play best with loud, persistent marking campaigns released on thousands of screens across multiple countries—people get excited about them, and distributors stand the best chance of a strong performance by making the project available on as many consumer-facing platforms as possible. By contrast, smaller art-house films with heavy drama or an intellectual twist do best in niche theaters and a completely different marketing approach (tailored press from vetted reviewers, word of mouth, festival recognition, etc.). An indie film or web series featuring a cast of all YouTube influencers would premiere best in its native YouTube platform. What distributors focus on with regards to genre is identifying where the largest number of potential end users will be—by what means they *prefer* to transact upon their content—then release accordingly.

▶ **Biggest Payer**—When distributors take a media property to a market or festival, they usually make a pretty large splash with their new content. That means all acquisitions executives see that a particular title is available at the same time. Those acquiring directly for a single media platform (a specific channel or VOD platform) are generally agnostic with regards to whether a title has properly passed through all appropriate windows; they know what content works and what their budgets are. For a distributor, if an SVOD platform is offering strong money whereas premium pay platforms or channels are low-balling prices (assuming they're even making offers), a distributor's going to go for the strongest offer on the table. Using the previous scenario, that would mean bypassing the premium outlets in order to go with an SVOD window first—which is not 'theoretically' the preferred route but makes the most sense in a dollars-and-cents world.

▶ **Timing**—Beyond predictable 'holiday genres' (e.g., Christmas-themed content, romantic comedies for Valentine's Day), there are numerous periods throughout the year that offer distributors time-sensitive content opportunities. In the US, 'back-to-school' is a very common programming stunt for a variety of consumer-facing platforms (a time period in late August where teen- and tween-themed content can garner strong numbers); other US periods include 'Black History Month' (inspirational content led by an African American cast or director can perform very well in February), 'Pride Month' (content focused on LBGTQ+ issues generally see a bump each June) as well as notable anniversaries (bundling content around a major anniversary of a significant human experience (e.g., 50th anniversary of the moon landing, notable deaths, etc.). These can be very different regionally and around the world. The holy month of Ramadan is observed by Muslims globally, and content is produced and distributed to coincide not with the 30 days of fasting but rather the 30 nights of *iftar* (when families break the fast at sunset, then enjoy a brand-new episode from their Ramadan 30-episode dramas that broadcast one new episode each night of the month). Examples of seasonal opportunities are limitless, and distributors regularly identify them for purposes of marketing and release strategy. As consumers shift from one month to the next, their interests naturally gravitate towards awareness months and significant anniversaries. Having a strong piece of content to accompany the spirit of the times always makes a good pairing. Timing can also play into the equation with something much more happenstance; perhaps a specific actor will be appearing in a major Hollywood theatrical release this August (a distributor can play off the major studio marketing to give a smaller title—with the same star appearing—a bit of a lift).

▶ **Competition**—Although generally a game reserved for the bigger studios and networks, the practice of releasing a title to purposely beat or play off another company's release can also factor in deciding when a title should go out. If a major studio (with name talent and a premium director) are preparing a massive WWII epic—one that's gaining a great deal of attention and buzz—a competing studio might be able to piggyback off this 'WWII hype' and release a similar title just weeks ahead of time. On the extreme low end, knockoffs and imitations also run rampant (micro-budgeted movies with similar titles and artwork to major studio releases can gain surprisingly strong numbers if placed the right way on digital platforms or in foreign markets). Another form of competition comes during a pricing war, only in the opposite direction you'd expect: perhaps the anniversary of a celebrity's death is fast approaching, and the networks each want a one-hour doc to commemorate; rather than pricing upwards, many distributors choose to price lower. The reason is that the networks only have so much budget to spend (and there's probably no shortage of one-hour docs if the celebrity is big enough); for distributors, sometimes any money is better than no money—meaning they deliberately undersell their title to guarantee a deal.

▶ COMMON NEGOTIATING POINTS

As discussed in Chapter 1, buyers attempt to acquire as many rights as possible, whereas sellers strive to license (dish out) the fewest rights possible. The exact purpose for this behavior is for sellers (distributors) to (i) maximize the profits of each rights category while (ii) ensuring future earnings opportunities. Although a major VOD platform or premium network might be placing a considerable level of cash on the table, there are still a few terms that can be tweaked that help future-proof a distributor's overall earnings.

▶ **Pre-Empting**—To pre-empt essentially means to 'go before'. If a distributor sells a TV series to a major premium network (e.g., Starz, Showtime or HBO), they can occasionally negotiate a transactional window to 'pre-empt' the network's premiere—putting up the exact same show on Amazon or some other transactional platform a few weeks *before* the television premiere. Networks generally feel comfortable with this model (or even encourage this); generally, the pricing on these early purchases is very steep—meaning only the very loyal will pay, which gives distributors an early bump in revenues before the premium channel takes over. The reason a transactional pre-empt is valuable for both parties is because it can serve as a form of awareness or promotion for the project (almost like a form of advertising). Not only can this help build an audience for the actual TV premiere, it can also serve to better brand the channel. The same can hold true for theatrical releases of movies; many indie distributors will release a film on limited screens—in select markets—primarily to market the film for 'preorder' or 'pre-buy' via TVOD outlets ahead of or simultaneously with the theatrical run. Distributors can negotiate for premium 'placement' of their title on the landing page of common TVOD platforms (e.g., if you open iTunes and see all those rectangular images of movies or TV shows (called 'bricks'), they aren't placed at random—nor do they simply go to the highest bidder). A 'pre-empt' window can also work in the case of a foreign-produced show appearing on a US network before it premieres in its native country. This is also seen as a major 'endorsement' for a project, the fact that a major US channel or platform was willing to pay top dollar for a title before it even played at home. Local audiences would definitely take note. The negative with a pre-empt is if the content is bad, then poor reviews or word of mouth can definitely ruin premiere ratings or box office; consequently, there's usually a bit of politicking to pull these pre-empt deals off. A common window for a 'pre-empt' is about two weeks (but the ideal is 30 days).

▶ **Day-After**—When a 'pre-empt' isn't permissible, many premium entities (channels, theaters, etc.) are open to the idea of allowing a title to be made available the 'day after' its initial premiere. This allows the premium consumer-facing platform and the audience a first crack while providing distributors a meaningful—non-competitive—right to exploit. If a feature film or first episode of a series premieres on a Friday, then at 12:01 am (the first minute of Saturday), the project can become available on iTunes, Vudu or any other transactional-based platform. That said, some contracts will require a minimum number of hours before the 'day-after' window takes effect—some will clearly require a 24-hour holdback, but others may only require two hours (allowing a full premiere block). Sometimes networks or theaters fear lost revenues for a 'day-after' digital release and will instead have a holdback for 48 to 72 hours (effectively getting the title through the weekend or pushing back for a second run). The price points for a 'day after' won't be nearly as high as they were if the title was available in a pre-empt window, but for well-rated properties, this can still generate very strong revenue.

▶ **Holdbacks**—A holdback prevents specific rights from being exploited for an agreed period of time. For example, a premium-pay channel like HBO is in direct competition with a SVOD platform like Netflix; they both have subscriber bases who expect to see unique—and quality—content in exchange for their monthly fees.

Therefore, if a deal were brokered with HBO on a film or TV series, a holdback would be included so that the distributor could not approach Netflix—or any other SVOD service—for a specific period of time. This allows HBO sole exploitation for a fixed period of time. The duration of a holdback is a negotiable item; a distributor would want to limit a holdback for as short a period as possible (HBO would seek to keep that holdback in effect for as long as possible). While we're only speaking of SVOD rights being held back, literally any right can have a holdback applied. This same hypothetical deal might be holding back all TV and VOD rights; in such an instance, the distributor would have to consider which rights have the best chance of pulling in the strongest second-window prices and focus to ease up those opportunities while still permitting the holdback against other rights. Holdbacks can exist for a duration as short as a few hours (as mentioned in the 'day-after' example earlier) or can stretch out for years—sometimes until the end of the agreement. In such cases, a distributor must carefully consider the license fee being offered in correlation to which rights categories they feel actually hold the most weight of bringing in additional cash (these variables are generally unique to each project).

▶ **Blackout Dates**—Blacking out a program is similar to a holdback, but it's generally used for programs that are already available in the marketplace. For instance, let's say a movie finished its theatrical run and is currently available in the market as both a TVOD offering and on select SVOD platforms. If a premium-pay entity (e.g. Starz) took an interest in the program and wanted to acquire it, they would most likely see the SVOD exploitation as too competitive to be worth their investment. But that doesn't mean the deal is off the table. During the negotiation, they could require the distributor to not only hold back the SVOD rights during the term (removing the title from current platforms and restricting additional platforms) but require the title to be removed no less than 30 to 60 days *before* the start of their term. The purpose for this is to allow a period of four to eight weeks (sometimes longer) where the title cannot be viewed unless paid for via a TVOD platform. This process is referred to as 'blacking out' the title (or erasing the title) in the market. The purpose is to encourage subscribership; if a title on a premium network is also available on an SVOD platform, where's the value in obtaining yet another subscription?

▶ **Limited Runs or Transmissions**—When brokering a deal, any limitation on its overall exposure can help maintain the value of a media property for future windows. For a feature film entering its TV window, limiting the number of times the network is permitted to broadcast the title is a common strategy. For very high-profile titles, the runs can be limited to a handful of airings (two or three), but generally, networks are allowed a number in the realm of ten to 15. When brokering such deals, a distributor must also be cautious of price points. In the basic cable or free-to-air TV space, content is seen as 'filler' between ad breaks (which is really where these platforms make their income); each ad that plays during a title's broadcast puts money into the network's pocket and should therefore be compensated. Limiting a feature film to five transmissions versus 15 or 20 plays a huge role to reigning in overexposure in the market as well as the risk of underselling it. A distributor needs to allow a bit of flex to make the title 'efficient' in the eyes of the acquirer while not shortchanging themselves.

▶ **Exclusivity vs. Non-Exclusivity**—An exclusive deal means that only the party acquiring the rights is permitted to exploit those rights within the territory for the agreed-upon duration of time; a *non*-exclusive deal allows multiple parties (an infinite number) to exploit the same set of rights in the same territory simultaneously. Having a title available on a variety of platforms—for the same select rights—is a great scenario for distributors (multiple revenue streams); but for consumer-facing platforms, it's difficult for them to make noise in the marketplace if other companies are already selling the same content. Therefore, consumer-facing platforms generally request exclusive rights so that they 'own' that title for their specific subset of rights. But to obtain exclusive rights, a consumer-facing platform must be willing to pay a reasonable sum of money to warrant fully taking those rights off the table. Occasionally, deals can have an exclusive period for a select set of rights followed by a non-exclusive period. Earlier we discussed this notion with regard to 'holdbacks', but in the case of 'holdbacks', the acquiring party isn't necessarily buying those rights; they just don't want others to sell them. In an exclusive-to-non-exclusive shift, a VOD platform might require a 90-day exclusive period—so that they can claim first dibs on a show's performance—but then allow their competitors to join the party on day 91 (only after that initial VOD platform has siphoned off a large percentage of the likely end users). For a distributor, this is a happy medium; as long as there's incentive for this first company to be granted an exclusive period (generally via increased license fee), then the move can be justified.

▶ Everything Is Negotiable

If you are new to many of the concepts regarding distribution, then this chapter might have been a bit tough to digest. Don't sweat it. When I was starting out in distribution, it felt as if every new deal presented a definition, right or concept I didn't even realize existed. The truth is they still do; that's because terms, definitions and release strategies change all the time, but the *principles* of media distribution are constant.

Whenever these concepts start to feel as if they're going over your head, simply return to the core principles discussed in Chapter 1; they explain at a high level the logic behind these workflows and why such tactics exist. Even though we covered some complicated windowing strategies and rights valuations in this chapter, all we were really discussing were two core principles: (1) media rights devalue over time, and (2) buyers acquire the most they can for as little money as possible, whereas sellers grant the least while holding out for the most revenue.

Thereafter, the complex back-and-forth (e.g., what goes first, what gets held back, etc.) ends up being different from one project to the next regardless of size. Distribution is a bit of a guessing game, one that sometimes has stringent rules while other times seems open to interpretation. And although it might seem as if distributors have ingeniously mapped out what will occur when, the truth is they're just going with the flow and following the money. From this, distributors will negotiate terms and orchestrate release ideas based upon the inevitable truths that their media project will devalue over time and that they need to price each right—across each window—to the best of their abilities based upon what's available to them in the present moment.

6

Global Media Distribution

Films, TV programs and new media content are not limited to generating revenues from one single market, territory or country. They can travel, garnering sales from around the world. However, the global media marketplace is not a level playing field. The values generated from each category of content—as well as the dealmaking strategies applied to broker content deals from one country to the next—can vary drastically on a title-by-title basis. This makes sense, and we can see this reality in play within other verticals: when the economy of one quadrant of the world is booming, another is in recession; a war or political crisis in one region can have bizarre effects elsewhere; and, cultural tastes and social sensitivities are all over the map. Throw in government regulations, international sanctions and good ole third-world bribery and doing business on a world-wide scale is a daunting task. But there is a method to the madness.

Because the international marketplace operates differently than domestic ones, companies must generally hire experienced sales representatives to manage overseas territories. It's not that the international marketplace is harder to work within, but foreign deals do require a different approach (and depend upon individuals comfortable adapting to language barriers, regional nuances and different business workflows). Although all of these things can easily be learned from experience, companies prefer to hire veterans who can simply get the job done on day one rather than train individuals from scratch.

Junior sales reps—individuals still getting their feet wet in the international market— usually oversee lower-caliber territories (ones that pay less and have simpler terms to negotiate). More senior sales executives will handle the larger territories (the ones with the strongest financial values and more complicated deal terms). These individuals are usually assigned 'regions' of the world to oversee (collections of countries and territories geographically or politically grouped together.) The number of regional divisions—and

DOI: 10.4324/9781003357902-7

how such regions are split—is usually determined by how many employees are in the company along with each individual's level of experience (smaller companies might only have two or three people managing international deals, while larger ones might have dozens).

Although the standardized deal structures are quite common to those previously discussed (in Chapters 2, 3 and 4), what does differ is that there are four styles of content deals that get brokered in the international marketplace:

1) Finished content deals

2) Repurposed content deals

3) Reproduced content deals

4) Foreign 'presales'

▶ **Finished Content**—'Finished' content, sometimes described to as 'ready-made' content, refers to completed media properties that are licensed 'as is' and imported into a foreign territory for local exploitation. Although these properties must go through a process of adaptation—for example, being dubbed or subtitled into a foreign language, potentially getting re-titled so the concept translates better to local audiences, etc.—the changes are relatively low-key, meaning the property itself remains essentially the same as the one which premiered in its country of origin.

▶ **Repurposed Content**—The cultural expectation of how a film or series should be structured differs from one country to the next. In example, the expectation of how long a program's duration should be can vary greatly; ITV in the UK occasionally broadcasts 90-minute episodes, Antenna in Spain prefers 70-minute episodes and channels in Brazil have long-running afternoon blocks (lasting three hours or more) whereby a local talent—in a 'talk show' format—will introduce a new series. Many programs are hosted; however, a popular host in Norway won't always click with the viewers in Romania, Japan or South Africa. But unlike 'finished content' where programs or films are released 'as is' and simply dubbed or re-titled for international exploitation, the 'repurposing' of content allows local buyers to acquire foreign properties and dismantle or rework them for better acceptance at the local level. Foreign hosts can be replaced with local ones; a 90-minute UK episode can be cut down into two separate 60-minute episodes in the US; and clip-oriented titles (e.g., *America's Funniest Home Videos*) can be spliced and intercut with local 'gag' or 'blooper' programs. Although the process of 'repurposing' is much more common in the television space, this process is used with features as well (especially when local buyers must excise problematic scenes or sequences to meet regional censorship demands or ratings approvals).

▶ **Reproduced Content**—When the concept of a media property is very strong, but the cast language or locations make it feel 'too foreign' to license as a finished program, there is the option to simply reproduce the program at the local level. This is exactly how the obscure Colombian comedy series *Yo soy Betty, la fea* became the US megahit *Ugly Betty* or the Dutch singing competition *The Voice of Holland* evolved into the multinational entertainment series *The Voice*. Although this process can occur across any type of media property (e.g., the Hong Kong action film *Infernal Affairs* (2002) getting adapted into Martin Scorsese's *The Departed* (2006), or Alejandro Amenábar's *Open Your Eyes* (1997) into the Cameron Crowe film *Vanilla Sky* (2001)), this workflow is much more common in the realm of television, where the easily replicable 'format' of a successful series (or its structure) will be sold to international broadcasters and production companies. Formatting a program is very similar to franchising a storefront or restaurant (e.g., Starbucks or McDonald's); the process 'distributes' a media property backed by a strong brand while allowing it to be localized in a more organic-feeling manner (with local hosts speaking in a local language rather than a foreign host overlaid with a choppy dub). Check out Appendix II for a full contract sample to get a sense for how the 'format' rights in a media property are brokered internationally.

▶ **Foreign Presales**—Preselling foreign territories is the process whereby a distributor will pitch international clients—on a territory-by-territory basis—with 'in-development' projects in order to fund each project's eventual production. Preselling via foreign clients allows a distributor to incrementally build the funds necessary to produce the project while never requiring one single client (representing one single international territory) to commit funds above or beyond normal market values from that region. Not only does this process allow international clients early access to premium content (placing them ahead of their competitors), it also allows distributors the opportunity to reduce the financial burden required from their local buying partners. For instance, if a US company secured 65% of the funds necessary to produce a feature film via foreign presales, they would only have to lock 35% from a local US buyer (rather than 100%). Although foreign presales can be used for television series and/or new media projects, it is most commonly used to fund independent feature films.

▶ DEFINING DISTRIBUTION 'TERRITORIES'

When distributors engage in business with the international marketplace, they do not specify geographical boundaries simply by commonplace country names, continents or even governmental definitions; instead, they divide the global marketplace by 'territories' (which bundle international regions based upon commonly understood *needs*).

There are a multitude of reasons for this practice, but it usually—as with everything else in commerce—boils down to money. For some countries, their individual buying power is so small it makes more sense to partner with larger neighboring countries to create a more regionally functional workflow. India, for instance, is a massive country with over a billion citizens, yet its buying power is actually quite low. Although an 'emerging' market, India can certainly stand on its own two feet fiscally and far surpasses its economically unstable neighbors (e.g., Sri Lanka, Bangladesh, Nepal, etc.).

Therefore, the deal terms India can offer would warrant a direct one-on-one deal (the license fees would be reasonable and would justify the materials expenses); that's not the case with India's neighbors. A one-on-one deal with Bangladesh would be complicated for a Western-based company; the money would be tiny, and the logistics would be complicated. However, the deal terms offered by Bangladesh would be reasonable for an Indian-based distributor. Because of this, smaller 'satellite' nations like Bangladesh, Nepal and Sri Lanka can partner with India and band together as a territorial region—led by an Indian distributor representing them all. As a result, a Western client can make a one-time deal with an Indian-based distributor and grant that client rights not only to India but also additional countries (ones deemed appropriate based upon regional proximity, language capabilities and/or cultural understanding) wherein they're permitted to exploit the title. The Western distributor gets to close more countries (for a slight bump in revenue) and allows their Indian-based acquisitions company to handle to the smaller players—and the less financially capable neighboring countries get to engage in business with a regional player who understands their budget capabilities and payment schedules. This is why a sale to India is commonly referred to by its territorial definition: 'India and the Subcontinent' (generally defined as India, Pakistan, Sri Lanka, Nepal and Bangladesh).

Whereas India's territory is etched out by low-paying bordering countries, the territory of France has a different type of financial burden: dubbing costs. A deal is never really closed with the country of France alone; its territory is defined as 'French-speaking Europe' (which includes France along with French-speaking Switzerland, French-speaking Belgium and occasionally reaches into French-speaking Africa or even gets defined as 'French-speaking world'—which includes regions ranging from French-speaking Canada, Haiti to islands as remote as French Polynesia in the Pacific Ocean). Therefore, securing a deal with France includes a multinational or potentially global geographical territory united by a common language. The reason is that French is one of the most expensive dubs to produce (the ideal Parisian dialect is required, translations of scripts into the French language are held to extremely high standards by regulatory boards and the French unions are in full force driving up the costs). And because of this heavy investment, France-based acquisitions executives want as many French-speaking territories to help recoup their expenses.

As for other examples, Scandinavian countries (Denmark, Sweden, Norway, Finland and Iceland) usually partner together as the territory of 'Scandinavia' to offset costs; the countries of Belgium, Benelux and Luxembourg commonly band together as the territory of 'Benelux'; and the Middle East covers 19 nations (stretching from Morocco in Western Africa to Iran in Central Asia); because of this wide reach, the Middle East is often territorially defined as 'the Middle East and North Africa' (or simply 'MENA' for short).

Of the 196-ish countries in the world, the international marketplace of media distribution uses 160-ish geographical territories. (I say 'ish' because new countries do pop up and dissolve from time to time (e.g., Sudan's 2011 split into North Sudan and

South Sudan), not all countries, commonwealths or sovereign territories are recognized (e.g., Taiwan, Palestine, etc.) and the designation of a country versus a principality can sometimes be up for grabs (e.g., 'the Vatican' versus 'Italy including the Vatican').

Although 'territories' seem like a constantly evolving collection of puzzle pieces, their definitions remain quite consistent across both the film and television landscapes. There are occasions of regional rights conflicts or disputes over contested territories; however, distributors around the world work by a commonly understood framework of how the geographical world is carved up in relation to the entertainment business. Although one might assume 'new media' content does not adhere to traditional territories—especially given the exposure many YouTube influencers have globally— territorial definitions are still applicable. VOD platforms are still bound to respect territory specific holdbacks and rights restrictions, and even 'global' entities like Netflix, Facebook and Google are completely banned or restricted in certain territories (namely China).

▶ UNDERSTANDING INTERNATIONAL TERRITORIES

To give a bit of insight as to how distributors approach the international marketplace, then consider the following 'snapshot' overviews covering a few of the world's major media territories. Please note, this list is not focused only on the largest revenue-driving regions; I've instead opted to highlight an array of territories to offer readers insight into how drastically individual regions within the international market differ from one to another. And since this list is not intended to rank any specific territory, I've opted to list each of the following in alphabetical order:

Australia and New Zealand

Due to their close proximity—and use of English as a native language—Australia and New Zealand are generally lumped together as one single territorial definition (commonly referred to as 'Aus/NZ' or simply 'ANZ'). There are, however, many instances in which distributors might license film or television rights to either Australia *or* New Zealand separately (especially for deals involving first-run television series or international coproductions utilizing the tax credits of either country). But in the realm of standardized indie film, television, and new media distribution, usually 'Aus/NZ' is licensed all at once. Occasionally, several of the Pacific Island nations filling the waters between Australia and Southern Asia will be included, which is often defined by the territorial name of 'Australasia' or sometimes 'Oceana'.

What makes the business of media distribution unique in this part of the world derives from the geography of this continent; Australia itself is a massive country with a very sparse population (less than 30 million citizens). Most reside in Sydney, Brisbane or Melbourne on the country's eastern side, or in Perth on the country's far western side— which leaves over 2,000 miles of seemingly uninhabited land in between. Aus/NZ also resides in the Southern Hemisphere—meaning its warmer months take place in the winter, and its colder months take place in the summer. This is important to note because many seasonally focused properties (e.g. a Christmas film taking place in a snowy land-scape) don't resonate down under.

The bulk of the country's business decisions are made in its capital city of Sydney, which is where the major television networks (e.g., Foxtel, Nine, Seven and its public chan-nel, Australian Broadcasting Corporation (ABC)) are based. Major home entertainment giant Village Roadshow is also based in Sydney, as are several of the major production facilities including Village Roadshow Studios and Fox Studios Australia.

Way in the South Eastern region of the country sits Melbourne, which is where the majority of independent distributors operate (especially in the home entertainment space). Melbourne certainly has a production hub with Dockside, but not nearly at the level of Sydney. Ironically, Australia was one of the 'DVD holdout' nations in the world. The reason for this slow adaptation to digital is a direct result of that giant 2,000+ mile gap between the country's east and west coast population hubs. Wireless capabilities hit this nation late; major cities had reasonable connectivity, but the rural areas in Central Australia were still reliant on traditional forms of media (e.g., free-to-air TV and DVD) well into the mid-2010s. Although VOD is now commonplace—even outside major metropolitan hubs—this western nation is still considered a bit slower to adopt new forms of media exploitation.

The major competitor to Netflix in the region is Stan, the homegrown SVOD platform owned by Nine Networks. Amazon's Prime service moved into the territory officially in 2017, adding the triple layer of global digital expansion seen in multiple major territo-ries: Netflix as #1, Amazon as #2 and a local player (in this case Stan) serving as #3. As of this writing, Stan is still working to find its identity among the giants.

Australia, especially Sydney, has a surprisingly large Asian community—not so sur-prising when you consider its closest geographic neighbors. As a result, many channels are catered to the content needs of this population (as are theatrical screens showing Southeast Asian content).

And regarding New Zealand, don't discredit the Kiwi nation's strength based upon its size. Although Australia generally leads the Aus/NZ territory as the stronger interna-tional buying and production partner, New Zealand can stand on its own two feet when the timing is right. For proof, consider the US megahit *American Idol*. Although directly evolved from the UK-produced *Pop Idol*, the *Idol* franchise traces its origins back to the 1999 New Zealand series *Popstars*. Throw in Flight of the Conchords, its base of media aggregators and the fact that its main channels—the government-owned Television New Zealand (or TVNZ) and Mediaworks New Zealand (owners of TV3)—pay healthy money for outside content, and this tiny nation is a country taken very seriously by distributors.

But despite the fact that both Australia and New Zealand are English-speaking, it is rare for natively produced content to cross over into the international market. In theory, content produced in this part of the world should enjoy the same success experienced by US-, Canadian- and UK-produced programming (that sells easily worldwide); but for some reason, Aus/NZ content rarely breaks out. That said, some of its talent has found great success internationally: Peter Jackson, Nicole Kidman, Russell Crow and Baz Luhrmann, just to name a few.

China

China is formally defined as the People's Republic of China (or PRC) and usually includes regions it identifies as falling under its 'One China' footprint (e.g., Taiwan, Mongolia) and occasionally includes its 'Special Administrative' regions of Hong Kong and Macao (territories that can also license content independently). China's sheer size, it's 3,000+ TV channels, it's massive population of over 1 billion people and its current ranking as the world's second largest economy—after the US—give many people the false impression that this nation stands as a huge revenue driver for foreign-produced media content. Truth is it doesn't.

China is bound by quotas, which block out a large number of foreign-produced films and series; government regulations make Internet access problematic, which has become a major obstacle for new media platforms like Instagram, YouTube and Facebook; and piracy, corruption and copyright infringement are rampant.

One of the first major obstacles media industry outsiders must deal with is that foreign producers or distributors are not allowed to operate independently, nor are they permitted to create their own companies or partnerships with Chinese companies (which is how the business is done most everywhere else). Chinese companies must lead these moves. And whatever content is created must go through an extensive evaluation process—starting at script stage—with the State Administration of Press, Publication, Radio, Film and Television (SAPPRFT, or occasionally referred to as SARFT for those dropping the 'Press, Publication' components of this administrative board). Feature films that are eventually approved to move forward are required to be distributed by a Chinese entity, generally one of the two state-run majors: the China Film Group Corp. or Huaxia Film Distribution.

Television and VOD distribution is no different; only an authorized Chinese company may acquire rights to foreign-produced content (and it still must go through the appropriate censorship approvals process). Of course, SAPPRFT or the Ministry of Culture can still blacklist a property—and have it removed—even after it's been approved. Although such instances are most commonly a result of controversial political themes, a foreign-produced title can also be forcibly taken out of circulation simply if it gains 'too much' popularity and outperforms Chinese productions.

And SAPPRFT isn't the only censorship board distributors must work with; based upon the subject matter of a given media property, other government offices might be required to review it as well. An action film dealing with spies or covert operations might require approval from the Ministry of State Security; if a film addresses socio-logical issues (like woman's rights or civil rights), the State Ethnic Affairs Commission will have to review. And anything delving into topics of religion or spirituality will have to gain approval from the State Bureau of Religious Affairs. The list of administrative boards is staggering.

Then there are 'blackout' dates, which are seemingly random periods of days or weeks whereby censorship boards ban foreign-produced content from broadcasting or screen-ing anywhere in the country. Why would this occur? To allow Chinese-produced titles an opportunity to gain critical box office revenues during peak consumption periods (e.g., Chinese New Year).

That all said, there is big business to be done provided the right approach is taken. China became a member of the World Trade Organization in late 2001, which allowed private mini-major studios to be created, opening doors to foreign investment and collabora-tion. This is why major Hollywood films started rolling cameras in China during the mid-2000s as opposed to more traditional foreign havens such as Canada or Australia. Although major studio films still get rejected by Chinese regulatory boards—for exam-ple, the Marvel hit *Deadpool* (2016)—Hollywood has implemented clever ways to gain nods of approval from these organizations—*The Martian* (2015) and *Arrival* (2016), two great American science fiction films interestingly embedded plotlines showcasing Chinese characters coming to the rescue of the United States (an appealing theme to the Communist nation).

And even though piracy and copyright infringement are major topics of concern, branded intellectual property is a very well-respected commodity across Mainland China. Comic book heroes and other similar 'branded' IP can garner strong investment from China, and formats can be acquired and produced within the nation, allowing cen-sorship approvals to be future-proofed from the concept phase.

Although a very tough nut to crack, for those large entities that have the means to play ball in China—which essentially limits the field to major studios—the revenue can be extraordinarily large (even if a bit of it is more than likely getting skimmed off the top).

France and the French-Speaking World

As previously mentioned, deals are rarely closed with 'France' alone; French acquisi-tion execs prefer to define their territory as 'French-speaking Europe'—which encom-passes France, Luxembourg, Monaco, French-speaking Belgium and French-speaking Switzerland—or expand this definition to include the entire French-speaking world (often written as "France including DOM-TOM"—an acronym for Départements d'Outre Mer, Territoires d'Outre Mer which translates to 'Overseas Departments and Territories'). While the French-speaking 'world' includes all nations using French as a national language (ranging from French-speaking Canada in North America to Cote d'Ivoire in Africa), DOM-TOM includes all of the tiny islands scattered across the globe that France actively represents—e.g., French Guiana, French Polynesia, Martinique.

The reason for this stems from the fact that in France, its language is a major part of its identity. Consequently, foreign-produced content deemed worthy of theatrical release or broadcast must go through a very rigorous adaptation process and be dubbed not just into the French language but specifically into its *Parisian* dialect. And given the extremely high standards required by regulatory boards coupled with the French unions driving up the costs, French stands as the most expensive language in which to dub media content. A low-end dub for a single hour-long episode of a TV drama can average $25,000 to $30,000 (and once you add in some well-known talent and make it a long-running series, you can easily add a zero or two to each broadcast hour. And because of this heavy investment, France-based acquisitions executives want as many French-speaking territories to help recoup their expenses. A solution sometimes employed by distributors is to dub the content into French themselves, but there is a great deal of risk involved considering the dialect and regulated translation procedures are so particular (along with the cost of undertaking such a move).

One of the unique aspects of France—which can prove to be quite challenging for indie distributors—is that France has a rather infamous Media Chronology law (government-mandated rules on how titles were to be windowed). The initial concept was to ensure that any foreign film that received a theatrical exhibition in its native country would be treated equally in France, but there were also strict windowing rules against forms of home entertainment (stretching windows to extreme two- or even three-year periods between Free TV and SVOD). But in that technology tends to move faster than legislation—and the grip of streaming giants like Netflix had the influence and resources and find loopholes—the rigid rules of Media Chronology fell under increasing pressure to change.

One of the major public moments that helped bring about this change occurred during the 2017 Cannes Film Festival. That year, Netflix had two films at Cannes in competition—Bong Joon-ho's *Okja* (2017) and Noah Baumbach's *The Meyerowitz Stories* (2017)—that were to follow Netflix's normal original content workflow of first being made available on its service to be later released into other rights windows later on (including theatrical). This was seen as undermining the regulated French process of releasing content to the point that—after attempting to have both films removed from the competition unless they were released theatrically in French theaters—France's political system instead pressured the festival into requiring *all* films going forward from 2018 to receive a French theatrical release in order to be eligible for competition.

The Media Chronology laws were finally revised—a bit—in 2022. Although still eye-rollingly rigid, the mandated windows are at least now a fraction of what they once were.

In addition to producing their own media content, French majors (e.g., StudioCanal, Pathé, Gaumont) often coproduce international films and TV series—which allows them to obtain early access to French-speaking world rights in a way that allows them to manage their forced Media Chronology windows (which explains why France remains a strong nation for format development). With this high-level access to first-run content, coupled with 'European content' minimum quotas, France can feel quite difficult to penetrate for foreign-based distributors. What's most important to note is that although the money can be extremely strong, deals in France are much more sporadic. Many foreign-based distributors choose to work with locally based exclusive agents—native French speakers who are generally based in Paris—but the French territory remains quite receptive to closing deals with outside entities (it just needs to be the right content worthy of the extreme expense of working within France's rigid system).

Latin America

Distributors have different lenses with which they view the geographical scope of a Latin American deal; most common would be 'pan-regional Latin America'—which is usually shorthanded as 'Pan Lat Am' and is defined as the following nations: British Guyana, Central America (specifically Belize, Costa Rica, El Salvador, Guatemala, Honduras, Nicaragua, Panama), French Guiana, Mexico, South America (defined as Argentina, Bolivia, Brazil, Chile, Colombia, Ecuador, Paraguay, Peru, Uruguay, Venezuela and Suriname).

Note that this definition excludes numerous Spanish-speaking islands located within the Caribbean (e.g., Bahamas, Cayman Islands, Cuba, Dominican Republic, St. Barts, etc.) as well as Spanish-speaking United States of America (including US possessions such as Puerto Rico). Some distributors will try to squeeze both of these 'add-on' territories into their assumed definition of pan-regional Latin America, but the Caribbean and Spanish-speaking United States are technically separate. Whereas Spanish-speaking US—often called 'US Hispanic' or simply USH—is technically included within the 'North America' territorial definition, the 'Spanish' language is often stripped out of North American distribution agreements (it can be very advantageous for rights holders to offer US exposure to pan-regional Latin American deals); the Caribbean, however, exists as its own territory but with its low buying capability, its geographical reach is often absorbed by either North America or pan-regional Latin America yet sometimes remains 'nonexclusive' and is shared between the two (see 'Disputed Territories and Possessions' later in this chapter). But because of these differences of opinion on what constitutes 'Latin America', nearly every distribution agreement will define the territory by listing out each nation.

Latin America is a dubbing territory, meaning any foreign content licensed will almost certainly be dubbed into the local language(s). Occasionally, for some higher-profile films or series, subtitles are acceptable, but the vast majority of content gets dubbed. Generally, Pan Lat Am distribution deals grant two languages by means of dubbing and/or subtitling: neutral Spanish (meaning a dialect of Spanish that is easily under-stood throughout pan-regional Latin America and is very different than Castilian Span-ish spoken in Spain) and Portuguese (specifically 'Brazilian Portuguese' aka 'BPORT', which is also quite different than the European dialect spoken in Portugal).

The vast bulk of Latin American content is produced in Mexico, Colombia or Brazil. The biggest media giant in the region is Televisa; headquartered in Mexico City, this massive telecommunications company produces tens of thousands of program hours each year. Not only can they spread this content across the multitude of channels they own and operate throughout the Pan Lat Am footprint, they also own the film dis-tribution and production giant Videocine. Televisa also has an ongoing relationship with the North American network Univision to cover US Hispanic rights along with BLIM, the #2 SVOD platform—next to Netflix—available throughout the region. Although most known internationally for their high-profile soap operas (known as telenovelas)—which export well throughout the world—they also produce movies and factual content.

Most in the world of distribution describe Latin America as one of the toughest markets to work within; this is true. But this complication is primarily due to the fact that there are really two types of deals that can be closed in Lat Am: (i) pan-regional deals (mean-ing a deal encompassing the entire territorial definition) or (ii) select territory deals (meaning a direct deal with a specific country—e.g., 'Argentina only' or 'Brazil only').

The big money can be found closing a pan-regional deal (meaning selling a feature film to a massive Lat Am distributor or licensing a TV series to a pan-regional broadcaster—such as Discovery Networks Latin America or AMC Networks Latin America). These distributors will pay a healthy license fee and handle all of the dubbing and localiza-tion expenses. But with major players like Televisa supplying such massive quantities of locally produced content—coupled with the fact that most pan-regional theatrical distributors and broadcasters are provided the bulk of their content by means of output deals from the US—there tends to be very little room left over for independent acquisi-tions. Therefore, only a handful of titles will be seen as valuable enough to take on the effort to acquire, dub and distribute locally.

Smaller money can be found licensing deals directly with distributors or broadcasters in each country (e.g., a direct deal with network Telefe in Argentina). Although it is quite common to sell directly to buyers in Brazil—for the country of Brazil only—other Latino nations are a bit more complex. The reason boils down to dubbed language expec-tations and the very tiny license fees usually offered by each country. In Brazil, Portu-guese is spoken; because this contrasts with its Spanish-speaking neighbors, Brazilian buyers have grown accustomed to licensing and dubbing content. And although Span-ish is spoken everywhere outside of Brazil, each country tends to have its own dialect; because of this, the 'neutral' Spanish language referred to earlier is used for purposes of dubbing. And although neutral Spanish is a comparatively cheap dub to produce, for smaller nations, especially very poor ones—Honduras, Peru, etc.—they require the content dubbed in advance (otherwise they wouldn't be able to cover the costs of both the license fee and the dub with the ease the pan-regional buyers can); because most foreign distributors aren't used to dubbing in advance, these smaller countries tend to resort to buying from the major pan-regional players and the closed-off cycle repeats itself. However, for the companies willing to take on this dubbing burden—and who are comfortable with the surprising volume of paperwork required by local buyers—strong money can be generated.

The other major complaint most distributors have with regard to Latin America is the painstakingly slow turnaround time with agreements. Even after all terms to a deal are agreed, it can easily take months for the Latin American side to return the agreements with signature. Payments can be equally slow, sometimes requiring distributors to send materials in advance of payment (which is something that makes third-party distributors incredibly nervous). But this is how the region works. It's overwhelmingly bureaucratic and requires a distributor to take a leap of faith on occasion; this is why most Lat Am buyers tend to gravitate towards buying content from distributors they've worked with in the past (the required trust and workflow has already been preestablished).

But this does offer a glimpse as to why most outside the region find Latin America to be a very tough market to work within. Because of this 'barrier', most companies work with territorial agents—ones who have a lifetime of close buying contacts throughout the region and who speak the language. Although Lat Am agents can be based anywhere, most are located in Buenos Aires, Argentina or within the US city of Miami, Florida (which is where many US networks house their Lat Am divisions, for example, HBO Latin America, AMC Networks Latin America, etc. and where Lat Am media conferences commonly occur). Common media trades include Prensario, Senal and Cveintiuno.

The one realm where foreign-based distributors have found a silver lining is with formats; all of the major Lat Am channels send formats acquisition teams to the major markets to bring home new content ideas. Since the style and approach of content is very different throughout the region—generally requiring much larger numbers of episodes per season (e.g., a season of 39 episodes versus a US season of 13), or use of regional hosts to present a full afternoon of content rather than single hours, etc.—it's much easier for networks to simply acquire the format rights to a successful international property and produce the exact content their unique market demands.

Middle East and North Africa (MENA)

Distributors define the Middle East differently than classical or governmental definitions. In the film and television industry, the general understanding is that this territory covers all of the classic Arabic-speaking Middle Eastern nations (Bahrain, Egypt, Iraq, Jordan, Kuwait, Lebanon, Oman, Qatar, Saudi Arabia (aka the Kingdom of Saudi Arabia, or simply 'KSA'), Syria, United Arab Emirates, which includes Dubai (aka UAE) and Yemen), while also including the Arabic-speaking nations of Northern Africa (Algeria,

Libya, Morocco, Sudan (North and South) and Tunisia) along with the Farsi-speaking nation of Iran. As a result, the 'Middle East' is sometimes referred to as 'Middle East and North Africa' or simply as 'MENA'.

The nations of Cyprus, Israel and Turkey are almost never included within distribution deals for the MENA territory. Cyprus is generally included in the 'Greece' territorial definition, whereas Israel and Turkey are classified as individual territories due to their respective language needs and economic strengths. Also, the political tensions of both Israel and Turkey with their Middle Eastern neighbors makes it difficult—or in some cases illegal, as with Israel—for select Middle East–based distributors to engage in direct business.

In that this region is in a state of continual change, disputed areas such as 'Western Sahara', the 'Palestinian territories' along with the partially recognized State of Palestine, non-recognized areas like 'Kurdistan' or 'Kurdish-Speaking' regions covering Northern Iraq and Southeastern Turkey, and/or failed states which use the Arabic language that sit extremely close to the 'MENA' footprint (e.g., Somalia) are usually included but get defined in a variety of different ways (e.g., 'Arabic-speaking Africa').

When distributing foreign content into the MENA region, the primary languages granted are English, Arabic and Farsi by means of subtitling and dubbing. Occasionally 'Kurdish' or other regional dialects are included—which would classify as an example of cleverly including 'Kurdistan' into the territorial footprint—but these are rare requests. French is occasionally requested since French is used in a variety of MENA nations—especially in Lebanon and select African nations—but this language is usually negotiated out of the deal to prevent conflict with potential 'France' territory deals (which often require 'French-speaking Africa' exclusively). The allowance of English is due to the extreme variations in the spoken dialects of Arabic. For example Tunisia, Egypt and Oman speak almost entirely different oral languages (nearly incomprehensible to one another) but all use the same written form of Arabic. This results in most films and television programs simply getting subtitled into Arabic (with the program's native language remaining) rather than getting formally dubbed, since all countries—excluding Iran—read the 'classical Arabic' text. Only a handful of nations (e.g., Egypt, Qatar, Saudi Arabia) would consider spending the money to dub content, which would still only be reserved for high-end Hollywood titles. As with most countries, content aimed at younger children (e.g., animation) must be dubbed since little ones cannot yet read.

In that MENA covers several countries, each with its own cultural, economic and political sensitivities, it's most common to work with regional acquisitions agents (or regional distributors) rather than licensing rights to each country individually—especially given the variations in buying power when comparing Saudi Arabia or UAE to Yemen (one of the poorest nations in the world). These distributors will acquire film and television rights for the entire territory, take on the costs associated with subtitling (many of whom own their own subtitling facilities), then repurpose provided artwork to create posters and sales sheets that better appeal to the various regulatory boards and channel censorship committees (e.g., translating titles, billing blocks and synopsis details). These distributors will then sell the rights of the content on a right-by-right basis to each respective country. As a result of this burdensome work, most MENA distributors require all available rights and push for lengthier term lengths (averaging five to seven years, with some extending far beyond the ten-year mark). Most distributors are based in Beirut or Dubai.

Major US studios (and other international powerhouse content providers) will enter into exclusive deals with regional distribution companies. For the studio or content provider, this serves as a valuable output deal which guarantees lucrative business in a less financially stable region of the world; for the regional distributor, acting as an 'exclusive agent' on behalf of a major US studio or international content provider secures direct business with the region's best-paying clients and allows leverage for better license fees—regional distributors often proudly display these relationships on their business cards or company websites. Medium-level and smaller distributors (e.g., mini-majors or indies) rarely secure these output deals.

While each country has its own assortment of government and private channels offering Free TV content, most citizens prefer accessing the major satellite Free and Pay TV channels offered by OSN (named from its merger of Orbitz and Showtime) and MBC (the Middle East Broadcasting Center Group)—both of which are headquartered in Dubai. Most citizens throughout the territory access both companies' Pay TV channels illegally—one person in an apartment building will purchase the subscription and then take cash payments from the other tenants for access to their feed. This is known and tolerated by all major players in the region; the richer Gulf nations more than cover the loss and allow these channels to remain profitable. Also, most locally produced television shows have incorporated their ads into the program itself (during my last visit to the region, *Project Runway Middle East* felt like I was watching *The Truman Show* with how the principle talents spoke about products and merchandise).

The three largest headquarters for the theatrical business are Beirut, Cairo and Dubai. The largest chain of cinemas is Dubai-based Novo Cinemas followed by Cairo-based Renaissance Cinemas. However, since this book was first published, Saudi Arabia has since ballooned into a major production hub in the region.

The most popular types of content continue to be Hollywood films, European productions and Bollywood content—there is little space (or demand) for regional or independent films, but they can be found locally.

Contrary to popular assumption, censorship demands aren't too rigid (and graphic sex scenes can be found as frequently on MENA premium pay channels as they can on North American or European networks); that said, most broadcasters have strict policies toward carving out any negative stereotypes about the region (i.e., removing 'terrorist' jokes or references to political leaders). In example, while jet-lagged, channel surfing one night in Beirut, I was shocked that *Basic Instinct*'s infamous vagina shot played uncensored while *Back to the Future* received heavy edits due to Doc Brown having bought plutonium from Libyan terrorists.

There is no home entertainment market. Pirated DVDs and Blu-rays are openly sold on streets or as 'side businesses' in back rooms of legitimate businesses or even at people's homes. With weak Internet connections coupled with a cultural complacency towards piracy, the VOD market is virtually nonexistent. Although the major Pay TV channels (OSN and MBC) offer SVOD services, these exist more as 'upsells' or 'add-ons' for current subscribers of the satellite feed. Other moves in the VOD space have been attempted by outsiders (e.g., Starz's launch of Starz Play Arabia in 2015 and Netflix's push for Arabic subtitled content for its 2016 global launch), but the real financial opportunities in MENA remain in the linear space of major theatrical releases and television broadcast deals.

United Kingdom and Ireland

The United Kingdom is comprised of Great Britain, Wales, Scotland and Northern Ireland—with the actual Republic of Ireland (the island) existing as an independent nation and formally part of the European Union. For the purposes of a media territory, the United Kingdom stands on its own (as the 'UK') but can occasionally—especially in 'all-rights' film deals—include Ireland under its umbrella (which is then referred to as 'UKIE'). There are a few coastal islands that are commonly used as tax havens—the Isle of Man, Guernsey, Jersey, etc.—although not officially a part of the United Kingdom, they are often included in most definitions (especially by companies with offshore bank accounts).

With a mainland population well over 65 million people, use of English as the national language and major production capabilities booming in the global city of London, there's no question some amazing content passes through this region. Second only to North America, content from the United Kingdom travels best throughout the English-speaking world (and therefore retains a very strong value in many foreign-speaking nations).

As a part of Western Europe, the United Kingdom is a powerhouse territory for a distribution company—one that is generally handled by experienced sales executives who understand how to negotiate and window detailed distribution agreements.

The UK's mass media giants BBC, Channel 4 and ITV produce both film and TV content (many of which are repurposed into major American TV hits like *The Office* or *Shameless*). UK original titles are also finding very strong success internationally via SVOD deals. Platforms like Hulu, Netflix and Acorn TV have dedicated fan bases of Anglophiles eagerly searching for UK-produced content. Programs like *Black Mirror* (2011),

The Crown (2016) and *Downton Abbey* (2010) have become megahits in the US despite their very UK-centric themes, dialects and pace.

What is unique about doing business with the UK are its subtle differences, especially with regard to its duration of content running times and episode counts. A typical US-produced series will have 13 or more episodes, whereas the UK might only produce four or six (and they have a constant output of one-hour factual specials). Major US networks—along with most international broadcasters—prefer an hour-long program, whereas the UK will still produce 90-minute episodes for miniseries. If a program is successful in the US, they'll produce season after season; in the UK, it's not uncommon for a successful series to skip a year or two before returning (or concluding simply because the story has reached its natural resolution).

One other interesting component in the UK, which also exists throughout much of Europe, is that the major networks—specifically the BBC—are public service broadcasters (PSBs). Unlike PBS in the US—which does receive government funds—the bulk of their cash comes from donations. By contrast, citizens of the UK are required to pay an annual license fee (essentially a tax, equivalent to about USD $200), which goes directly into the BBC's pockets. As a result, the BBC, on one hand, is expected to produce amazing content (that makes the UK look great globally), while, on the other hand, it shouldn't be *too* successful or profitable—at least not in the eyes of the public. The reason for this paradoxical thinking is that if the BBC's commercially successful, the public should no longer pay their annual tax; however, if the content isn't high-enough quality, then consumers feel they're paying an unnecessary fee. Although counterintuitive to an American mindset, this is the kind of understanding distributors must have in order to be successful in the UK (they must sometimes pitch content so that for a UK public broadcasting buyer, it fits that comfortable 'middle' zone). This is why from those who know the UK market well, they understand that the major branded companies aren't necessarily the most lucrative—or easiest—deals to secure.

Independent distributors and private channels, on the other hand, are much more in tune with profit margins. These are the entities that coproduce, codevelop and deficit finance local and international projects that get major UK films and TV series green-lit domestically so that they can be exported and released globally. As an example, that annual BBC tax does bring in a great deal of revenue, but it's not enough to produce all that high-quality BBC scripted content; the BBC will still coproduce these projects with indie distributors (ones who can deficit finance the budget). In exchange for this, the BBC gets its program funded and manages all UKIE rights, whereas the independent—and profit-driven—distributor has a 'BBC branded' program that it can exploit globally.

Exclusive 'UK agents' are almost never used for this territory; the UK is a very open region ready to acquire and broker deals with the international world. This trend will continue as ad-supported streamers (e.g., Roku and Pluto) cement themselves in the territory. The thing that can make the UK difficult to crack is that they have strong output deals in place with major studios and networks that make the quality of film and television content very difficult to compete against midsize independent distributors.

► DISPUTED TERRITORIES AND 'POSSESSIONS'

Whenever a major territory is listed in a distribution agreement, it is generally followed by some variation of language stating the territory header (e.g., the United Kingdom, the United States of America, etc.) followed by language akin to 'and including its territories and possessions'.

Without getting too historical, the bulk of today's major global powers have at one time—or presently—occupied or attempted to colonize sovereign foreign nations. Whether for economic gain, political stance or strategic military presence, smaller regions or specs of land throughout the world have been 'acquired' by the major players and are presently defined as 'territories' or 'possessions' under the flagship of these major powers. For example, the US, UK, and Netherlands (among other nations) each claim specific islands located throughout the Caribbean (e.g., the 'US Virgin Islands', the 'UK Cayman Islands' and the 'Dutch (Netherlands) Antilles'). 'French-speaking world' extends deep into Africa as well as out into the Pacific Ocean (e.g., French Polynesia); and in the case of the United States, 'possessions and territories' extends to military bases located throughout the world (technically on foreign soil but claimed as 'US property' during its military stay).

But how are the disputed regions defined? What happens when a Chinese client blindly assumes Taiwan should be included into the definition of China but the Taiwanese rights have already been sold? Or what happens when both South America and North America are claiming rights to the Caribbean?

The film, television, and new media business follows its own rules regarding what 'possessions' belong to whom. Such disputes are solved by whichever party defines the territory first (or whomever pays the most). Regarding China, if Taiwan is sold, then it's gone, and the Chinese client will adjust his or her offer accordingly (you won't see any political discussion about 'one China' as you hear on the news). For the Caribbean Islands (and their claim of ownership by multiple global powers), the best answer has been to clearly define specific islands (e.g., US Virgin Islands), but use the all-encompassing phrase 'the Caribbean' to simply remain 'non-exclusive' within the deal.

This also comes down to a distributor's talent and experience in brokering deals coupled with the quality or long-term value of the content being licensed. For example, an acquiring party representing Russia might try to include the Baltics (Latvia, Estonia, Lithuania) or Ukraine into the deal, claiming that these make up the true Russia 'CIS' territorial definition; in reality, these countries are sovereign from one another but can be grouped together based upon the overall terms of the deal (as 'CIS'). In short, the deal could go either way, and the seller negotiating the deal has a choice to make. Within this example, an experienced distributor will know whether 'the Baltics' and/or Ukraine are worth carving out *or* keeping in the deal (to satisfy the clients' ego). Some television programs and films can close in the Baltics and Ukraine directly (and offer direct revenues); other media properties don't stand a chance or would require a Russian dub or subtitled version in order to sell—meaning you'd have to sell Russia/CIS first, which would make it far simpler just to place it with your initial client.

On the point of Russia/CIS, the Russian invasion of Ukraine in February 2022 has caused a dramatic slowdown in business connected to Russia/CIS (including Ukraine). Aside from the fact that sanctions were imposed, blocking direct business with Russia, the economies of both nations are in shambles. But that isn't to say business still isn't being done behind closed doors. Russian companies are still acquiring media content but are buying them via shell companies established in places like Cyprus (a small Mediterranean island-nation with an interesting 'banking' industry). Same is true for Ukraine; media content is still flowing in and out, but everyone has revised their financial expectations from the deal.

Bottom line, the politics of international land disputes do make their way into the media distribution game—but most in the business of film, television, and new media brokerage turn a blind eye to the rhetoric and get down to dollars and cents. The party willing to pay more will take on the disputed region, and truly contested zones (e.g., the Caribbean) are usually placed into a definition of non-exclusive since both parties are targeting different clients within the area.

▶ VALUING TERRITORIES

The definition of a 'major' country means something different in the realm of international media distribution. For example, China stands as the world's second largest economy and proudly boasts its massive population (by far the largest), yet for a media distributor, the tiny European territory of 'Benelux' (comprised of Belgium, the Netherlands and Luxembourg) might actually pay *more* money than China for an indie film or TV program—and, dare I say, will probably be much easier to work with.

Global territories are not created equal; they are often ranked and sorted by their buying power. The continent of North America represents the largest media player on the planet, followed by countries comprising the 'English-speaking world' (e.g., UK, Australia, etc.) and thereafter a collection of foreign-speaking nations with heavy infrastructure and technologically advanced capabilities (e.g., France, Germany, Japan, etc.). At the bottom of this list are those countries and regions making up the third world—often more positively referred to as the 'developing' or 'emerging' world—including regions such as Africa, Southeast Asia, Eastern Europe and Central America.

When distributors and producers consider the market value (or total worth) of a media property, they must take a very realistic view of how much total revenue is likely to be generated from each international territory. Although the total revenue in dollars varies drastically from one title to the next, the percentage each international territory is likely to contribute to a media property's bottom line is quite consistent.

To offer some perspective, then consider the below chart which offers a ballpark understanding of the assumed value of a media property's total valuation when split out across each international territory. Please note, the territory of North America (comprised of the United States of America and Canada (both French- and English-speaking)) is *not* included; instead, we've applied generalized estimates of what the rest of the world's value represents by territory:

REGION	%
EUROPE	
Benelux	2%
France	10%
Germany	10%
Italy	5%
Spain	8%
United Kingdom	10%
OTHER EUROPE	8%
EASTERN EUROPE	
Croatia	1%
Czech Republic/Slovakia	1%
Latvia	1%
Lithuania	1%
Poland	2%
OTHER EASTER EUROPE	5%
FAR EAST	
China	1%
Hong Kong	2%
India	1%
Indonesia	1%
Japan	3%
South Korea	3%
Thailand	1%
OTHER FAR EAST	5%
LATIN AMERICA	5%
AUSTRALIA/NEW ZEALAND	7%
SCANDINAVIA	5%
MIDDLE EAST	1%
AFRICA	1%

Just so we're clear on this, if a film generates a total revenue of USD $1 million during its first sales cycle, then the amount of revenue secured via the Middle East (which is valued at 1%), would likely land at USD $10,000 (or 1% of the $1 million budget); by contrast, France is valued at 10% and would therefore rake in USD $100,000 (10% of $1 million). Again, it's important to note that it's extraordinarily rare for every territory to be licensed—which is why the major territories have 'other' applied (e.g., 'Other Eastern Europe'). Also important to note is that multiple deals can be closed within a specific territory; in the UK, a television deal might be closed followed later by a second deal focused on SVOD; the assumption here is that both deals when totaled together would equate to an approximated 10% of total international revenue from that particular region.

▶ CURRENCY EXCHANGES

With hundreds of currencies traded daily, one would assume when engaging in the international world that deals will always be done in the local currency. Not true. Although the US dollar (USD ($)) is the most commonly used currency, deals are often brokered in Great British pounds (GBP (£) or pound sterling) or the European Union 'euro' (EUR (€)).

It's important to note that virtually every global buyer knows the value of their local currency against the US dollar; it is one of the most stable currencies on the planet, and most international banks have preference to trade using dollars (it is the world's reserve currency). Europe can be a bit more finicky on this point, which is why the GBP and EUR are also common currencies. For a US company to be brokering deals internationally, it is not really seen as presumptuous to establish prices as USD figures. In example, the first deal I ever closed was a TV series on sports cars for a South Korean channel; I made the novice mistake of carefully calculating the prices in South Korean won. The buyer appreciated the gesture but responded in dollars (the currency she preferred to negotiate in).

When brokering deals into Canada, the Canadian dollar is often used as the main currency upon which to make a deal—as is Australia with the Australian dollar. But both countries will work in USD if requested. I point these out as separate occurrences because this only applies to deals closed directly with these countries. For instance, a TV content deal between a US company and China wouldn't use Aussie or Canadian dollars as a point of negotiation, whereas they might use GBP or euros.

Occasionally there are advantages to using one currency over another, even for American companies. For example, the great recession of 2008 tanked the value of the US dollar. Suddenly the world preferred trading in GBP or EUR since they had 'more value'. Americans didn't mind this point. A single British pound was suddenly worth more US currency (as was the euro); and Americans knew that the US dollar would eventually go back up. For deals that had to pay out over a longer term, the value of the money actually increased just because the US dollar climbed back over the next few years. Same is true for the euro as several EU member states have started experiencing instability; the euro, which once had a cost of USD $1.25, dropped to $1.10. And in June 2016, when the UK formally 'Brexited' from the EU, the Great British pound (which normally cost about $1.50 or higher) dropped to $1.25—and for a few terrifying days was almost break-even with the US dollar during the 2022 inflation spike. While this might not feel impressive at the single-dollar level, multiply these numbers by hundreds of thousands—or even millions—and the currency one uses can have a dramatic effect.

One of the more unique components when using alternative currencies is that there is always some form of bank fees associated. Banks charge a commission to exchange currencies (and usually add another commission to wire the fees internationally). As a hypothetical, let's say a content deal was brokered at USD $10,000 for a film deal; when the buying company (let's say in the South Africa) wires the $10,000 funds to the American company, the first bank will take a small fee to initiate the wire transfer (let's say $25). Then they'll charge a 1% commission for 'exchanging' the currency (since the initial funds would be in South African rand). And on the other side of the planet, after that $25 fee plus $100 exchange fee are sent over, the US bank will charge another bank fee of $25 (average) to 'receive' the money. The deal was worth $10,000 on paper yet only $9,850 is actually received. Again, at this level, most would let it go, but when extra zeros start getting added to those larger deals, this USD $150 loss can turn into several thousand dollars in lost revenues. To battle this, it's quite common to see the total license fee figure followed by language akin to 'net of any taxes or banking fees'; therefore the client would have to add these numbers into the amount being wired so that a flat $10,000 is received on the other side.

Another common problem are withholding taxes. Several countries require a blanket tax to be withheld from every wire transfer leaving their soil. Canada has a blanket 10% withholding tax (if $10,000 Canadian dollars are wired to a client abroad, the Canadian government will simply pocket $1,000). Germany, Japan and many others play the same game. Unlike banking fees and exchange commissions, withholding taxes are trickier to avoid. However, since the monies are being sent overseas, the party receiving the money generally has the right to request a refund (they just have go through the—sometimes arduous—task of filing tedious paperwork in a timely manner).

▶ TAX HAVENS AND PROBLEMATIC COUNTRIES

When brokering a deal with an international client, it's not uncommon to receive a contract whereby you're doing business with a completely different entity (located in a completely different country). For instance, a deal between the US and UK might conclude with an agreement listing the 'acquiring' company as one formed in Panama, the Cayman Islands or the Isle of Man. While it might seem shady at first, there are a number of legitimate reasons for this occurrence.

Most commonly, it's to avoid excess taxation. When taxes go up, acquisition executives must pay more to acquire content (which limits how much content they can buy). So instead of doing business directly, the deal will pass through a tax haven that does not require excess taxes to be applied. Also, for the same reasons, a great number of companies—especially ones residing in very bureaucratic nations—can avoid tedious paperwork (notarized documentation, specialized double-taxation forms, certificates of residency, among other documents which slow down the acquisitions process).

In other circumstances, there are a number of countries where it is simply illegal to engage in direct business. As an example, the United States has applied sanctions against nations like Venezuela and Iran (countries that have legitimate media infrastructures). This doesn't mean a US-based media company wouldn't license these territorial rights to a Venezuelan or Iranian client; it just means they won't be able to do *direct* business. The deal could easily be routed through a third-party entity established in a neutral country—or have those territories included into a pan-regional or multi-territorial deal.

▶ SPILLOVER AND GEO-BLOCKING

In the city of Toronto, if one flips through local free-to-air TV stations, they'll inevitably come across Buffalo, NY stations sandwiched in between the Canadian networks. Makes sense; the city of Buffalo is only about a two-hour drive from Toronto (and that drive is geographically exaggerated because you must drive all the way around Lake Ontario which sits between the two); but it's not just a lake separating these two cities; there's also an international border—one that satellite transmissions cross (or 'spill over') unintentionally.

While the notion of Canadian's accessing Free TV content spilling over from the US market might not seem like a big deal, it does impact content value. For major players like Discovery Networks or Turner (who own channels on both sides of the border), this scenario isn't a problem since they can schedule the 'start date' of a series to transmit on the same date (within the same time slot) in both countries. However, for a distributor securing a program with a US-centric channel (such as PBS), the stakes are much different; if a program broadcasts on PBS first (for US broadcast rights only) yet is unintentionally made available to Canadian viewers by means of 'spillover', then the content has effectively—by default—'premiered' in Canada. This poses a real problem for distributors because after such spillover occurs, a Canadian network will no longer pay a first-run higher-value license fee for the content; since the program has already technically exhibited, they'll only pay reduced 'second-run' rates.

Such spillover is not limited to the US and Canada; many countries around the world experience such spillover scenarios.

Contracts will include stipulations that clearly define a geographical territory, but often permit 'reasonable' spillover (the type that is truly unintended and occasionally unavoidable, as mentioned earlier).

Geo-blocking, on the other hand, is a much more controllable means of keeping media rights secured within the boundaries of a territorial definition. Geo-blocking capabilities exist within digital content deals, where very clear regions of exploitation can be contained. Geo-blocking technology is able to allow Netflix to keep 'Canada-only' titles from being seen in the US (and vice versa). Of course, one's use of a virtual private network (VPN) can allow seamless access to media content even from locations where such content is technically not permitted. And the EU's adoption of General Data Protection Regulation (GDPR) has complicated the EU landscape in terms of streaming company's ability to track users. Bottom line, even as the industry shifts toward a digital distribution medium, spillover will continue to be an ongoing problem.

▶ DUBBING, SUBBING OR PARALLELING

There is no simple rule used by all regions for how media is to be imported and localized into regional languages or dialects. The reason is because culturally, languages work in dramatically different ways depending on where one speaks.

When acquiring media content, international acquisition executives will usually specify within the agreement whether they'll be dubbing, subtitling or paralleling the audio tracks for purposes of local adaptation. Here's how each works:

▶ **Dubbing** is the process of stripping out the actual audio tracks of the original actor's voice and replacing that voice with the voice of another actor (speaking in a foreign language, translated and adapted from the original script). A common material request when delivering a title to a distributor is that audio tracks have separate 'M&E tracks', a simplified way of saying Music and Effects tracks. These audio tracks have absolutely no verbal language on them but have all the sound effects and music— listening to them is like watching the movie as you'd expect, only when the actors 'speak', no words come out. This allows foreign distributors to add in their dubbed language tracks right into the soundtrack without having to remix any of the other audio tracks. Interesting Fact: major American A-list talent (e.g., Tom Cruise, Arnold Schwarzenegger, Meryl Streep, etc.) have foreign language versions of themselves working abroad (meaning, there is an actor in Germany who is the only artist performing the German-speaking voice of Tom Cruise for every one of his films that arrives in the territory, and there is an actress in Italy who is the Italian-speaking voice of Meryl Streep). This phenomenon stretches to B-listers as well and even to television content. Imagine watching an animated series like *Family Guy*; if after being an avid viewer of the program for years, how shocking would it be if a different actor suddenly performed Stewie's voice? One that might be very talented but is simply different than the 'Stewie' you'd always loved? Most would stop watching the show, making the content less valuable. To keep revenues strong, there's major interest from US-based studio execs to keep 'foreign speakers' attached for potential sequels or future seasons (this is a common stipulation within agreements).

▶ **Subtitling** is when the original actors' voices remain on the audio tracks, but a visual text of the translated words being spoken appears in sync, allowing a foreign-speaking individual to 'read' the dialogue or audio cues they're hearing.

▶ **Paralleling** (or sometimes called parallel tracking) is when a foreign-speaking actor speaks directly on top of the native-speaking actor—but in a way where you can still hear the native-speaking talking. For instance, if a US program is being parallel tracked, a viewer might hear the English being spoken very softly with a French actor speaking in French on top of the same audio track (so that the English would be hardly audible but still present). Paralleling is hardly ever used in feature films or scripted series (only in situations of piracy or with third world countries). However, it is quite common in the world of factual content (documentaries and non-scripted programs). For instance, Discovery Networks in France might broadcast the US crime programs found on the US-based Discovery ID network; however, instead of a full-out dub—which is very costly—they'll just hire a male and female voice-over artist to speak on top of the American on-screen personalities (the male will speak all male parts, and the female will speak all the female lines). You'll occasionally hear the people on camera start their sentences, but very quickly the local foreign talent begins speaking right on top of them, providing a generalized translation.

▶ LANGUAGE VERSIONS AS *ASSETS*

When a US-based distributor brokers an English language series with a French channel or buyer (or any foreign-speaking client), it's understood that the license fee might be priced a bit lower than normal market rates since that French distributor will need to spend additional money producing the French language dubs.

But one party's burden can be the other's business opportunity. There are two approaches that can be done in this instance: first, the client (in this case the French buyer) can acquire the property, then invest in creating a French-language dub themselves, but include language in the agreement related to 'Language Access' whereby they agree to sell the French-language dubs at 50% the cost incurred to produce them—this is incentivizing because the French buyer gets half their money back, whereas the US seller can have access to an extremely expensive dub at half the cost it'd be to produce it themselves. What would a seller do with a French dub? Use it as a marketing tool.

Languages like French and Spanish 'travel' well, meaning there's a great number of countries on the planet that speak these languages. In the case of French, there are numerous channels in Quebec, Canada that are required to broadcast in French but have limited funds to dub—so if a distributor can 'include' the French dubs on content, they'd garner sales they wouldn't normally be able to secure. In the case of Spanish, only the major 'pan-regional' channels (e.g., NBC Universo, A&E Ole, Turner Latin America, etc.) have the funds to acquire and dub; but if a distributor were to access these dubs after they were created (or potentially invest in producing the dubs on behalf of these channels in advance of a deal), then there are real opportunities with all the smaller Free TV channels in smaller countries throughout Latin America (in places like Honduras, El Salvador, Uruguay or Bolivia—countries that have strong TV markets but limited budgets). Access to a free dub would guarantee a sale, whereas a non-dubbed English language show would be too great a financial burden).

Take a company like Netflix; in early 2016 it launched a 'global' offering, where literally everyone on the planet (excluding only nations like Iraq and North Korea due to government restrictions and lack of infrastructure) could have access to its service. As

Netflix began to acquire content on a global scale—or at least a multi-territorial scale—language versioning was a major point of negotiation. For audiences in foreign-speaking regions, they'd need either dubs or subs to enjoy the newly released entertainment (and be incentivized to become a Netflix subscriber). A distribution company—even with more independent content—that had language dubs and subs of its content readily available suddenly had more to offer Netflix than some of their bigger competitors. And as Amazon and other entities begin expanding into the foreign world, distributors that can provide language assets have an upper hand in the marketplace.

▶ RACE AND CULTURAL DIVERSITY

I questioned writing this section. (And after writing it, I considered deleting it.) But I kept it because there's no point in sugarcoating reality:

The international world's 'first glance' and blunt approach to race, ethnicity and cultural norms can be a bit of a shock; and as a person born and raised in a culturally diverse country (and living within a culturally diverse family), it's still at times a bit difficult to digest. And despite the fact that races, cultures and societies are more interwoven today than ever before, stereotyping and racial preference remain very real 'filters' for buyers in the global media marketplace.

I have been asked point-blank about the racial makeup of programs (e.g., if it was a predominantly 'Black' cast or 'Asian' cast); I've even been asked 'on a scale of 1 to 5' how 'gay' a program was. In the realm of international distribution, things considered seemingly taboo or off the table as inappropriate talking points can suddenly become worthy of open discussion.

Here's the surprising thing: the territories you'd expect to be overly conservative (e.g., the Middle East or Latin America) can be surprisingly liberal, and the territories you'd expect to be completely open-minded (e.g., North America and Western Europe) can be shockingly homophobic and racist.

But don't in any way think this somehow means films or content with minority cast members or alternative subject matter don't stand a chance in the international arena; they must simply be pitched in a specific way in order to find their ideal target audience—and asking direct questions is the only way to get there.

I highlight these points only to acclimate readers to the very real fact that entering the global marketplace requires a certain objectification on the part of filmmakers and producers; they must look at their projects in a way that is outside of their normal comfort zone (and this makes sense; you have to leave the cultural norms of your own country in order to dabble in the international arena). A question from a foreign buyer that is seemingly racist or sexist is simply an exercise in info-gathering; by knowing the racial demographic or sexual overtone of a title, a buyer can make a more educated guess as to a property's potential release strategy.

Consider Turkish dramas (some of the best-produced and most well-received programs traded in the non-English-speaking world). Turkey is a majority-Muslim country with a language used only within its borders—two factors that tend to limit one's Western opportunities. However, Turkish distributors took an objective view of their dramas and saw them in the way the rest of the world would see them: non-English-speaking dramas with a non-white cast members. So instead of setting their sights on Europe or North America, they shifted their aim to the parts of the world where people 'looked' and socially interacted in a similar way (which allowed them to find huge success in Latin America, the Middle East, Africa and Southeast Asia).

This isn't just an international phenomenon; here in the US we've coined politically correct filters in an effort to categorize content. Even though terms like 'urban content' (which is a polite way of describing majority-black movies like *ATL, Straight Outta Compton* or *White Chicks* while excluding more 'serious', wider-audience-appealing majority-black titles like *Moonlight*, the series *Black(ish)* or the global hit *The Black Panther*) feel more mild in their delivery, they are just as seemingly racist from the outset. However, as with the example of Turkish dramas earlier, being realistic about the ideal demographic of a property's target audience only aids a distributor in better achieving a cash positive release.

Rest assured: the world is very much open and ready to experience stories of the human experience; but in order to deliver those stories to the right audiences—to give those stories the merit they deserve and their best opportunity of success—distributors must ask blunt questions.

7

Marketing, Ratings and Audience Cultivation

Although end users have no shortage of choices when it comes to accessing new media properties, they do have a limited amount of available cash and time. Yet despite the fact that distributors and consumer-facing platforms are careful to invest only in content that stands a strong chance of performing well with a pre-identified target audience, there's two major hurdles they must overcome: (i) their targeted audience needs to be aware the content exists (along with when and where it can be found), and (ii) that audience needs to be *excited* to spend their money on it.

This is where the role of marketing enters the picture; marketing is the process whereby information campaigns are created to reach out to targeted audience demographics with the specific goal of getting that audience to engage with a product. The objective of a marketing team is to get the widest margin of people familiar with a media property, then convert the largest number of those individuals into engaged consumers by getting them to effectively click the 'buy now' button.

The transition of audience members from being informed end users into ones who've made the 'buy now' transaction is what transforms a media project into a profitable title—one that generates a profit margin for its investors which allows them to invest in future media projects.

But media content isn't only marketed for mass audience; although we primarily associate 'marketing' with huge public awareness campaigns (e.g., theatrical trailers, billboards of movies, on-screen ads for new TV shows, etc.), the initial financiers of media content—namely distributors and acquisition executives—must also be informed and excited about a new project's potential before they're willing to invest (which is what's required to kick-start the whole process).

DOI: 10.4324/9781003357902-8

Although we will discuss strategies and techniques applied to reach mass audiences (direct-to-consumer marketing), the primarily focus of this chapter will discuss how distributors 'market' titles in a business-to-business approach—focusing on reaching targeted groups of acquisition executives and negotiating marketing strategies with consumer-facing platforms.

▶ MARKETING FOR THE PRESALE

In essence, the function of marketing is the same across both the direct-to-consumer (D2C) and business-to-business (B2B) models. While direct-to-consumer platforms must sell their consumer base on a new title being released, distributors must equally sell their pre-buying clients on a new project that's in development. Although many of the same techniques are used—promotional trailers, blast messaging, etc.—what separates the marketing strategy across both models is the information that's relayed.

In Chapter 2, we discussed how media content gets pitched and distributed before it exists. Just as end users want to 'see' what a movie or TV show will be like before they make the commitment of purchasing a ticket or downloadable copy, acquisition executives too want to know what the final product will 'look' like (especially at the pre-buy level). And since there's no finished content to screen, distributors must get very creative to properly convey the mood, scope, style and tone of the end result—from very minimal resources—in a way that gains traction with their pre-buy clients.

This is accomplished by providing acquisitions executes with information about the project that answers critical questions before they've had a chance to ask them; examples include

- ▶ category of the project

- ▶ production or distribution partners

- ▶ on-screen talent attachments

- ▶ creative talent attachments

- ▶ verifiable audience

- ▶ budgetary expectations

- ▶ time frame of delivery

- ▶ call to action

Laying out details and explanations for each of these categories provides a seasoned acquisitions executive with enough clues to visualize—with a great deal of accuracy—what the end result of a given project will be; here's how:

▶ **Category of the Project**—Commercial forms of content are primarily classified as feature films, television or new media; from there, most apply the standard genre headings such as drama, comedy, action or horror. But for distributors and acquisitions executives, these vague labels offer way too little information to calculate a project's potential release strategy or real-world market value. Therefore, distributors break these genre headers down even further into *very* detailed content groupings—or 'buckets'—that hone in on key variables which allow them to quickly evaluate a given project's margin of profit, potential out-of-pocket costs and its shelf life for potential sales (a process which allows executives to quickly generalize a realistic ballpark figure for how much should be put down as an initial minimum guarantee or advance). To give readers a taste of this process, consider that for a distributor, a dramatic feature film is never thought of as just a 'drama'; instead, a dramatic feature film might be defined as 'a cast-driven drama' (which would infer a higher-budgeted film led by bankable leading star(s)), a 'TV-movie drama' (which conveys limited theatrical or TVOD opportunity, B-level cast and most probably melodramatic in style—therefore female skewing) or as an 'indie drama' (which relays minimal commercial value, most likely unknown talent and limited opportunity outside of festivals). While these descriptions might sound negative—and while it may seem as if each of the examples earlier has very few commercial options—to an acquisitions executive, such explanations offer a road map toward calculating critical numbers quickly and effectively. The process of bucketing content is really used to answer common questions acquisition executives and distributors ask when being pitched new content. Producers and writers often focus their pitch on story themes, characters and plot points; but this doesn't answer the question distributors need to know ('what kind of product will this be?' and 'what marketplace need will it serve?'). So when a producer or writer begins their pitch by describing its plot—"it's a *drama* about a guy who . . ."—it leaves distributors in the dark about what kind of a drama they're hearing about. Acquisition executives need to know what grade level of actor this 'guy' will be portrayed by (and how much money will this actor's attachment to the project cost versus measurably generate) and which third-party companies—if any—would be most likely to acquire the rights of the end product.

▶ **Distribution or Production Partners**—Listing third-party companies that are already supporting a project—that have already put some skin in the game as a coproduction or commissioning partner—can greatly elevate a project's stature. For a prebuying client, seeing that other entities are already behind a project can help assure them other claims about the proposal have been verified. That said, these third-party companies must actually be on board ('interested' or 'considering' companies cannot be mentioned—at least not in writing). In the absence of coproduction or commissioning partners—which is inevitable during every project's early days—the next best approach is to validate the production company (or production teams) that will be responsible for overseeing the project. This is accomplished by highlighting other projects they have developed and fully produced—especially those that have been financially successful. Another interesting point is that attached third-party distribution or production partners can also help new clients better visualize the project as they review materials because each distribution and production company has its own signature look, feel and tone to its library of work.

▶ **On-Screen Talent Attachments**—As mentioned in previous chapters, one of the first questions acquisition executives and pre-buy clients ask is 'who's in it?' It's a valid question since it will ultimately be the leading cast members whose faces are plastered on posters and key art and who appear in trailers. A strong cast—with recognizable names and faces—is what makes a project pop in the minds of end users (which makes them equally appealing to investors and distributors). And because strong cast converts audiences into wallet-opening end users, consumer-facing platforms need to know the level of names they're gaining access to. But 'name' talent is not limited to multimillion-dollar Hollywood A-listers; 'name' talent means an appropriate choice for that specific project category. A niche feature film could find a cast member that resonates well with that particular genre (one who's unknown by most but clicks very well with a core audience); a documentary feature could boast access to a very high-profile interviewee (such as a politician or known activist); a series could feature an up-and-coming stand-up comic who has become a social media hit and therefore brings a fresh audience to a network. But it's not all just name recognition, it's a cast member's ability to help vet a project as worthy to watch (and help convert audience members into engaged end users); this is why on-screen talent has started sourcing YouTube, Instagram and TikTok influencers as they would traditional actors. It's not just about 'who is in it'; it's about how many audience members they can bring to theaters (or tune in on TV) when the property is released.

▶ **Creative Talent Attachments**—Not all 'marketable' talent is on screen. During a project's very early stages—when many other marketing categories are uncertain—a veteran creative talent attachment can be just as effective with acquisition executives. Since most projects require a commissioning party or pre-buy client to put some skin in the game very early on—long before on-screen talent can be confirmed—acquisition executives and pre-buy clients will look for other means of valuing a project's potential. In the media business, scripts are a dime a dozen (treatments and loglines are in even more abundance); but a script written by an Emmy Award–winning writer—who has a career of major hits under their belt—is an easier sell. Having a strong creative talent contributing to the project in development can help open a great many doors that otherwise would have remained shut. Writers get a lot of credit here, but 'creative' attachments can easily include or range from directors, producers or showrunners. And don't forget, companies too can be seen as 'creative' attachments—as mentioned earlier—since each company has its own style or flavor it brings to each project.

▶ **Verifiable Audience**—Since distributors and acquisitions executives primarily make decisions based upon targeted audiences that already exist—that consumer-facing platforms will be able to target and convert into engaged end users—offering proof of a verifiable audience is critical. A great example of showcasing a proven audience stems from the process of licensing the format rights to a foreign-produced television series. To sell a format, a distributor must showcase to an acquisitions executive the concept is based upon a successful program that's already yielded strong audience engagement in a foreign market. If the format has already been produced in other countries (the more replications the better), the reliably strong ratings of those foreign-produced episodes coupled with repeated seasons would help make the case that the format offers a stable investment opportunity (that comes with minimized risk). However, if the format has never been produced—and exists only as an idea on paper—then using the ratings and production history of *similar* programs would be the next best option (which is the route most indie feature films and TV programs are required to take). But copy/pasting strong performance metrics from similar media properties won't 'verify' that an audience is already out there. That is why other aspects of a media project's marketing campaign become so critical, including but certainly not limited to the following: (i) the utilization of 'creative casting' (e.g., using social media influencers with strong follower metrics) can assuage hesitant executives that a core audience demographic is ready to potentially transact; (ii) the choice of director—especially if the project taps into a niche audience and the director brings a cult audience following—could help home in on an audience demo; and/or (iii) if the project is an adaptation of a book, video game or other media property, then the IP could also have a provable preexisting audience (e.g., retail sales would paint a picture of audience reach (or lack thereof)). Any lack of verifiable audience is a major red flag for an acquisitions executive.

▶ **Budgetary Expectations**—The real assessment of 'budget' is to estimate how much investment is required for the acquisitions executive and—based upon other factors (such as release windows, cast and partners)—what margin of revenue required to generate a reasonable profit. The out-of-pocket costs required to produce a sellable project can be all over the map, ranging from a few hundred thousand dollars to tens of millions. As an example, a standardized straight-to-TV or straight-to-VOD feature will most likely have a budget under $1.5 million (and usually much less), but that's not to say there aren't legit reasons it can be larger. A TV-movie for a major network, such as Nickelodeon or Disney Channel, could easily cross the $5 million mark (and the audience reach of both networks would justify the total). But a straight-to-VOD movie with little cast and a price tag of this level would be a red flag that it's a poor investment. When an acquisitions executive asks about the budget level, any number existing outside that pre-calculated range would require a logical explanation.

▶ **Timeframe of Delivery**—Is there a locked production schedule with a tentative start date? Or even more importantly, is there an anticipated *completion* date? How long is postproduction expected to last? Although these dates are never finite until they've occurred, a generalized time frame can help an acquisitions executive balance the potential of a new project. An acquisition executive thinks in terms of 'slates'; they know about how many media properties they need to release each year (and know the ideal windows for when they'll need new content to be delivered). Therefore, a media project that's good but not great (meaning it's an affordable and interesting but not a runaway 'gotta have it' title) can suddenly become much more appealing if it's delivering at a crucial time for a buyer. Since it's impossible for a distributor to know the annual corporate objectives for each of their pre-buying clients, what they can do is lay out the high-level bullet points for when production will commence and provide a realistic estimate for when the project will be delivered as a sellable and exploitable product. Obviously, plot and genre are very important, but acquisition executives, investors and pre-buyers have output schedules to maintain; being accommodating to this need can greatly elevate a project's appeal.

▶ **Call to Action**—The element often lacking in a distributor or producer pitch is stating a clear 'call to action' (or a clearly defined expectation for the investing party). All too often, the party presenting the project assumes the other party knows what's needed; consequently, the investing or pre-buying party—even if very interested in taking next steps—is left a bit unsure of what those 'next steps' might entail. The 'call to action' will most likely be a financial commitment, to which the pre-buying party might inquire how much the distributor is seeking—but more than likely, the answer is either vague or places the burden of making a 'first offer' on the part of the investor (which immediately puts them on the defensive). A clearly stated expectation—either in writing or as a prepared verbal answer—allows a pre-buyer to know what level of financial commitment they'll be expected to put down. However, a call to action doesn't only need to exist as a financial figure; securing key cast members to perform within the project, negotiating product placement deals or incentivizing first-window distributors (such as a theater chain or VOD platform) to gain some kind of preferred placement can also be forms of 'action' desired by a distributor.

▶ PRESENTATION MATTERS

When pitching projects at the presale or development stages, distributors must offer the earlier informational points in a manner that effectively relays the brass tacks while also presenting the overall 'image' of the final product. Numerous pitch conversations take place via phone or in person—especially between clients with a history of working together—but a lot of this can also be accomplished via email or video conferencing (via Zoom, Microsoft Teams or Google Meet). But eventually, the 'selling' party must present materials that the acquisition executives can pass around within their companies for internal review. Here are the most common examples:

▶ **Pitch Decks**—A pitch 'deck' is essentially a PowerPoint-style presentation, one that's usually branded by the distribution company (so that it's clearly established they're the ones presenting the project). All of the earlier-mentioned informational points (cast, production partners, verifiable audience, etc.) are presented within the deck by means of company logos, cast headshots, measurable audience data (in the form of graphs or other 'visual' representations). These decks are also very stylized—using color schemes, fonts and graphic arts that reflect the genre, mood, tone and style of the project being pitched (so that even if a temp form of key art doesn't yet exist, the buyer can still visualize the end product). These decks are often sent around in advance of a scheduled conference call or in-person meeting to familiarize teams with a project—so that they can bring the right team members in to get the most information gathered as possible. Pitch decks can be used for single projects as well as 'slates' of projects (whereby several films or programs are presented at once). They're generally six to ten pages in length but can sometimes stretch well beyond 20 pages. Information is primarily presented as bullet points. Although the plot and story are revealed, the real purpose for a pitch deck is to relay the informational points in order to accurately present the project as a vehicle for reduced risk.

▶   **Mood Boards**—When content doesn't yet exist—and no cast or key art have been created—a PDF copy of a script doesn't exactly elicit an instant emotional response. Even after a strong verbal pitch, the potential buying party must still read through all the documentation (scripts, treatments, etc.) before understanding the full 'feel' of the finished product. But tapping into a buyer's emotional sector can certainly help gain their interest while making the project pop when placed alongside others. But for this internal connection to take effect, distributors need something that instantly relays the emotional response the producer and distributor hope to achieve—one that can take hold without extensive reading or explanation. To tackle this, marketing teams will sometimes create 'mood boards' or 'look books'. These are similar to pitch decks (in that they function like PowerPoints or some other easily 'skim-able' document), but rather than using bullet-pointed word descriptions, mood boards are collages of still imagery or other visual works that convey the desired emotional feeling of the project. Imagine a book of landscape photography or key art created for one of your favorite songs or albums; consider how these images can emotionally take you to another place. The collections of images within a mood board can equally take the acquisition executive or pre-buy client for an emotional ride (which allows them to better understand and connect to the project). This provides them a visual palate from which to imagine and 'see' the story. These are not always used but can be very effective when the time and energy is placed to create them. The imagery used can range from recognizable stock photos used purely for emotional engagement—meaning content that will not appear in the final program—or exist as a compilation or real-world locations the producers intend to secure for production (or as a combination of both).

▶   **Scripts or Treatments**—Eventually, the treatment—and ideally the script(s), assuming they exist—will need to be handed over for formal analysis. Although pitch decks and mood boards can grease the wheels in advance of a pre-buying client's review of these materials—allowing them to be absorbed with more enthusiasm—ultimately these will be the documents that require sign-off. But when forwarding such documents, distributors will often include the production details listed earlier (cast, genre, budget expectations, delivery time frames, etc.) in the same email. The reality is that scripts and treatments are almost never read without a clear understanding by acquisition executives as to what role they will serve (defining what need they fill within the acquiring or pre-buy company's overall mandate). Therefore, distributors need to constantly remind acquisition executives and pre-buying clients why this specific project is worthy of their attention and potential investment. Treatments and synopsis details are often augmented or revised so that it's specifically tailored for a client—in a way that syncs with how they prefer to be pitched content. Distributors also understand that when these documents are sent—generally via email—the party on the other side will often forward these materials to dozens of people within their organization (which allows distributors a great opportunity to choose their words wisely to best present the projects).

Although the final decision will ultimately rest on the strength of the written materials, even without a formal pitch deck or mood board, distributors will still add as much 'spin' as they can when sending over these documents.

▶ **Client Preferences**—Some buying companies prefer to review projects that are further along with their development—that have more talent attachments and committed production or distribution partners. Other companies, by contrast, prefer less developed projects (ones that allow them more creative input with casting, story or release strategy). Distributors will often approach both buyer types regardless of a project's current status; they'll simply 'present' the project in a manner that best caters to the needs of each buying client with whom they're speaking. It's not that distributors are misleading potential acquisition executives; they're simply highlighting select attributes of a property while downplaying others. As stated in Chapter 1, a project is never truly complete until it's released (which allows ample time for any party contributing money to add their own unique spin or touch). A distributor should always reach out to a wide audience of potential acquisition executives to secure the best possible deal—even if that means focusing on certain aspects of the project over another.

▶ UNDER-THE-TABLE DEALMAKING

At the early stages of the development process, there can be certain 'sideline' dealmaking strategies and blind faith loopholes used to bypass traditional legal requirements. The assumption many have is that a fully formalized 'acquisitions' agreement has already been secured before the distributor is permitted to present the title to potential acquisitions executives, but in that distribution is a business of relationships, there are many instances when a producer grants a distributor permission to present a new project to a targeted buyer in advance of a long-form distribution or representation agreement.

This would only be done with a very clear understanding between the parties; a distributor would never send an unsigned property (claiming ownership) without clear approval from the rights holder—not unless they wanted to deal with a major lawsuit and loss of reputation. But during 'the fog of development', producers and rights holders must occasionally liaise with a few different parties—and even send scripts or other materials ahead of crucial meetings with key executives (who might have to send the project to potential buyers to verify if there's indeed a marketplace need in advance of putting down a formal written or financial commitment)—in order for a traditional acquisitions deal to take place.

While this seems scary, there are protections put into place to prevent anyone from sending confidential or sensitive materials blindly. These protections are usually created in the form of simplified legal documents that focus on preventing damages from preemptively sending out materials—that hold the same weight as a fully formed acquisition or distribution agreement without all the excess terms. Examples would be non-disclosure agreements (NDAs) that pre-buy clients and acquisitions executives must sign, assuring the materials will never leave their organization or binding letters of intent (LOIs) that clearly state the parties are in discussion on a project and—if things move forward—will sign a long-form agreement (but allow for the strong likelihood that a deal might never come to fruition).

Some consumer-facing platforms will first enter into a 'master' agreement (or 'bridge' agreement) that is not focused on a particular project, but rather spells out how the parties are expected to work together. A separate amendment will be added for each film or TV series that consumer-facing platform wishes to acquire, but the terms of that amendment are governed by the master agreement. Generally within these master or bridge agreements are clauses serving as an NDA—that clearly state the acquiring party will keep any presale pitches confidential.

None of these workflows are meant to be mischievous; they are simply well-intended conversations to get quality projects into motion. Although most lawyers would wave a major red flag at such behavior—which is their job to do—the reality is that such under-the-table pitches and content conversations occur all the time (and generally this is how the bulk of indie content finally lands a secured home).

I've personally worked with numerous companies following this type of approach. This process allows both parties (buyer and seller) to have an open conversation about needs and opportunities. The buyer can clearly express what their ideal projects would be, and the selling party—us as the distributors—can present the content we have that fits (even if we 'invent' a few concept loglines on the fly with the intention of having them written down the line).

▶ MARKETING AS A SELLABLE ATTRIBUTE

After a distributor has piqued the interest of an acquisitions executive or pre-buy client, the next phase of the negotiation gets more granular.

For buyers, just because a project has a major on-screen talent attached doesn't necessarily mean a consumer-facing platform will be able to openly exploit that talent's name and likeness without restriction. And for a seller, just because one company is offering slightly more money doesn't mean another company wouldn't be able to do a more effective job—generating more money over the long haul—by strategically building audience awareness and converting a higher number of end users into paying customers.

Although distribution seems only to be a numbers game from the outside, both sides of the equation (sellers and buyers) actually benefit most from the projects that will be marketed most effectively. Therefore, the up-front financial figures need to be in alignment with market value, but the *treatment* of the property—how it will be marketed and presented to the world—is ultimately one of the leading decision points during the early negotiation process (well before preproduction and sometimes before a script exists).

These deal points can be negotiated in a variety of ways, but here are some top-line examples:

▶ **Preferred Placement**—The placement of a leading actor's name on the poster of a film or the placement of the title on a digital platform's landing page is not random. These specifications are negotiated in advance. Generally, on smaller projects, such discretion is simply given to the consumer-facing platform (allowing them carte blanche in terms of marketing decisions), but for higher-end projects, the distributor along with other attached parties will have a clear say in how the title will be presented to audiences. Therefore, a bargaining chip that can be played by both sides is including preferred placement stipulations. Although the specifics can sometimes be vague, language is usually carefully crafted to indicate minimum parameters (that a title has to be placed alongside content of perceived equal value; that it must appear at certain shelf levels at a retail or digital store; or that a select actor's name can be used within the synopsis but not in any press releases, etc.).

▶ **Minimum Marketing Commitments**—Talk is cheap. A buyer can verbally present the greatest marketing strategy in the world to lure in a distributor or producer, but if such deal terms are not included within the written agreement, then they are not legally obligated to follow through. That is why certain minimum requirements are sometimes placed into deal memos, including terms such as 'minimum marketing spend' or even defining the exact number of online ads or billboards required for a campaign. The legalese on these can range all over the map, but the concept of a party placing the nuts and bolts of their marketing strategy within the agreement is quite common—especially for higher-end content.

▶ **Talent 'Shout-Outs' and Socialization**—Marketing conversations and strategies can be crafted well before a production commences photography. Language can be negotiated requiring that production teams capture (film or shoot) a minimum number of client-promotion 'shout-outs' while on set. For instance, if a movie is being shot for a specific TV channel or streamer, then the marketing executives at that outlet can craft scripted language such as "watch (film title) only on (name of outlet)", and production teams can ensure top talent are captured—in costumer, on set—saying these sound bites are specifically for network/outlet promotional purposes. Social media strategies can also be derived (games, interview questions, etc.) that can be captured while on set, then saved and staggered out in a buildup to release date. Agreements for talent to participate in a minimum number of panels at certain conferences or livestream Facebook interviews can also be woven in.

▶ **Marketing Reserves (aka Marketing Caps)**—Marketing costs a great deal of money. From simple Google ads purchased to drive online traffic to massive national TV spots advertising an upcoming movie during prime time, the costs can quickly add up (buying the 'background' landing page on IMDb or Deadline Hollywood can be *tens* of thousands of dollars for a single cycle). And since these monies—whether pre-negotiated or not—require out-of-pocket expenses before profits start to roll in, many buying parties include a marketing reserve (where they can hold on to a certain level of first monies in to offset the expenses). Although we'll dive much more into this when tackling the finances of distribution (in Chapter 8), what's important to understand here is that the party buying a media property would ideally like to expense every ad dollar spent; therefore, selling parties attempt to limit this as to not allow an endless list of recoupable expenses held against the title.

▶ Consumer-Facing Marketing Strategies

After a media property has been formally acquired by a consumer-facing platform (and all of the details regarding how the property can/will be marketed to audiences have been ironed out), the direct-to-consumer marketing strategies commence.

Unlike the B2B models—that focus more on assuring potential acquisition executives that a property is a stable (or lucrative) investment that aids their overall content strategy—the D2C method is all about making noise and getting people excited for a new piece of entertainment. Audiences aren't looking to spend their cash on stable investments; they expect on-demand entertainment value in exchange for their money. Therefore, the call to action during the D2C phase is to assure members of a core audience that this particular media property will provide them the emotional escape they seek.

To achieve this, consumer-facing platforms use a three-step approach for their direct-to-consumer campaigns:

1) Build or identify a core audience.

2) Schedule a targeted release date, and make the core audience aware.

3) Convert core audience into engaged end users.

Each of these steps has a variety of procedures (that can differ greatly depending on the level of the media property being released). And these three steps are often repeated to correspond to the start of each new rights window (e.g., theatrical window moving into a SVOD window and later moving into a free-TV window); each window has a different set of end users—who utilize different resources to gather information on new content. Consequently, a fresh or unique marketing push will be implemented to maximize each window.

Build or Identify a Core Audience

If you're working on marketing a franchise, there are already predetermined pathways to reach a core audience. But for new indie titles (that might not have a clearly defined audience), marketing teams need to get a bit creative with how they first identify a core group that might have strong interest so they can later encourage them to click the 'buy now' button.

Here are common steps:

▶ **Approach With a Wide Scope of Marketing Tactics**—Consumers all 'discover' new content from different sources. Some people seemingly live through their Facebook feed while others deactivated their accounts years ago. Some people have cut the cord while others prefer their cable bundles. For marketing teams, they must first figure out who it is they're interested in talking to. Once they figure out that step, marketing teams can then identify the most plausible locations and resources where they can interact with their core audience. For larger media properties—with larger marketing budgets—they can cast a very wide net, but for indie content, they must be very careful to focus on the outlets with the largest grouping of their anticipated core audience. The process here is to hook and hold on to audience interest. This is where websites, twitter feeds and other platforms come into play; a focus on growing a subscriber base will begin the process of consumer-facing platforms directly interacting with their core audience.

▶ **Support What's Working, Drop What's Not**—The trend marketing teams often see is that they'll release a variety of ads, press and info to multiple outlets and that most come back yielding very minimal click-through. While that might seem counterproductive, it's important to note that the outlets that do show feedback and interaction tend to show these results in very high numbers. This is why casting a wide net is very important; sometimes these core audiences stem from areas no one would suspect. But rather than simply saying 'there's our audience, let's try to find other groups', they instead funnel nearly all of their remaining efforts toward that core group (to cultivate it and keep them engaged). The objective here is to identify a group, focus on catering to their needs heavily and keeping them not only interested but, more importantly, very aware—and excited—about the project in motion.

▶ **Augment and Support**—Once a core audience is identified, marketing teams must 'speak' to them in order to keep them engaged. This cannot simply be a single tweet or shared link to a trailer (that might work for a few days, but interest will fade quickly and then the title will get lost in the shuffle). As you'll read below in the 'Socializing' section, this is the phase where 'sneak peeks' and influencer interaction is widest at play. The idea here is to grow the fan base and their enthusiasm to click the 'buy now' button once the option is made available.

Schedule a Targeted Release Date, and Make the Core Audience Aware

After the core audience has been gathered—and while it continues to grow—the marketing conversation (or messaging) starts to shift with the new objective of relaying the property's official availability or release date. Whether it's a feature film appearing in theaters or a brand-new original series on TV, the goal here is to let audiences know when and where they can have access to the final product.

This is generally accomplished by feeding the core audience new and updated information (by means of cast interviews, behind-the-scenes footage, sneak peaks or 'leaked' footage). As the content spreads, the release date can be peppered within. Influencers or other big names can be included to help build momentum; they can lead audiences directly—via links or other calls to action—to pre-buy tickets or pre-sale VOD access. All ads, messages or communications made to targeted audiences during this phase must reenforce the release date and build hype to further excite—and grow—the audience.

The choice of release date is another strategy altogether, one that juggles a variety of factors. Release dates aren't random. Although there's no end to the reasons why a distributor chooses one date over another, the preselected 'timing' of a release date plays a major role in its potential for success.

The media business is cyclical (e.g., the summer months tend to be filled with major studio releases (generally large-budgeted franchise releases) whereas the autumn months offer more serious dramas, gaining exposure in advance of the major award shows' nomination periods, etc.). This extends to television and VOD as well—where the autumn months tend to be the biggest in terms of major network releases. But content can be released year-round; and indie titles tend to perform better when released in times the studios aren't making too much noise. As an example, the period around late August into early the early days of September tends to quiet down—a period that's great to release a new film or series onto digital platforms before they're overwhelmed with new fall lineups. The post-Christmas season (in mid-January through February) is also a quiet time that can be a great release period for smaller titles. Holiday weekends throughout the year tend to be a major release period for studios, where they can capture three full days of strong returns; you'll notice some of their biggest releases are announced on these dates. Other timed releases can focus on similar content—where the 'mood' of an audience has gravitated toward a certain subject matter—or the release of another property featuring the same cast (a technique widely used for straight-to-VOD releases due to search engine optimization). And then there's the strategy of counterprogramming (e.g., releasing horror titles at Christmas), which allows reduced competition while offering audiences an alternative to holiday themes or serious studio fare.

Convert Core Audience Into Engaged End Users

All roads in marketing lead toward getting audiences to click the 'buy now' button. The objective is to convert as many audience members into cash-paying end users during a title's initial release date. And it pays to be in first place. If a title wins the weekend box office, it will likely see strong returns the following weekend. If a title wins a digital window, it can be lumped into a 'most popular' category, which hooks even more viewers.

And if a title is successful during its premiere window, distributors will have more leverage to negotiate stronger deals on future release windows.

But after the opening day—which generally covers the first full weekend or occasionally the first full week after a media property has been made available—a new phase in the marketing strategy begins. All of the messaging and language start to shift. Since there is no more drive toward clicking the 'buy now' for maximized sales on day one, the new approach is to maintain a steady level of traffic and maintain the positive placement. Generally, a high volume of 'updates' and informational feeds are released to the core audience, with a new emphasis on how well the project performed. As a result, the messaging around the title's performance tends to shift toward a 'what are you waiting for?' approach.

This strategy is twofold: First, no matter how large a core audience has grown—or how excited those audience members might be to see the property—not all of them will have been able to access it on day one. And second, audiences who were on the fence about transacting on the project—who might have otherwise waited until a later (cheaper) window to commence—might be persuaded to transact in the present.

▶ MARKETING TOOL KIT

'Hype' is what ultimately sells a media property. If a project is marketed well, audiences feel as if they'd be missing out by *not* experiencing the media property (which compels them to click the 'buy now' button during earlier release windows). To achieve this phenomenon, ads and trailers aren't enough; to build legitimate hype, the marketing teams utilizing consumer-facing platforms have to ensure the vehicles used to propel their messaging truly captures the attention of their core audiences:

▶ **Titles Matter**—A distributor changing a film or property's title is nothing new (and existed long before the movie camera in the realm of theater and literature). Screenplays are often polished with new titles applied, films are often re-titled after production to make them more 'punchy', and it's not uncommon for media properties to have both a domestic title as well as an 'international' title (which can allow it to travel better overseas). But it's not just about a title sounding 'cool' or being witty or tongue-in-cheek; there's a real strategy at play here. As Video-on-Demand consumption became a more commonplace manner to view content, distributors noticed that titles beginning with numbers or the letters 'A' performed dramatically better than titles beginning with letters in the middle of the alphabet. The reason is simple; most platforms alphabetized their offerings—with numbers preempting letters. As a result, viewers would begin scrolling through a large collection of titles and would tend to get hooked by something within the first batch of titles. It's important to note that revenues also spike (though not as high) for titles starting with the letters 'Z' or 'Y'; this is due to the same consumer behavior, only resulting from audiences starting from the end and working their way backwards through a list. But it's important to note that titles were changed for the exact same reasons in the straight-to-video era (because VHS tapes were placed in alphabetical order on store shelves, and theatrical titles were often listed in alphabetical order in newspaper show times). Plot, cast and content aside, a title that's simply visible to an end user ahead of the competition's project holds an edge (and therefore a stronger chance of capitalizing on additional revenues).

▶ **Socializing**—The concept of 'socializing' was first broken down for me at a coffee shop in Toronto during the Toronto International Film Festival (TIFF) circa 2010. A close contact at Hulu was explaining why some projects were extraordinarily successful on their platform—including small indie docs that were outperforming major studio titles—simply because their distributors 'socialized' the right way. In essence, socializing uses a multitiered approach going well beyond a website or Facebook page; media properties now have Twitter handles and Instagram accounts—where influencer cast members can 'share' updates and information directly with audience members. While distribution companies send out press releases and notices to traditional media outlets (gaining formal write-ups in trades, magazines and online publications), influencers and social media managers can 'leak' behind-the-scenes footage, gag reels, sneak peeks and other information in a very off-the-cuff way. The lump sum of both efforts was to clearly state where the project could be found online. Getting individuals to 'like', 'subscribe' or 'follow' a single influencer is quite easy. And once an influencer has a strong audience, they can very easily relay targeted information to core audiences. This process has become so commonplace that 'socializing' a project is now woven into standard boilerplate agreements. Exact dates can be announced for releases; links and ads can be deliberately placed within a video, guiding a viewer directly to an Apple store, Amazon or Vudu pre-buy page.

▶ **Spin**—'Spinning' the positives of a media property is an art. The objective of spin is not to trick an audience into watching a property, but rather to gain revenue from a previously unexpected audience demographic. In today's world, trickery will quickly be found out (too many audience members will spot fake reviews or identify an online troll). Spin, on the other hand, gets an audience that would never traditionally watch a property and transforms them into converted end users. To give an example, let's look at documentary content. Traditionally, filmmakers are taught to be 'objective' when making a documentary (to show both sides and allow the viewer to draw their own conclusion)—but this is not what makes a documentary sellable. For an average non-scripted property to be successful, it should ideally pick one side of a debate and defend that stance to the fullest. The audience members who share that view will always enjoy seeing a new reason why their opinion is correct. But 'spin' will allow the opposing side to take interest. A marketing contact of mine routinely took very conservative docs and would post its links on very liberal websites, saying 'can you believe this garbage?' He would equally take very liberal docs and post them on conservative forums with comments saying 'can you believe this garbage?' Never once did he try to hide the fact that the program represented the opposing view—in fact that would have worked against his strategy—but by simply presenting that final product to an alternate audience with a clever dose of 'spin', the revenues increased.

▶ **Artwork and Imagery**—Everyone judges books by their cover; everyone also judges media content by their key art (the poster images and stills used in advertising, trailer, etc.). This key art is generally skimmed in a fraction of a second and must achieve a very large amount of the 'selling' work in that short time. In a blink of an eye, a quality piece of key art should convey the genre, the tone, the cast and indicate to a degree the general conflict driving the storyline. Many will argue this is the job of the project's title, but in reality the title is there to simply augment or support what the imagery in attempting to sell us. In the early years of Hollywood, a film's poster (followed by select stills placed into major magazine cover stories or printed as lobby cards for theaters) would do the trick. When home entertainment came along, stills were required for the box art. And in the digital space, stills and other preconceived imagery are must-haves—for example, if you click on a TV series (via Netflix or Tubi TV), you'll notice stills populating various regions of the program's landing page(s) as well as a single still or frame grab representing each of the episodes. But the power of key art and imagery go beyond these surface-level examples; on a user-generated platform like YouTube, if two identical videos are posted (with the exact same title), the video with more appealing artwork will receive more clicks—the number of views quickly becomes exaggerated if the individual posting the video has a large following of subscribers and even more so when YouTube begins placing the more 'popular' of the two videos on 'recommended viewing'—a process that is curated algorithmically by identifying it as the more popular of the two videos. Distributors and consumer-facing platforms are very aware of this phenomenon and take a great deal of time designing their project's imagery to best place the title.

▶ THE 'RISE' OF SOCIAL MEDIA INFLUENCERS

In 2012—which really wasn't all that long ago—I was literally laughed out of a production meeting (actually asked to leave the room) because I'd suggested that we use YouTube influencers in supporting roles of a TV movie aimed at tweens. My argument was that YouTube influencer cameos would replace the 1980s 'what's-his-name' sitcom-star-type roles in indie movies, but the logic wasn't well received at the time.

But in 2014, a few months after *Camp Takota* (2014) hit the market, Hollywood was suddenly obsessed with YouTube influencers. The big agencies rushed after these online personalities in a frenzy, seemingly signing anyone with a few thousand followers. I recall receiving several large (very expensively printed) catalogs from multiple agencies, each showing off the hundreds of 'influencers' they'd signed (with detailed stats of followers, etc. at the bottom of their pages). An insane rush of 'influencer' mania became the craze, but there was one little problem: most of these influencers couldn't act. They had very little stage presence and could hardly carry a believable scene. (Sidebar: even as TikTok has outpaced YouTube in terms of influencer popularity, the lack of acting chops is still a recurring issue.) What social media influencers could play best was themselves—and when using the *Camp Takota* model of user-generated marketing to their own circle of followers, they were much more successful at bringing in audiences.

What came from this craze was two interesting workflows: first, a new 'market' had been created where influencer callouts could be monetized (meaning rate cards had been calculated so that a clear dollar amount could be paid in exchange for a high-ranking influencer's curated 'tweets' or 'shout-outs'); and, second, select influencers' stories could be told in a more fleshed out and formalized way (as was the case with *This is Everything: Gigi Gorgeous* (2017) which, on one hand, exists as an uplifting story following the courage of a young transgendered man evolving into a woman (asking her YouTube audience to watch); while, on the other, simply honed in on allowing a real influencer to more formally tell their story—while pulling in millions of followers and a few notable sponsorship deals in the process.

But the notion of an 'influencer' is, again, nothing new. Sports figures have served as influencers for corporations for decades; for a predetermined dollar amount, contracted athletes will embrace a specific product and appear in commercials promoting it. Aging actors will appear in films knowing their name is being used to sell it. Famous A-listers will even lend their names to political causes to help raise awareness and donations. Talent drives audience attention (even if that 'talent' isn't from a traditional acting background).

▶ METRICS

In media distribution—as with all businesses—executives base their decisions (to the best of their abilities) on available data and metrics. Media metrics (e.g., ratings, box office, etc.) offer insight to audience demographics and historical financial averages. For a distributor, such insights can allow them to not only value one offer against another but also weigh in the possibility of an alternative distribution path.

In the media content business, there are generally two major metrics that reveal the most information about audience behaviors: theatrical box office and the Nielsen ratings (the latter of which can be broken down into audience ratings and ad ratings).

Although theatrical box office numbers tend to be discussed at a high level (weekend gross, etc.), they can actually be quite precise—identifying very specific zip codes, regions or cities where a title performs better. This type of insight can easily allow marketing teams and theater chains to better target their core audiences (and reshape the messaging to increase numbers in similar demographic areas).

But the Nielsen Television Index (NTI) is even more in-depth and stands as probably the most well-known means of measuring an audience's viewing habits. Despite the fact that the Nielsen ratings are primarily limited to television, in July 2017 they added Hulu and YouTube TV to their scope of measurement and reporting (which finally started to pull away the vail of secrecy VOD platforms had shrouded themselves with). Although NTI had been tracking digital viewership for some time, the inclusion of Hulu and YouTube was a game changer in terms of how digital platforms were being recognized as equals to major traditional television networks. And in late 2022—when Netflix adopted an ad-supported option—Nielsen ratings brought much needed visibility to the giant's actual viewer performance.

Today, unlike box office reports, broadcast networks have more minute-by-minute ratings information than they could have ever dreamed of just a few years back. In addition to steady displays of viewership spikes and dips, they also have countless third-party resources from which to glean a vivid image of their true 'target audience' (e.g., Twitter, Facebook, etc.) as well as how this audience responds to a variety of media. Long gone are the days of simplified Nielsen ratings—that gave an end result, allowing generalized buckets of demographics; in today's Hollywood, a network can see precise cause and effect from what they broadcast to viewership turnout.

And as more media starts getting viewed and consumed via connected devices (or purchased via a traceable means such as a credit card or online platform transactions), the metrics behind the end use (at every stage) is more advanced and refined today than at any point in media distribution history. And since this process is only getting more detailed (with the laws aiding the process), the degree to which metrics play a critical role in the green light, distribution and marketing process will only become more important.

Although we could go down a deep rabbit hole on digital metrics—which can be frighteningly detailed—the Nielsen ratings offer a pretty good snapshot at how distributors and consumer-facing platforms read the information. NTI works by strategically targeting and monitoring a very specific matrix of viewing households; based upon the information gathered, Nielsen is then able to extrapolate the viewing trends of a cross-section of demographic 'buckets' (e.g., 'Women 18–49', 'Children 6–11', etc.). For a top-line understanding, there are really two key numbers to understand when discussing Nielsen ratings, 'Audience Share' and 'Audience Rating':

▶ Audience 'Share' is the total percentage of viewing households actively watching or receiving the broadcast signal of a specific program. It's important to note that this number does not compare the viewership with all households, only those homes that actually have their televisions or select types of connected devices turned on. Audience Share helps determine the popularity of a program within its specific time slot and identifies the targeted demographic makeup of that program's audience (by means of location, economic status, gender and age).

▶ Audience Rating, on the other hand, calculates the percentage of viewership against *all* households actively or inactively viewing (meaning households are included whether their TV sets are turned on or off). This number is important because it can display the growth of a time slot, meaning if a show's audience rating increases, it could signify that it drew in a certain volume of audience that previously weren't watching anything at all.

Because of these splits, a program with a low rating but a high 'share' of the viewing audience can actually be seen as a more valuable program to advertisers—who will be able to identify a very targeted demographic to advertise to. But not only are Nielsen ratings useful for advertising, their information can be used to pitch similar programming or allow networks or VOD platforms to alter their schedules. It's important to note that ratings numbers are often casually thrown around (and can be morphed in a way to always sound positive). Same thing applies to other media metrics (such as box office totals, content views, 'likes' or shares and even into consumer-facing rating processes like Rotten Tomatoes or Metacritic). But when all is said and done, distributors and consumer-facing platforms are constantly combing through real-world data to gain a better understanding of their consumer base's tastes (so that they can produce more curated content for them).

▶ WHAT'S REALLY FOR SALE?

Let's take a step away from movies and TV content to explore branding within the music industry. And for a fun example, let's talk about Sub Pop Records: Sub Pop is a record label from the mid-1980s that was majorly influential in the explosive growth of the Seattle Grunge movement. The company was formed by Bruce Pavitt and Jonathan Poneman; two hopeful musicians who found success on the business side of the music equation. Their organization was quite small and simple; it operated in turn key approach. They had rules for their bands to follow; for instance songs couldn't use more than a limited number of chords (they had to be simple and digestible); they used one staff photographer with a very simple and unique style (which made all of their albums have a distinct look and feel, 'imagery' that made them cool to buy even if you didn't know the band).

In short, Sub Pop was not just in the business of finding and developing musical talent in late 1980s Seattle, it was trying to create *itself* as an appealing label to its core audience (transforming themselves into a company that sold products that made teenagers feel 'cool' when they bought them). Well, it worked. Before long, local indie bands like Soundgarden, Pearl Jam and Nirvana—that had arguably little hope of expanding beyond their local neighborhoods—became global sensations. And for a few years, the midsize American town became the musical mecca of the world.

In no way does this undercut the very real talent all of these bands possessed, but talented bands can be found in every major city around the globe. What Sub Pop did was identify a target audience that was being underserved by the major labels, then fed into their pulse. Since most of the bands they were pushing had zero fan base outside of local audiences, Sub Pop's marketing team needed to make their product appealing in an alternative way—so they made the *product* cool. The records themselves looked great, which allowed them to serve as vehicles for the consumer to feel confident clicking the 1990 version of the 'buy now' button (which was a mail order catalog).

This same logic can be said of The Criterion Collection; art house titles are notoriously tough to sell, but while Criterion Collection's aim was to expose great cinematic treasures to the home entertainment audience, what made their product pop was the vehicle in which they presented it. The artwork of a Criterion Collection box 'felt' important and could seemingly make any random old movie feel like a masterpiece. Movie lovers acquired them in droves, proudly displaying them on their bookshelves (they looked very sophisticated and became a symbol of one's appreciation of great cinema). I'm not arguing about any of the choices of films Criterion released; I'm simply commenting on the method they used to increase sales.

This same logic applies to the logos of distribution companies, the face of a popular actor on a poster or the tweet of a YouTube influencer; audiences simply feel more assurance when they see a property has been 'verified' by someone they follow or that it carries the branded logo of a company they feel meshes with their tastes. In other words, audiences must feel content has been curated for them in order to feel confident spending their money on it (a principle of marketing that has existed throughout the history of commerce).

8

Accounting Practices, Monetization and Business Structures

▶ THE COST OF DISTRIBUTING CONTENT

Money flows in two directions: out and in. Monies going out refer to expenses (or to the *costs* of doing business), whereas monies coming in refer to receipts, recoupments and profits (or the *gains* of doing business).

While it's easy to focus on a single title and digest how its development and production cost money (by means of development, cast, crew, equipment and location expenses) and later gain a profit via distribution (after the direct out-of-pocket production expenses are recouped), this process provides minimal insight to the indirect costs distributors must incur to make this workflow function. And similarly, although there are numerous distribution-related expenses for each individual title (e.g., costs associated with marketing a property or delivering it to acquiring parties, etc.), there are multiple expenses that are indirect—meaning they cannot be specifically allocated to only one title—despite the fact that no title would be 'sellable' without them.

We start with this point because this core concept is where several misconceptions about the financials of the distribution process originate. Many have a preconceived notion that distribution companies are simply out to siphon off as much money as they can (and are falsely accused of pulling 'creative' accounting tricks to effectively steal money). Such misunderstandings generally derive from word-of-mouth stories about films getting 'shelved' or producers getting screwed on royalties (and such stories often leave out critical details about terms agreed to within the acquisition or distribution agreement). Although there are certainly a handful of shady companies peppered throughout the media distribution landscape—as there are in every industry—the vast majority of media distribution companies operate in a very reasonable and ethical manner.

DOI: 10.4324/9781003357902-9

That said, this misconception is only reinforced when a rights holder or content producer is first presented with a distribution agreement that, at first glance, seems filled with fees, recoupments and protections that are advantageous to the distributor and not the rights holder. But this blind assumption fails to consider the numerous financial burdens placed upon distributors to keep their business model in motion (e.g., those indirect costs that cannot be applied on a title-by-title basis). And since distributors are making a mere fraction of each dollar earned, these indirect expenses need to be recouped along the way. While many jump to the notion that distributors should simply increase their prices when selling content (passing the burden to their client base of 'buyers'), one must remember the principle that a media property is only worth what a consumer-facing platform is willing to pay (meaning there is a ceiling for how high their returns on a property can be). And adding expenses to their profitable sector only hurts a distributor's bottom line (which decreases their ability to acquire future content); therefore, distributors apply these expenses to an area of their business that also costs them money: acquisitions.

As previously stated in Chapter 3, it costs a great deal of money to acquire a title (even if no advance or minimum guarantee is being paid). Since acquiring titles exposes a distributor to financial risk, it makes the most sense to apply such indirect expenses toward this internal workflow (which is why the fees and recoupment costs are always included within an acquisitions agreement). By understanding a bit out how distributors incur expenses in order to later sell media projects, one can gain a real understanding behind the protective language listed within their acquisition agreements.

Let's first cover a few examples of indirect costs (expenses incurred that are agnostic of title):

▶ **Markets, Festivals and Travel**—As one of our principles states, the media distribution business is one based upon relationships. In order for those relationships to thrive—and drive new business—distributors must be in front of their buying clients. Whether attending the major markets (which can cost tens of thousands of dollars in airfare, hotels, booth space and transportation expenses per event) to connecting one-on-one via simple business trips, distributors must be present. While the costs of placing specific titles into a festival or buying ad space in a trade magazine can be linked directly to a single property, the mandatory cost of 'being present' and representing the entire catalog at a market falls squarely onto the distributor's shoulders. Although one can argue this is a normal business cost, each producer benefits greatly from these efforts.

▶ **Staffing and Overhead Costs**—When we picture distribution, we tend to focus on the buyers and sellers; we rarely give much thought to all the other roles required to the make the process of 'buying' and 'selling' possible. Distribution companies require accounting teams, legal and business affairs teams, marketing teams, operations teams (who manage the quality control (QC) and delivery of the content being sold) along with other general roles such as office managers, receptionists and IT specialists. Without individuals performing these roles, the basics of any organization would fall apart. It goes without saying that—at minimum—all of the individuals must receive an income. On top of personnel costs, the distribution company must either exist in a physical office space—generally in a major global city, which further increases the costs—or must provide adequate equipment to support an employee's virtual work-at-home office. One must also factor in basic insurance policies required to rent or buy office space, phones, general utilities, and server capacity along with general office supplies. Without these individuals and elements in place, the sales team could not effectively pitch new content, the legal team could not properly process agreements and the accounting team could not report profits back to the rights holders. Although they might be indirect, every rights holder benefits.

The earlier examples leave out other basics—like maintaining business licenses with the state and city, payment of taxes, banking fees, interest fees or employee incentives (e.g., bonuses, commissions and other perks that keep a sales team motivated to broker bigger content deals)—that again benefit all producers.

By no means am I implying that all indirect costs are simply passed on to the producers or rights holders; distributors pay a large chunk of cash toward operating their businesses. But there are several expenses incurred that directly benefit all of their clients equally—and these are the ones that are subtly built into each acquisition contract (and explain why distributors include fees and recoupments into their acquisition agreements).

There is also an argument to be made regarding the value—as a branded company—a distributor can offer each rights holder or producer. When an established distributor takes on bigger projects (incurring greater financial risk), the press and publicity of these major acquisitions can elevate the overall market presence of the company. Such major tentpole projects can also increase business—bringing up the overall value of deals while increasing the number of opportunities for its entire library. For example, a massive feature film (with major cast) could drive a package deal that allows a distributor to include 19 other films into the same agreement (ones that otherwise would have gone unsold); should the producers of the major title alone bear the burden while the other 19 benefit from the deal without added expense? Should the distributor—who invested major risk acquiring that massive feature film—alone eat the additional costs?

From here, the larger question starts to evolve into 'where does the direct versus indirect line cross?' What legit out-of-pocket expenses should be shared by the content providers (producers), and what should be eaten by the distributor on their own?

There really aren't easy answers to such questions; every project offers a different set of variables to skew what their 'share' of the burden should be. But there is a reasonable method successful producers use to decrease many of these additional fees. Let's first examine what motivates the need for the sharing of indirect expenses so we can better understand the common ways in which they're divvied up—and occasionally avoided—among rights holders.

▶ CARVING OUT MISCELLANEOUS EXPENSES

There are three major expense categories distributors oversee in order to make a newly acquired project 'market ready' (and by 'market ready' we mean the point at which the property meets the minimal workflow requirements to be reasonably exploitable in the marketplace); it's important to note these expenses are incurred *regardless* of how much money—if any—was paid to acquire the title (via minimum guarantee, advance, license fee, etc.):

▶ Avoidance of Liability

▶ Assurance of Deliverability

▶ Marketplace Awareness

▶ **Avoidance of Liability**—In Chapters 2 and 3 we discussed the notion that distribution companies mitigate financial risk by focusing on projects that have verifiable audience (therefore possessing a higher likelihood of recouping their expenses and generating a profit margin). While such risk avoidance strategies can help reduce the impact of a poor investment, they do not prevent unanticipated damages from mismanaged—or deceitful—production practices. Such expenses incurred from third-party claims, copyright infringements or inadequate material deliveries fall into the liabilities column. As distributors invest into media properties—either as a pre-buy or as the acquisition of a finished product—they are inadvertently taking on all of the legal responsibilities associated (something they do not want). If anyone claims their name or likeness was used without permission or that music was used without clearance, the financial penalties would fall into the lap of the distributor. This is why in acquisition agreements there are several clauses stating that the producer or rights holder shall take on all liability claims (leaving the distributor harmless). But to further ensure avoidance to potential liability, distribution companies generally own Errors and Omissions (E&O) insurance policies—which they can use should a credible third-party claim ever pop up; distributors also require each producer to secure a title specific E&O policy as part of the delivery schedule. Additionally, prior to an acquisition, distributors will run title clearances and copyright checks (procedures which cost money but verify that a project is fully 'clean' from any potential snags). All of this costs money, which is why these costs are often seen as recoupable expenses within an acquisition agreement's fine print. These title clearances and copyright checks appear as slightly inflated values due to the time required by the business affairs team to produce them; adding a property onto the distributor's active E&O policy—if the producers never secured one for their project—carries an added annual fee (even though the distributor's premium would be paid regardless). And materials delivery schedules (as outlined in Appendix II) include multiple paperwork requirements—including copyright documentation, certificates of origin and cast appearance releases.

▶ **Assurance of Deliverability**—Distributors are often in a position to acquire content that's not yet finished. Whether acquiring a title during its early development process or deficit financing a property that ran out of money during post, distributors must first pay to acquire a project before all of its loose ends have been ironed out. And as a project gets closer to completion, the elements of the production itself (e.g., master digital file, audio tracks, etc.) must meet very specific technical standards in order to be 'sellable'. But in that distribution companies need to showcase 'fresh' content to their buyers, there can be a great deal of pressure—especially in public companies—to meet quarterly revenue markers. Therefore, even when a new project is still in its final postproduction stages, sales teams are often already in motion brokering deals. In theory, there should be no issue with this, but in the real world, Murphy's Law reigns. There are numerous scenarios—involving major projects alongside shoestring budgeted indie titles—where materials arrive late or don't pass their quality-control review. If a distributor has presold a title that does not meet the technical minimums of the consumer-facing platform it's selling to, the deal can fall apart (which costs the distributor money and can tarnish their reliable reputation, impacting future business). Additionally, the distributor now must pay to bring the deliverable elements up to a market-ready level. Technical specs are changing all the time, and distributors must keep their libraries up to par. Although these can exist as direct costs, such scenarios become indirect when they stall package deals or affect major driving titles. And if a trusted buying client suddenly becomes wary of acquiring content from a distributor (as a result of a botched delivery), the opportunity for other titles—belonging to other rights holders—become diminished.

▶ **Marketplace Awareness**—Marketplace awareness is much more macro than targeted trailers or banner ads—which would all classify as direct costs allocated to individual titles. Distributors must make their *entire* library visible to potential buyers. At minimum, they must maintain a website, tidy their catalogs and release press announcements ahead of major markets and events. While the direct costs of placing each individual title into the catalog can again be allocated on a title-by-title basis, the execution of the entire catalog becomes indirect (same with a website; the upkeep on each title is clear, but the maintenance and functionality of the entire site is indirect). Yet, for any title to sell—big or small—the entire catalog and website are required (as are the press announcements and company branding used within the marketplace to help direct the attention of potential buying clients).

The bulk of miscellaneous charges, fees and recoupments that distributors withhold from the rights holder's share of the profit margin stem from the earlier expense categories. During the negotiation phase of acquiring a new media property, one back-of-mind consideration for acquisition executives is how easy (or problematic) a project would be to take on given the earlier categories. A problematic title would be one that lacks clear documentation regarding liabilities (such as not having E&O insurance or performer release forms) or basic material requests (such as a digital master that fails initial rounds of QC checks).

Such issues are not grounds for rejecting a title; programs with high potential to sell will still be acquired. However, the acquisition agreement will include far more contingency fees and recoupment language to protect itself from issues down the line (such as fees to add the rights holder as an additional insured on policies or including a blanket 'market' fee allocated to adding the title to the company's website and catalog—or to cover an unexpected 'takedown' if the project is later deemed undeliverable.)

By contrast, a producer or rights holder who can deliver a project that assures a distributor of such concerns (e.g., having all legal documents in order, delivering QC-approved files and having all elements which will be utilized in the catalog and website promotion process) will be able to negotiate their way out of such miscellaneous fees. In other words, by helping a distributor avoid liabilities and assure technically sound materials, producers are able to access their proceeds more quickly.

▶ STANDARD RECOUPABLE EXPENSES

Direct costs associated with the distribution of a media project are unavoidable. But that's not to say there aren't loopholes regarding how the recoupment is managed.

Examples of unavoidable direct costs include

- ▶ recoupment of minimum guarantees (MG) or advances

- ▶ directly related marketing costs

- ▶ directly related material fees

- ▶ distribution fees

▶ **Recoupment of Minimum Guarantees or Advances**—If a distributor pays any money out of pocket to secure rights to a media property, it makes sense they should be able to recoup such expenses off the top (or from the first monies it receives after sales commence). In rare circumstances, such as very strong blockbuster films—ones that will surely drive package deals or improve sales on smaller titles—the MG or advance required to secure the title can be recouped over a longer period (where the rights holder is obtaining payments from dollar one). But no matter how you slice and dice this one, a distributor will require recoupment of its down payment.

▶ **Directly Related Marketing Costs**—Those ads in trade magazines cost serious cash, as do billboards and trailer creation. The size and scale of a marketing campaign is completely dependent upon the scale of the property being sold. But those expenses will need to be recouped by the distributor since they're the party taking on the risk. However, 'marketing costs' do not need to be ongoing; savvy producers and rights holders always request a 'cap' (or a ceiling) to these costs. Applying a cap does not mean the distributor will cease its marketing efforts; it simply means the distributor will have to eat its marketing costs after the recoupment cap has been reached. Caps on marketing costs can vary, ranging from $15,000–$50,000 on smaller-budgeted titles up to hundreds of thousands on larger-budgeted films.

▶ **Directly Related Material Fees**—There are minimum delivery requirements, and then there are 'add-on' material needs. The add-on fees are related to the creation of dubs, closed caption files, subtitles or uncommon delivery specs (used in delivering to new VOD platforms requiring unexpected file configurations or third world clients relying on out of date technology). Since these are not required to sell to most of the world, they are usually not included as 'mandatory' in material delivery schedules. However, distributors will generally apply language that permits them to create these materials in the event a deal requires them. As with marketing caps, there are limits that can be applied so that distributors do not fall into a habit of creating materials on a whim. Additionally, during the negotiation phase, rights holders and producers will generally require that they approve any such material creations in advance (to further prevent unnecessary expenses getting recouped against their proceeds).

▶ **Distribution Fee**—For every dollar a distributor brings in, they are entitled their cut (generally an overall percentage applied to the gross earnings of a title). This is a crucial point to consider because the distribution fee is where the distributor truly earns their income. Even though these percentages can range from tiny to massive—depending on the title—it's almost always taken off the top (from the gross figure). Distribution fees are scalable. Major titles can command low distribution fees (in the 10% to 15% range), average titles fall into a moderate distribution fee range (20% to 30%) and smaller titles— ones that offer more liability or up-front expenses—generally require a high distribution fee (30% to 50%). When producers or rights holders negotiate down the distribution fee, they inevitably see fees, caps and recoupments rise elsewhere in the agreement; and to reduce fees, caps and recoupments, generally, the distribution fee must rise.

▶ GROSS VERSUS NET

Receipts and proceeds are defined as either 'gross' or 'net'. The difference between the two is where in the financial workflow the monies are being defined as gains in relation to distribution-related expenses, recoupments or withholdings.

Gross receipts or proceeds are defined before expenses (meaning this figure represents the total value of a deal or recognizable intake of cash—such as we weekend's ticket sales). Net receipts or proceeds, on the other hand, are defined as the total amount of cash that remains after all permissible expenses, recoupments or withholdings have been applied.

Where this concept can be confusing is that monies received from the same deal can be defined as both gross and net for differing reasons to differing parties. In example, the distribution fee is generally taken off the top from the gross receipts, whereas the producer's share of the same monies would be paid on the net (after the distributor has withheld the agreed amount of allowable expenses).

But it's important to note that any of the standard and miscellaneous expense categories are negotiable and can be rearranged within the recoupment timeline. For instance, producers of high-end content can negotiate for a portion—sometimes all—of their receipts to be paid out as a gross percentage while keeping the remainder as net; or they can require receipt of a threshold minimum amount (above the MG or Advance) before withholdings can take effect. All of these terms are open for discussion. That said, rights holders and producers should take time to understand the total workflow as each dollar arrives into the hands of a distributor and how such monies pass through various permissible expense categories in relation to payouts.

▶ FINANCIAL WATERFALL

The concept of a financial waterfall is to systematically recoup expenses in the most beneficial order for the distributor's bottom line.

Although the model can be different by company—and the exact applicable expenses can be different from one title to the next—a waterfall provides an instruction manual to the entire company (as well as visibility to the rights holder or producer) as to how the financial gains of a property will be internally managed in correlation with its costs and expenses.

After a sales agent has brokered a deal, the distributor's accounting team carefully tracks the monies wired from the acquiring party. If the title is the only property in the agreement, then 100% of the funds will enter that title's contractual waterfall; if the agreement includes multiple titles, the monies will first need to be allocated to each title (so the accounting teams know how much to apply to each producer's account).

Once the money has been consolidated, the accounting teams must take the gross distribution fee and later deduct preapproved standard deductions and miscellaneous fees. (Banking fees and other wiring expenses incurred during the receipt of the funds will also be included as a 'direct recoupable expense'.)

To give a visual example of this process, please consider the following:

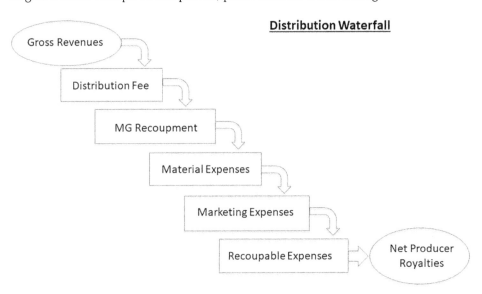

Distribution Waterfall

Figure 8.1 As gross revenues are allocated to a single title, accounting teams will deduct the gross distribution fee from the total monies received. Thereafter, any advances or minimum guarantees will be recouped followed by material and marketing expenses. Whatever monies remain after traveling down the entire financial waterfall—hitting each 'expense rock' along the way—equates to the producer's net take.

As a hypothetical, let's assume a distributor has acquired a feature film from a producer for a $50,000 advance against a 25% distribution fee and a marketing cap allowance of $10,000. Then let's assume the first deal this distributor closes with a consumer-facing platform is for a total $100,000 license fee. And—although incredibly rare—to simplify this example, let's assume this consumer-facing platform is paying 100% of its license fee up front. Here's how the money would waterfall down to the producer's pocket:

Gross receipts:	$100,000
Less 25% distribution fee:	–($25,000)
Less MG recoupment:	–($50,000)
Less marketing cap:	–($10,000)
Net receipt	$15,000

However, if all of the earlier hypotheticals were the same yet the consumer-facing platform only paid 50% of their $100,000 license fee up front (with an understanding they'd pay the second 50% installment six months down the line), the producer would see a large negative number in their receipts column—especially if wire transfer fees further reduced the distributor's gross receipts.

Then again, this is not to imply that a rights holder would only gain 15% of each deal; once the full MG and marketing cap have been reached, future monies would be split into 25% to the distributor and 75% to the rights holder (assuming no required materials or banking fees).

▶ REPORTING

Distributors should regularly update producers on the performance of their titles (something we touched upon in Chapter 3). Although different companies approach the reporting process in different ways, the general rule of thumb is that a quarterly report is mailed, emailed or made available via direct portal access showcasing deals closed and revenues generated. It's important to note that some companies only report biannually, and others do not present a report until a threshold level of money has been generated (e.g., after full recoupment of the MG or some other benchmark).

Provided that a producer hasn't signed away their rights to have access to a report—which is occasionally required when a major license fee is paid—clear language within the agreement should indicate how often a producer will receive a report and clear parameters regarding what actions a producer may take if a report is not sent. Not sending a report doesn't necessarily constitute as a breach of contract unless it clearly states when reports will be automatically sent and that a written request to receive an overdue report wasn't purposefully ignored (the latter could be a breach depending on how other wording in the contract is written).

Many producers are miffed to see an alarmingly negative number for their first few reports; the waterfall process earlier explains why this occurs (along with how a producer has negotiated down additional expense categories.)

Another factor to consider is that just because a distribution company has closed a distribution deal on a film, that deal might not appear in the producer's statement until the distribution company has actually received funds from the buying party. For instance, using the $100,000 waterfall example, this deal might have closed in March (at the end of quarter 1), but in April (when that producer receives their Q1 statement) they might be alarmed that their major six-figure deal isn't appearing. One must keep in mind that during the first 30 days after a deal is signed, the accounting team might only be initiating the invoicing process. Monies might not even be due until Q3, which means the deal wouldn't appear in a producer's statement until Q4.

▶ ROYALTIES

Monies generated based upon a title's actual performance during the exhibition period—meaning the revenues actually earned/generated (and separate from any MG or advance payment)—are generally referred to as 'gross receipts'. After the gross receipts trickle down the distributor's financial waterfall, a net remainder will then be payable to the producer. These producer payments are the producer's 'royalties'.

Depending on the agreement, royalty monies can arrive on a quarterly basis, biannual or even monthly basis. But after all the 'active' work has been completed, these inactive payments—or passive payments—become the liquid cash producers gather to pay back investors or save for a future production.

Royalty payments are not exclusive to producers; distributors also receive royalty revenues, primarily from consumer-facing platforms (especially those in the transactional space—for example, TVOD platforms, theaters, etc.). However, just as producers receive royalties after all expenses and recoupments have been deducted, the same holds true for distributors. This should be a point of caution for producers to ensure that any exploitation is being handled as much as possible by the distributor directly (otherwise the producer's cut will be a percentage of the distributor's share).

Royalties can also be paid to creative talent in the form of 'residuals' (or prespecified amounts due based upon a media property's exploitation in specific rights categories). For instance, an actor who is a member of the SAG-AFTRA union is required to receive a residual based upon what type of platform a feature film is being exhibited—therefore, the distributor or rights holder is required to pay these sums to the union (similar to a tax). Residuals are deducted from a media property's profits as an 'expense'.

▶ CROSS-COLLATERALIZATION

When a deal is brokered involving one title, the revenues are pretty straightforward; however, when a collection of titles (a 'package' deal) is pieced together the costs and profit margins get a little bit more complex.

Let's assume a package of ten movies is licensed together. One of the films is a major title—a driver title—that allowed the distributor to tack on nine additional films. Although the license fee might be a lump sum divided equally among all ten movies, the costs and revenues associated with each film might be radically different. Let's assume the majority of the movies are in great shape—ready to sell and quick to earn a profit—however three other films might have minor technical problems that require the consumer-facing platform to pay additional monies to make them 'market' ready. Since the major 'driver' title will be the largest revenue generator, it will require the consumer-facing platform to pay out royalties well in advance of the other titles. But even with the success of this one title—and the medium success of the ready-to-deliver six—the three problematic titles are keeping the consumer-facing platform's overall revenues from the deal in the red. Since this is a major financial risk, many acquisition executives request all of the miscellaneous and standard recoupment expenses get 'pooled' together so that they're only responsible to pay out royalties after the entire deal has recouped.

This process is called 'cross-collateralization' (or simply 'crossing'). This is very much a one-sided benefit to the buying side of the party—it greatly reduces their risk, makes the accounting process much simpler and prevents them from paying out royalties if other titles have burdened them with unexpected costs. That said, there is a benefit to the selling party. There are many occasions when distributors are put in the position of accepting cross-collateralization versus not doing the deal; in such instances, as long as the up front monies are reasonable, it's to everyone's benefit to move forward with the deal. There are occasions with major driver titles where the notion of cross-collateralization is a non-starter, at which point the deal is incapable of moving forward (or the acquiring party agrees to only 'cross' on the other titles).

For Producers, this is a bit of a catch-22. On one hand they're title is gaining revenues it otherwise might not have, but on the other their potential royalties might be reduced due to expenses incurred by other titles. Then again, for the rights holder of a problematic title, having other producers eat the expenses of your title could be beneficial—especially if the up front payment was meaningful.

▶ AUDITS

All distribution agreements should have a clause allowing a rights holder to conduct an audit of the distributor's books.

In general independent distribution agreements grant a rights holder the ability to conduct one audit per year—to be conducted at the rights holder's sole cost. A rights holder must give prior written notification (usually ten business days or more) so that the distributor can reasonably gather all the paperwork and redact (censor) any terms in their agreements that have no relation to the title being investigated.

If the audit reveals a miscalculation—generally of 5% or more—then the distributor will be granted a limited window of time to pay the rights holder their rightful share. Occasionally, a miscalculation can require a distributor to also cover the expense of the audit and can sometimes allow the rights holder the option to terminate the agreement early.

While shady practices of 'skimming' or hiding monies off the top can occur, the majority of miscalculations derive from accounting teams unintentionally misallocating revenues and expenses (e.g., not realizing a select title doesn't require certain material expenses, not realizing a marketing cap as been exhausted, etc.).

After the term of rights exploitation ends—when the distributor no longer has the right to sell a media property—monies can still be received in its name (from agreements with staggered payments or back logged royalties); as a result, the right to audit is usually permitted for a window after a deal has expired (usually 1 year after expiration).

▶ BUSINESS STRUCTURES

If you've ever worked on a professional media project (e.g., serving as a crew member on a feature-film or TV show, etc.), you might notice the 'payee'—or paying company—sending your earnings is sometimes different than the production company producing the project. To give an example, let's use a few made up names: a production company called 'Industrial Images' is producing a movie you're working on called *City Story*; when you receive your payment after a hard week of work, the payee might read something akin to 'City Story Movie, LLC'.

This is not a mistake; the production company has actually created a brand new company in the name of the movie. The reason for this comes back to the notion of avoiding liability and risk. If a distribution or production company were to invest in a new project and use funds from their main bank account, a legal claim made against the new project—even for actions outside of their control or knowledge—could potentially put *all* of their money at risk (including those related to other projects). To protect themselves—along with their other media assets—distributors, producers and production companies will instead isolate the monies by creating a brand new company (one that exists purely to pass all investments, expenses and gains through).

The name of the company can really be anything, but most commonly it's simply the title of the project (something everyone in the company is familiar with). This also helps the accounting teams track monies and the business affairs teams to better manage paperwork.

Although there are numerous types of business structures such projects could be organized under, the most common is a Limited Liability Company (or LLC).

The production or distribution company behind the development of the project would serve as the LLCs 'operating manager' (and would be responsible for maintaining records and filing taxes). The distribution company will actually enter into a contract with their own LLC (meaning the CEO of the distribution company could apply their signature as both the Licensee AND Licensor) where all rights to the title-specific LLC are clearly granted to the distribution company to manage.

It is very common for a single production or distribution company (itself organized as either a corporation or LLC) to own dozens of LLCs—especially companies that produce large annual slates of content.

Companies or individuals investing in media projects can actually 'own' a percentage of the title-specific LLC. To use the rich dentist concept, they could put down enough liquid cash to buy a 50% stake of the movie (but on paper, they'd be acquiring 50% of the company or title-specific LLC which owns the movie). When a profit margin is secured and royalty checks are sent, our rich dentist would file their tax return with these profits listed as income (or claim the investment as a loss if no monies were returned). And by investing into the single LLC, our rich dentist would have zero access to the profits of any other media project owned or developed by the production or distribution company. But other companies can be 'owners' as well as financial institutions such as banks—who can claim ownership if the distributor is seeking a loan to produce the project.

By contrast, when the distributor is licensing rights to a media project—even in a pre-sale scenario—these deals are brokered as license agreements with the distribution company (meaning there is no ownership stake offered in the project).

LLCs are able to have their own bank accounts, which is where presold or early-invested money will be placed until a pre-agreed threshold is hit to permit preproduction related costs being spent. Clear agreements are drafted that stipulate under what circumstances select parties are able to pull money from the accounts—e.g., meeting minimum financial levels, with written permissions, etc. This is to protect investors from our 'operating manager' production or distribution companies from running off with the cash as well as preventing third parties from having access to profits or funds related to other projects—and other banks accounts—the distribution or production company might own.

LLCs cost money to create and manage; these are one of the common expenses during the development phase of a new project as well as throughout the project's existence.

Although sales executives work for the distribution company—as salaried employees—they're job is to sell the intangible rights to each of those LLCs. If a sales exec has a single film in a contract, the monies are clear to follow; if a sales exec sells a package (or group) of titles, each dollar of that contract will need to be properly allocated so that each title—or rather, each LLC—has a clear value of earning associated (that amount is what's 'recognized' or visible to the LLC and its investors; they have zero visibility to the values of the other projects).

As distribution companies grow and evolve—generally taking on some ownership of the production process—they often 'incorporate' (which really just means they're taxed differently). And usually, they incorporate as two separate entities all under the company branded umbrella; the first corporation manages the distributor's distribution business whereas the second manages the distributor's production business.

▶ INTERNAL ALLOCATIONS

Each acquisition agreement contains different deal points with regards to MGs, distribution fees and other miscellaneous recoupable expenses. Consequently, there will inevitably be titles that become more advantageous for a distributor to push as opposed to others. For instance, a title that required a sizable MG would be seen as more important to push than a title that required zero down payment simply because recoupment of an MG directly impacts the distributor's bottom line. Same applies for titles with higher distribution fees and titles that have higher recoupable expense allowances because both permit the distributor to hold onto a higher volume of cash as monies pass through the accounting waterfall.

In instances where a title is sold on its own—with no accompanying programs—then the distribution waterfall offers a straightforward workflow. However, sales teams love to add extra titles in order to beef up a deal's overall value. And since these deals tend to be brokered for lump sum amounts—meaning a total value applied to the entire package rather than itemized valuations—then the distribution company has the opportunity to allocate differing amounts to each title in the manner that's most beneficial.

This process is referred to as 'internal allocation'; although it might seem unethical it's actually a very common practice.

When a content package opportunity exists, chances are it was a single—or small group—of title(s) that drove the deal. An experienced sales executive will always attempt to capitalize on the situation by including more programs in order to increase the total value (which often allows titles that tend to go unsold to receive an additional licensing opportunity). The notion that a distributor divvy's up the total lump sum to favor the driving titles does make a fair amount of sense and it is reasonable to reward the driving titles. In most circumstances, those driving titles would be the ones that incurred the higher levels of risk for the distributor (via MGs, marketing expenses, etc.) and should therefore be allocated to help reduce their impact.

Where this can get unethical is by what degree a distributor internally allocates. Allocations of a few percentage points higher or lower is well within reason, but shifting a 2-picture deal into an extreme allocation (such as a 90% to 10% allocation) should certainly raise a few eyebrows. While it's important to note that not all companies operate with such shady practices, a few certainly do.

There are very reasonable explanations as to why an internal allocation had to be made; for instance, a major title—driving the overall package—might require a minimum license fee to be sold into a specific territory (and the actual offer on the table is too small). By internally allocating monies away from other titles toward the major one, the deal can move forward (whereas without an allocation, no deal would be possible thereby negatively impacting all the titles).

The crunch of internal allocation for rights holders and producers is similar to that of cross-collateralization: on the one hand, there's an argument to be made that no deal would have been possible without cross-collateralizing, but on the other, 'crossing' could potentially siphon off money rightly earned by a single driving title.

Although producers and rights holders are not permitted to know the financial details or license fees applied to *other* titles, there are certain steps they can take to prevent having monies allocated away from their property. The most common is to require Producer Approval for any active deals. Although such a request can come with its own set of setbacks (see Chapter 3), provided a producer is able to make a quick decision that the value of a license fee is reasonable, this can be a strong safety net. Another way is to include language that essentially requires the license fee allocated to their project match that of all other titles (or at least the higher allocated titles) in a package deal. Such language can actually permit the fees of other titles to be visible during an audit, information that would otherwise be redacted. Please note, there is no one 'correct' way to phrase such preventative language; each contract is different and might require specific wording or placement to make the request stick. When considering the application of such language, one should always seek the advice of a lawyer or industry professional with strong legal experience; they would be able to accurately use terminology existing in the agreement to prevent excessive internal allocations from taking place.

▶ 'RECOGNIZING' REVENUE

Different companies 'recognize' the existence of gains and expenses in different ways. While this might seem abstract, the logic derives from the fact that a distribution company must report its sales and earnings to producers and rights holders as well as investment partners, parent companies and government financial departments (e.g., the Internal Revenue Service). While such a process would be unnecessary in a world where all third-party clients paid on time and never defaulted on their agreements, the real world of business offers a seemingly unlimited number of issues that can delay or prevent payments or cause deals to fall apart. Because of such potential snags regarding payments, distributors must exercise caution in informing their clients and partners of deals until they're confident either the monies will arrive or the option of legal recourse can be taken.

As a result, distribution companies officially recognize monies or deals at one of the following three stages:

▶ Upon full execution of a deal memo

▶ Upon receipt of revenue

▶ Upon license period start date

▶ **Full Signature of Deal Memo**—Although most deal memos or sales contracts include payment structures (meaning the total value of the agreement might be paid over three or four staggered payments—spanning a few months to potentially over a year), the total value is recognized by many companies on the date both the buyer and seller sign the agreement (when the agreement is fully executed). Where this can be problematic is when monies are booked as a locked sale, the actual cash might not come in for several more months and could never arrive in the event of a default or breach by the distributor. This workflow is very common for companies that have quarterly or annual targets—especially when they're owned by or are themselves public companies. Although the company might 'recognize' the revenue for purposes of accounting and reporting to investors, the producers and rights holders might not be entitled to their share of the revenue until the actual payments arrive.

▶ **Receipt of Revenues**—As stated earlier, fully executed deal memos are rarely paid in full; they are generally split across three or four payments staggered out over a period of time. The event which triggers a payment are usually one of the following: (i) an agreed upon date as specified in the contract (e.g., '30 days after execution of the agreement') or (ii) by some reached milestone of accomplishment (e.g., 'licensee's approval of material assets'). In either scenario, the distribution company does not 'recognize' the full amount of the contract; instead they recognize only the portion that has been wired in. Think of this as the 'cash' method (or 'bird-in-hand' method). There are no assumptions of how much will arrive in the future, only an emphasis on what exists in the bank at month's end. Smaller companies will work on this type of system, generally ones that do not have larger entities or investors in which to report. Nevertheless, even for companies that 'recognize' the total value on the date of full execution, the 'receipt of revenues' model is one all distributors use when making payouts to producers, rights holders and, occasionally, to their own employees with regards to commissions or bonuses. This notion of 'staggered' payments has become critical in recent years as more companies have stretched their payment schedules across eight to 12 financial quarters (e.g., quarterly across two or three years). Not only does this stretched schedule heavily impact when a rights holder will receive monies (and how much), but in a period of rising interest rates—such as 2022–2023—the value of the money decreases in terms of buying power quarter to quarter despite the fact that the banks are still owed interest on the outstanding balances for any loaned monies that initially cash-flowed the productions.

▶ **License Period Start Date**—The final type of 'recognition' is upon the license period start date or the commencement date of a contract. If a contract is executed in the middle of July, the license period might not start until October (this 'window' allows the distributor to deliver the materials required for the title's formal exploitation). Usually, the license period start date is the first date of valid exploitation that the acquiring party is permitted to showcase the title. Select accounting teams prefer using this event to book the total value of a contract because it's an undeniable action (the title either was released or it was not); if any future payment defaults exist after a title had been released, there is clear evidence that the distributor had fully honored its side of the deal. Although there is a sound logic to this approach, it can be problematic when involving presales since deals can sometimes close years before the project is ready to release.

With regard to recognizing revenue, there is no one better option; they all come with their positives and negatives. Nevertheless, a rights holder or producer should take the time to find out how a distribution company recognizes its internal revenues to better relay financial expectations to their investors and partners.

▶ COLLECTIONS

The ideal workflow for any accounting team would be one allowing them to simply draft the contractually stipulated invoices, send them to the appropriate client(s) and receive the proper payment on time without any issues.

But the world is an imperfect place. Late payments are common, even from major companies. In addition, consumer-facing platforms go bankrupt, go out of business or exist in countries that don't follow strict legal enforcement.

Since most companies recognize monies on the date of full execution, a delay or default in payment can cause a major burden on a company's books—especially at the end of their fiscal years, when the bulk of 'corrections' are applied (meaning a few bad deals can sink the final quarter of an otherwise successful year). To future-proof such mishaps, most deals are structured so that 100% of funds are paid before a distribution company releases the master materials (a workflow that effectively prevents a broadcast or release in advance of monies due). However, there are scenarios when clients are in need of urgent content and such rules must be skirted, which means distributors use other tactics to protect themselves.

In the event of delayed payments, distribution companies will occasionally apply 'interest' charges. These amounts can vary but are generally quite low (less than 5%). The idea is that for each 30-day or 60-day period of delayed payment, the amount due will become greater to offset missing revenue. Rarely are these enforced—most companies are just pleased to receive the initially requested amount and clear their books—but if such language was placed into the agreement and the distributor took the extra step of arbitrating or filing lawsuit against the acquiring party, the applied interest could be factored into the final settlement.

There are third-party companies that exist to oversee 'collections'. These entities can serve a wide variety of services but can be used as a pass-through entity to collect outstanding balances on behalf of a single distributor. They will invoice and receive the funds due, then—after withholding a fee for themselves of 1% to 3%–they will send the net amount to the distributor.

Although there have been attempts by organizations to blacklist companies or buyers with a poor reputation of paying its balances, most of these formal efforts fall short of enforcement. (It's very common for companies to simply file bankruptcy or change their company name, small efforts that allow them to bypass the formal blocks.) That said, in a business as small as media distribution, companies with a reputation for defaulting on payments are quickly 'blacklisted' in the worldwide court of public opinion; all companies have had a few unintended deals fall through, but when a buying entity attempts to play games, their reputation can be quickly tarnished.

▶ PROTECTIONS FOR PRODUCERS AND RIGHTS HOLDERS

There are a few outright tricks used in the distribution game, but it's not just distributors applying these against investors or producers; a handful of consumer-facing platforms and acquiring companies attempt to employ these tactics against distributors as well.

Creative Budgeting

A common example would be the practice of 'creative budgeting'; since presales and early buy-ins are calculated as a percentage of the production budget, many distributors or production companies will 'pad' their budgets with slightly inflated costs (e.g., cost of overhead or equipment) or pad them by including additional expenses. Bear in mind, the practice of padding a budget has a certain degree of merit; when required to 'cut' the budget down—per the request of a pre-buy client—a production or distribution team can easily target 10% or more from figures they artificially beefed up (a strategy that can help secure required funds). Where this can get deceitful is when costs having nothing to do with the project are included purely to launder money into the pockets of select individuals. Although there have been many scenarios where a certain picture car or high-end set piece was acquired for the purposes of the production only to end up in the personal possession of one of its producers, this can get much more shady when tens—if not hundreds—of thousands of dollars are being skimmed from the budget and paid directly to key individuals. To prevent fraud, a vetted third-party line producer (approved by all direct parties) is generally hired to create a non-biased budget of the production.

Sublicensing

Another example would be the practice of 'sublicensing' rights to a third party. Most acquisition contracts will have a clause dealing with the process of sublicensing (or licensing the same rights to a different company within the territory), but while this common deal practice has legit purposes, it can also be used to wrongfully take advantage of a rights holder or producer. As discussed in Chapter 4, there are occasions when a third-party distributor is building a large package of content for a direct client of theirs; in order to reach the minimum threshold, they sometimes must acquire rights from competing distributors. For a distribution company, selling these rights to another distributor would be considered sublicensing them to the other entity. Where this can get deceitful is when the expenses to be incurred by the distributor are passed over to the rights holder or producer's shoulders (whereby the sublicensing distributor takes the cash without incurring the expenses they're technically required to pay). Rights holders and producers can avoid this scenario by carefully reviewing any sublicensing clause and ensuring payments and expenses meet their expectations. Don't take this to mean sublicensing deals are in any way bad for producers or rights holders—often these deals allow for revenues to exist on a title that otherwise wouldn't have sold in the territory—but such deals should have a fair value in relation to allocations and permissible expenses.

Exit Clause

Every distribution agreement—whereby a producer or rights holder is licensing their content to a distribution company for territory specific representation—should always have some sort of exit clause (a block of text explaining how the relationship can be concluded in a way that will not result in either party being in breach). For a producer to pull a film or media property away from a distributor can be a costly process (especially if the property has only been in their possession a short period of time), therefore any inclusion of such a clause will undoubtedly come with some level of expense to the producer. And a producer or rights holder should only exercise such a clause if they truly feel their property is being misrepresented; pulling a title away from one distributor and handing it over to another will undoubtedly devalue the title in the marketplace due to double exposure. An easy alternative is to include some sort of performance clause, whereby the distributor is required to meet some financial threshold within a reasonably specified period of time; if the minimum number is hit, the deal continues, but if the minimum number is not met, the deal cancels.

The Financial Waterfall

The most common way producers and rights holders miscalculate their financials is by not understanding the recoupment of expenses that will be applied to their project. An agreement should clearly specify which expenses are recoupable and which are not; what financial caps exist if any; which revenues or receipts will be recognized as gross versus net; and in what order recoupable expenses and withholdings are placed within the distributor's financial waterfall. We mapped all of this out earlier in this chapter, but it's critical for a rights holder to actually take the time to truly map out how monies generated by their property will bounce through a distributor's financial waterfall.

All of the topics covered within this chapter are generally used to legitimately protect the distributor from excess liability; they incur a great amount of expense—and risk—when acquiring media projects and do reasonably deserve to protect themselves. That said, their protections should not take advantage of any rightful monies—after reasonable and logical out-of-pocket expenses—due to the rights holder or producer.

9

Practical Approaches for Kick-Starting Your Career

After eight chapters overviewing how established professionals and executives serve the Hollywood machine, it's now time to shift the focus of this conversation to your career objectives. Regardless of what position you hope to reach (e.g., director, writer, producer, editor, actor, etc.), the principles that fuel the business of media distribution—as outlined in Chapter 1 and described throughout this book—are just as applicable to helping you create a real-world game plan to kick-start your own Hollywood career.

▶ SEPARATING FACT FROM FICTION

At this very moment—across the entire global media industry—there are established producers, distributors and acquisition executives (with money in their pockets), looking to review new scripts, invest in new projects and green-light new content. Every studio (from tiny to major) releases dozens—sometimes hundreds—of feature films and thousands—sometimes tens of thousands—of television and new media content hours every single year.

The irony is that there are countless numbers of industry newcomers (many of whom have a few spec scripts in hand or even a completed feature film), yet they struggle to get their foot in the door. Even with an agent or manager, their professional hopes seemingly go nowhere. But it's not the talent department in which they're lacking (I'd argue that many of them are quite good at their craft); it's simply that they're approaching media's top decision-makers with the wrong content and in the wrong manner.

Although we will go into detail regarding ways in which novices should start to organize their overall game plan, let's first break apart three recurring 'myths' about making it in the industry that repeatedly hold back those eager to get their careers into motion:

DOI: 10.4324/9781003357902-10

Myth #1: I Do Not Need to Learn the Business

For many individuals with big entertainment dreams, they often assume that one day their talents will simply be recognized. And once this magical moment of recognition takes place, they believe their only responsibility thereafter will be that of 'creating' their next project (meaning all that complicated business nonsense will be handled by their agents, lawyers or an army of minions serving their needs).

This just isn't the way the real world works. Most bigwig writers, producers and filmmakers are very professional and astute with all aspects of their careers; they take an active role during contract negotiations and manage their careers as if it were their own small business (they don't just leave it to their agents and lawyers). Yes, vetted professionals generally have agents, but at the end of the day they use *their own* judgment, insight, and wherewithal to make the decisions that will affect their careers. And even after a high degree of success, most established entertainment professionals I've known carry pretty in-check egos; their current and continuous levels of success is not from a brash attitude of know-it-all isms and 'take no prisoners' contract negotiation, but rather one of compromise.

Brokering deals in the business of media distribution—as with all industries—is about focusing on what works, what doesn't and, most importantly, working to *get the project done*.

And consider this: if one were to be represented by agents, lawyers or managers, then at some point that person must sign their own name on the contract to secure the representation. And believe me when I say these individuals are *not* serving you; they're serving their own financial interests (meaning you'll exist simply as a line item on their clientele list). Although agents, lawyers and all other representatives are incredibly valuable assets to your career objectives, it's important to note that they are hired by you to serve your needs (it is not their job to drive your career).

If you want to truly succeed in entertainment, then you must fully understand the business behind the distribution of media. There are plenty of resources to grasp the basics—including the one in your hands—but your career will require your active participation throughout your professional life.

Myth #2: My Work Will Simply Be 'Discovered'

Regardless whether the fantasy is that your first feature will sweep the festival circuit, that your face will grab the attention of a director at a coffee shop to star in their latest project or that your script will be embraced after a blind submission to CAA, all of these involve the overly simplified 'discovery' myth (whereby one day your life simply changes forever).

Although many Hollywood novices can quote stories of such incredible luck, most of these are simply 'stories' (focusing on the aspects we love to hear while ignoring the less fun parts, namely *all the hard work*!).

For any overnight success story—whether in media or any other industry—you can blindly assume that individual contributed at least ten years of effort prior to achieving their shining moment. That's a decade of hustle, persistence, sweat equity and hard work (early mornings, late nights all without extra compensation while managing full-time jobs, family obligations and all other day-to-day responsibilities). And no third party was doing all this hard work for them (see Myth #1 earlier); they had to take the initiative to zero in on their goal and strategize ways to make the vision of their professional life become a reality (and then put in the effort to see it through). To offer some perspective on the 'story' of discovery compared to the reality of the hard work required to achieve it, just reread my breakdown of Diablo Cody in Chapter 2, or read the biography of any great director, actor or writer.

But let's say you wrote a spec script that's gained some attention, or produced a feature film that's really garnered some traction; the recognition from these projects will exist more as a 'stepping stone' as you build your career (offering you something to carry the momentum from which to build upon). The offers won't just start getting handed to you; you're still going to have to hustle and self-promote. For instance, that spec script of yours probably won't get bought 'as is' but might be enough to land you some 'writer for hire' gigs—sprucing up treatments, polishing other writer's scripts; or that feature film might be enough to secure you meetings with high-level producers capable of hiring you to oversee projects they have in motion (allowing you to build your directing credits).

There are obviously stories of outliers, where the fantasy seems to be the reality, but these are rarer in entertainment than winning the lottery. In the real working industry, one must prove they can do the job *before* they're given the chance to do it professionally.

Myth #3: I'll Let My Work Speak for Itself

A spec script or completed feature film should absolutely hold its own weight and reflect the talents of the individual(s) responsible for its creation. However, there is a ton of competition in Hollywood (and only so many available slots to fill). Although your completed work will be used to evaluate your future capabilities, you're still going to have to convince people to take notice. Therefore, in order to get your work noticed, you're going to have to perform a little self-promotion.

Here's why: people in the media distribution business are busy. On top of balancing major work objectives and getting bombarded by dozens of critical emails and calls at all hours of every day, they also have personal lives to keep in check (families, doctor's appointments, car repairs, etc.). And although they are indeed actively seeking out new projects—and never want to let a potential opportunity slip past—they simply lack the time to give everything proper consideration. Therefore, they use a third-party vetting process to help them focus on the projects that are worth allocating attention.

A third-party vetting process basically boils down to allowing other people to indicate or recommend which potential projects are worth the time to check out. In example, screenwriters submitting spec scripts are very familiar with 'readers' (whose only job is to read script submissions, then summarize their plot—and the writer's talents—into a short synopsis referred to as 'coverage'); this coverage quickly boils the script down into a few key factors (e.g., is the script good?; if the script is weak, is the writer at least good?; does this script fit our company mandate?, etc.). Completed feature films are also reviewed by juniors in the acquisitions department, who will watch enough of the project to make an informed decision about whether the submission is worth passing along to their superiors. Submissions from well-established professionals (or major media companies) might get more pressing attention than the works submitted by novices; but rest assured that everything will get reviewed sooner or later. (No one wants to be the individual responsible for passing on the next big title!) However, the individuals tasked with reviewing these submissions are people too—ones who are generally being pulled in multiple directions at once.

While it's a great dream to quietly send along your script, film, proposal, demo reel or headshot, it will need a bit of accompanying self-promotion to make it pop.

(Please note, self-promotion is not constant calls or obnoxious follow-ups; we'll get to the 'how-to' specifics on this one later, but at this point we're just expressing that notion that you will have to nudge your work (and yourself) a bit in order to get the attention you deserve.)

In short, to deconstruct the myths that unnecessarily hold back many talented newbies, you're going to have to learn the business and hustle your own talents. Not only will this double-step approach ensure your best attributes are represented, it also gives you complete control—and freedom—to promote and market yourself in the way professionals need to hear about you.

All that said, let's also point out that real 'foot-in-the-door' opportunities don't come in the form of prescheduled meetings or other situations that we have a fair amount of control over. Instead, they come from random interactions, leads and connections that align spontaneously. How these interactions develop can happen at parties, networking events, film and TV markets or just casually as two career-oriented friends catch up and mix business and personal talk over the same lunch.

The problem for most industry novices is that they are taught the overly formalized forms of pitching without learning how to subtly pitch their work (and themselves) during these everyday casual events. I call these moments 'soft-pitch' opportunities, and the vast majority of the potential work one might secure for themselves—especially in the early parts of their career—result from how well they've established a 'base' of professional contacts with whom they can communicate and share these soft-pitch announcements of their projects or goals.

Whether semi-planned (at a professional networking type event) or completely random (at a party or casual outing), there will inevitably be a time when you meet a professional who asks you point-blank 'So, what do you do?'. While some may see this vague question as yet another example of the shallowness of the industry, this is actually your moment to shine.

When you respond proudly with "I'm a screenwriter" or "I'm a director", that professional will immediately want to know whether (i) you're new to the industry but have a firm understanding of the business with the aptitude to grow professionally—aka someone who *can* help them—or (ii) whether you simply scoff at the real-world needs of the marketplace and blindly hold onto an idealized view of how the industry *should* be catering to your individual vision, needs and wants—aka someone who *cannot* help them. Let's make sure you know how to secure option 'i' regardless of what career objectives you have.

Just as the principles that drive the business of media distribution are unchanging, so too are the steps that will help you promote your talents and kick-start your career. What follows are three targeted objectives you can begin working on today—regardless of where you live or what position you hope to achieve within the business. By following these three steps (and actively incorporating them into your everyday life), you will start to see the doors of opportunity leading you toward your career objectives.

However, you cannot cheat. Following just one of these for a few weeks isn't going to yield any results; these steps must be applied so regularly and so often that they simply become habits:

Habit #1: Always Be Working

You should *always* have 'something' that you're working on (meaning you must be actively involved in a career-related project that is aiding your overarching career objective). For a writer it means you must always be writing; for an editor it means you must always be editing, etc. Isn't this a given? On the outset, of course. But the way in which this principle applies to entertainment 'schmoozing' is so that when you are asked that inevitable question of 'what are you working on?' (aka 'what do you do?') you'll always have a selection of intelligent—and situation-appropriate—answers to pull from. You should always be working because that's what professionals do.

Habit #2: Grow and Maintain Your Network

Habit #2 is not about pitching yourself or your talents to complete strangers (or the bigwigs running the studios); it's instead about making a conscious step towards consistently building and maintaining your own personalized professional social network of individuals that directly link you to established decision-makers. This means picking up the phone and actively communicating with people you know (and reaching out to those whom you don't)—not because you're a nice person, but because you (and your talents) deserve to be on the forefront of other people's minds when they suddenly find themselves in need of a person with your specific talents. Entertainment is an industry built on relationships; start growing your network *today*!

Habit #3: Expand Your Understanding of the Business

Where most books tell you to 'read the trades' and 'study the studios'—and other advice that will yield minimal results—Habit #3 is about encouraging you to learn everything you can about the business of entertainment that has *nothing* to do with your desired career path (even if only at a grassroots level). The reason, the more you know about how other people's jobs fit into the overall system, the easier it will be to find a way for you to pitch your work and/or talents to them so that you gain a foothold. Not only are there excellent books covering a variety of topics, there are also podcasts and other forms of new media focused on the subject (even to this day, I listed to Variety's Strictly Business podcast on my morning runs to not only stay informed regarding new business opportunities but also to continue my own 'understanding of the business' education).

▶ APPLYING THESE HABITS

A career in entertainment blossoms when one can prove they have the ability to deliver the industry a consistent and reliable output of steady work—all while making the job of others around them easier. Your most recent project showcases your value to the Hollywood system—and when you're starting out and don't yet have any credits to do this work on your behalf, you must be prepared to answer professionals with the industry-appropriate work ready to show (with more already in motion behind closed doors).

That way, when you do find yourself in one of these sudden face-to-face interactions and the casual 'what do you do?' or 'what are you working on?' questions pop up, you will always have a collection of work in motion that allows you to best *cater your answer* to them. And because you've taken time to learn about other careers in the business—and how other jobs fit into the overall business—you'll be able to pitch the work that best represents what *that* individual would be interested in hearing about (meaning what's most pertinent to *their* career needs and not just pitching the story you're most proud of).

By piquing their professional interest, the conversation can close more on a point of you asking 'so how can we work together'? For a screenwriter, this could be phrased as 'seems we have similar content interests, maybe I can flesh out one of your (or your company's) story ideas?'; for an editor, it could be 'seems like your company has a large output of work, maybe I could help organize some of the video files so your staff editors can work more efficiently?' Opportunities generally present themselves as problems.

But remember, it's not all about you; it's about your ability to support the needs of the overall entertainment industry, which is why when you reciprocate the 'what do you do?' question the other direction, you need to have an appreciation and understanding of what the other side's contributions (and needs) are within the system.

When you're starting out, it's very common to be interacting with people who serve—or are hoping to serve—very straightforward roles in the business. People want to be editors, directors, actors (among many other clear-cut roles). But as you begin to associate with people who are more established, they tend to have roles that are a bit harder to place: line producers, producer's reps, executive producers, acquisitions agents, etc. So the more you know about *their* role in Hollywood, the better your ability to find a way to wedge your foot into their professional world. If they're a line producer or producer's rep (purely as an example), they'd know which production companies tend to produce content in alignment with the scripts you're currently writing or the types of movies you're patch-working together. And if you have a strong attitude—one that shows 'you get it' since you're focused on serving the system—they might even be willing to make an introduction (which would 'vet' your talents).

The media business, like any industry, is purely a numbers game. Putting yourself out there, interacting with people in all facets of the industry (not just those interested in the same objectives as you) gets both you and your skill sets in front of new people. The more people you're in front of, the more opportunities there are for you to take the lead on. And the more opportunities like these you get yourself involved with, the more your name is slowly—and firmly—planted into the minds of people who can reach out to you when they're in a jam (which is how jobs across all industries are generally filled).

This is not an overnight achievement; it's instead a process of always keeping your work (and yourself) in shape so that you can (i) discuss and deliver 'fresh' content immediately upon request when you have these sporadic encounters, and (ii) so that you're ready to move when that big opportunity suddenly falls into your lap. As the old saying goes, "'luck' is when opportunity meets preparation".

But to reach this point, it takes a great deal of work. Not just to create your arsenal of presentable projects but also to develop your pitching skills to engage others to consider you—and your work—as a strong fit for their specific needs. But generic 'write every day' advice is not the same old 'Stephen King writes 2,000 words a day' approach, nor does it mean you literally need to sit at a computer and punch the keyboard for a blocked amount of time each morning. Working every day simply means not being idyll with your career objectives; you must always be consistently moving your current ideas forward (towards a state of completion). And 'pitching' doesn't mean only discussing your stories or career objectives in formalized boardroom meetings; it means being able to intelligently speak about your work—and yourself—in a way that engages the other party (and not blindly spouting out a forced or memorized logline).

In order to apply our 'habits' effectively, you'll need to focus on the following three objectives:

▶ Build an 'arsenal' of projects

▶ Hone your pitching skills (to cater to Hollywood professionals)

▶ Network, network, network

Build Your Arsenal

Your 'arsenal' will be slightly different depending on which exact role you hope to fill within the Hollywood system. If you intend on being a 'go-to' writer, then you'll need spec scripts that showcase your ability to deliver quality writing that's mindful of budget. If you want to direct, then you'll need visual examples of *real* projects you've directed (that verify your ability to work within a budget and deliver quality content on time). And if you hope to produce content, then you'll need 'market-ready' projects that actually meet the needs of consumer-facing platforms (with a business plan to support them as viable vehicles of investment). Let's give examples of each:

▶ **Writer**—A writer needs at least two (ideally *three*) fully completed feature-length spec scripts ready to show. In addition, they need a list of at least ten structured (meaning fully log-lined and broken down into key plot points or story reveals) ideas ready to pitch. If you really want to approach Hollywood as a writer, then you need to show them you've got what it takes; and that you are a *writing machine*. In addition to giving you a great collection of stories to pull from to best engage your immediate professional audience when those inevitable 'so what do ya got?' questions arise, having two to three completed scripts to showcase proves consistency, and the list of ideas shows stamina and preparedness.

Although this is a *very* large volume of work to achieve, it is an excellent target portfolio for you to work towards and to keep as a minimum. Also, this doesn't mean that once you reach this target you can simply press pause and wait until your career begins. Once you have two to three scripts you're confident in, you can then 'pluck' one of your solid ideas from your 'ten ideas list' and start fleshing it out as a new screenplay. Once fully finished as a completed script, it can then replace the weaker of the previous two to three spec scripts in your arsenal (and you can add a new concept/idea to your 'ready to go ideas' list)—and this cycle repeats itself.

Here's another interesting point. The spec scripts (and the list of ideas) should all be *the same genre type* (or, at minimum, very similar ones). Most people make the false assumption they should present a diversified slate, but the opposite is actually what garners results.

Let's hypothetically say you are in discussion with the development team at a mid-level production company. You get along, your ideas are in alignment with their way of doing business, you have a great script in front of them and they're impressed. Before they offer you a writing position for their new film, they'll want to make sure your current script isn't just some fluke anomaly (or random win). They'll want to make sure you can churn out a workflow that is consistent (and fresh). If they ask to see other writing samples, and all you have is work from a different genre, they might not be convinced. However, if you had a second example, completely unique to the first script yet from the same genre type, you would be able to prove dependability.

Also, it's important to understand that these specs scripts and ideas aren't for selling; they're for showcasing your ability to deliver. (Yes, they *could* sell—and you absolutely can sell them if offered the chance—but mentally understand these are primarily to showcase your talent and may never 'progress' beyond existing as samples.) The objective here is that after feeling assurance you can write what's needed, a company might offer you a writer-for-hire opportunity (either to polish something they're already working on or to draft a treatment for a project they're in early stages on).

Writers can create their own personalized website (e.g., www.yourname.com or similar) and can define their writing style, offer samples and list out loglines. Those seeking to find connections to build their careers can reach out to acquisition executives at production or distribution companies as well as seek out professional writer's rooms to network TV shows (offering to work as a writing assistant—I've known quite a few TV writers that got their start following this path). Another pathway I've seen is writer's actually writing novels—or novellas—then self-publishing them. The novels verify one's ability for writing output while also offering samples that shape a writer's 'brand' or genre style.

▶   **Director**—No one is just handed the job of directing. Although behind-the-scenes featurettes and movies about the film industry add to the allure of this role, directing a film, television project or any other form of media is grueling and requires a great deal of professional *management* experience. While most envision directing as only focusing on camera angles or the on-screen visual magic, they turn a blind eye toward how much pressure is placed upon the director's shoulders (much of which is *not* artistic in nature).

Media direction is really all about project management. A director is being handed a project (a script) along with parameters to work within (cast, shooting schedule, budget, etc.) and is expected to deliver the footage required so that a sellable product can be compiled together, marketed and released. One likes to imagine the director having a vital say in cast, script or budget, but in real-world indie Hollywood, many of these choices are made prior to the director getting hired on. To secure this job, a producer or distributor must know the individual being considered can reliably handle all the ups, downs and setbacks guaranteed to occur while still managing to get a quality product across the finish line that's within those financial boundaries and time constraints.

To accomplish this, a potential director's arsenal must include the following three elements:

▶ **Visual Examples**—A directing candidate must prove they are visually competent (meaning they must have a body of work created that showcases their ability to convey story ideas, work with actors and deliver despite tight time constraints). Short films and shoestring indie features can prove this, but only if these projects have been acquired by a distribution company for professional marketplace exploitation. An alternative way to build a portfolio of visual examples—that is less costly and time-consuming—is by shooting commercials (even if only spec commercials). Commercials have limited time constraints, must be respectful to the brand being conveyed and require a director to think outside of the box in order to relay an idea or message. A directing candidate with their own website featuring spec commercials or comedic skits *in addition* to professionally exploited indie features and shorts will be taken seriously; however, these will not be used to 'hire' your talents (the way a spec script will for a writer). Instead, these will be used to verify your visual talents after the next two 'must-haves' are achieved.

▶ **Verifiable 'Management' Experience**—By management experience we mean your ability to showcase evidence that you have been handed a project and led a team of individuals to complete and deliver that project in a timely manner. While most assume 'visual' examples (such as a self-produced short or feature) would cover this requirement, what we're really going after is proving your capability to be handed a project from a third party (meaning that another entity has instilled trust in your leadership and you fulfilled the required objective). Many directors in Hollywood are not brought on early to develop the creative; they're hired later in the game to 'project manage' the production and post; a great number of directors have also been brought in to replace a recently removed director. Project management experience showcases your ability to simply be plopped into a difficult situation (a project already in motion) and quickly organize the production to ensure an on-time and under-budget delivery. Great examples of jobs where such experience can be developed would be those of assistant director, producer (all forms) and showrunners. However, a more creative and often overlooked starting point—that also verifies 'visual' capability *and* verifiable management experience—would be the role cinematographer or director of photography (DP). A DP meticulously manages the camera crew and grip and electric teams to ensure a specific visual style and look for the media property. Additionally, DPs must be cognizant of budget, time constraint and have the foresight to understand how the work they're performing in the present will affect departments and schedules in the future. They're also not strangers to speaking directly with talent (which can be intimidating on larger projects). For a real-world example of how the DP role can evolve into that of director, consider the career of my friend Marco Fargnoli; having lensed dozens of shorts and indie features (with his fair share of camera operator and grip/electric jobs in between), he had secured a very strong reputation for his visual talent and leadership skills. From here, Marco was able to land the role of DP on the Adult Swim series *Children's Hospital* and later on the Mindy Kaling starrer *The Mindy Project*. After lensing four complete seasons on *Children's* and after a complete first season on *Mindy*, Marco began discussing the possibility of directing an episode of *Mindy* with its producers. Halfway through season two, Marco received his first 'directing' credit on an episode of *The Mindy Project*. And from that momentum, he was offered the director's chair for the season premiere of *Children's Hospital* (season five); he went on to direct multiple episodes on both series. No one just handed him the role of director, he earned it (and was only given the opportunity *after* he'd proven his ability to be effective wearing his DP hat.) He'd proven he knew the workflows, had developed a strong relationship with the cast and understood while respecting and understanding the demands of the producing teams. Although Marco's story is more likely to occur in a 'series-centric' scenario, this level of verifiable project management and leadership experience is just as necessary—if not more so—for a feature film producer to entrust their entire project onto the shoulders of a potential director. That said, most of the directors I've seen hired on—or the few I've personally hired on—primarily rose in similar fashion to Marco but stemming from the producer, acting or AD realm.

▶ **Vouch From an Insider**—Although verifiable project management experience and a strong portfolio of visual media projects will be utilized to judge your capabilities, the real 'must-have' is having a vetted industry insider recommend you and vouch for your talents. Just as our principles in Chapter 1 stipulate, distributors and heads of production seek assurances (to eliminate as much risk in their decision-making as possible); they won't take a blind gamble just because a novice director has a cool-looking reel. Therefore, they rely on close contacts to recommend strong directing candidates (ones who know several directors and can recommend the *right* director for the project at hand). Entertainment is a business of relationships; those relationships ultimately let producers and distributors know who they should bring in to 'project manage' (direct) a newly developed film or TV program (ones who will get it right).

I thought Tom Hanks actually summed up the job of director quite well when he was asked about the experience after his directorial debut of *That Thing You Do!* (1996); he described the job as being asked hundreds of critical questions every day and only being allowed to get a few of them wrong.

Since time and money are riding on a director's shoulders, a novice director needs to relay they are capable of answering all those questions—correctly—while also being vouched for and having a solid portfolio of visual work.

(Many of the earlier 'director'-related points should also be applied for obtaining other 'visual'-oriented leadership roles, including editor or cinematographer.)

▶ **Producer**—Although it might sometimes feel as if having money is the only viable way into building a producing career, it is not. Most successful producers working today did not start with money (or contacts). They built them following our three habits as outlined earlier in this chapter.

There is no prerequisite job for 'producers'; they literally come from all walks of life (and all conceivable backgrounds). But there are many experiences and character traits that nearly all successful producers have in common:

▶ **Business Experience**—Most producers have actual business experience and are well-versed in distribution. They understand how money is raised and how rights are divvied up and take time to learn the financial aspects. They can gain this experience in a variety of ways; for example, many producers are entertainment lawyers or have legal experience related to the industry, others are former executives who actively sold or distributed media content and others came from a production background and blossomed into line producers prior to taking on a project of their own. And others still are very new to the world of business—and the industry itself—but they have taken the time to learn the core basics of budgets and have made the pivot toward pitching projects as business opportunities. Bottom line, from somewhere within the industry, they learned the business and financial elements which drive media projects toward completion, and after gathering the information, they began developing and pushing projects of their own.

▶ **Well-Connected**—To produce content, you need a large network of professionals to put the whole project together. Generally from their involvement in the finer points of the distribution business, they have built friendships with individuals peppered throughout the entire media landscape (from actors to distributors to crew members). This is built from Habits #2 and #3 earlier—about always growing their networks and expanding their understanding of the business. From this, not only can they present and discuss projects to a variety of individuals, they also have direct access to people who can serve a specific role required as their project develops. This network is critical throughout the entire process of putting a project together (from the embryonic beginnings all the way to release date marketing strategies).

▶ **Willing to Shoulder More of the Work**—This is a character trait, one that can be learned; it's valuable across all professionals but is especially applicable in media. Producers must be capable of wearing multiple hats with a smile (many of which they're wearing at the same time). While many people have clear boundaries they refuse to cross (refusing to handle a specific job because it's not in their departmental description, etc.), a seasoned producer is always willing to dive in and tackle it. I've seen established producers—ones who've held Academy Awards in their hands—step in and grab a piece of equipment or help carry gear. A successful producer is willing to get their hands dirty and doesn't hold an elitist attitude. Although a great number of people believe they have this trait, it can only be found when it's hour 16 on set and there's still more to shoot (they'll be the ones helping to energize the team). This is true 'leadership' in action. But for a producer, this ability to shoulder more of the work stretches far beyond the shooting schedule; they're up late all nights of the week during preproduction, post and well after a project's release, keeping things on schedule and staff motivated. You'll often find producers performing the role of 'therapist' to writers, directors and talent to help them work through creative problems.

The most efficient path toward becoming a producer is simply focusing on the three main habits and then keeping projects in the pipeline that are relevant for discussion. Rather than writing spec scripts (as a writer does to build their arsenal) or shooting content for visual display (the way a director does), a producer must be constantly seeking out and building a collection of stories they have access to. This can be befriending authors, acquiring 'option' rights to a story or book they're passionate about or collaborating with writers they're confident in to develop story ideas. The concept here is that a producer constantly needs to be building a library of media projects that have legs for development opportunities (a wide range of projects they can quickly 'dust off' and make presentable—with attachments, budgets and other pitch-worthy elements). For more detail on what's required to 'produce' a pitch-worthy project, see Chapter 2.

▶ IMPROVE YOUR VERBAL COMMUNICATION SKILLS

Some people are naturally gifted at verbal communication; they seem to be able to gracefully enter a room, open their mouth and simply captivate an audience. But in truth, most people never started this way. Instead, they *learned* how to command an audience through practice and application. Many of us cringe at the idea of making small talk, cold-calling or public speaking. And there is no worse feeling than standing before someone, being asked to tell them about your script (or yourself) and having a total loss for words, followed by an immediate loss of self-confidence.

I've been there—we all have in one form or another—and for those who get overly self-conscious when pitching ideas, there are many ways to learn how to *fake* confidence and teach yourself how to handle any social encounter the media business might throw your way.

What follows are a few basic steps you can take action on today (while working towards building your arsenal of projects) that will not only aid you in how you view your own work but will also improve your self-confidence (so you can pitch your projects—and your talents—more effectively), expose you to other facets of the film and media business all while helping grow your social network (that's win-win-*win* thinking). Before you dismiss these, really read through how each of these can help you (not just to be a more effective writer, director or producer but also to more effectively manage your own career):

▶ **Improv Groups**—Improvisational acting is probably one of the best skills you could ever hope to acquire. Whether you live in Los Angeles or not, your town will have a band of actors with an improv group open to new members. What should you say if asked why you've joined the group? The truth! Tell them you are a writer who is trying to gain better confidence and public speaking skills, or a hopeful producer trying to learn how to better discuss your story ideas. Let loose. They'll have you perform all kinds of weird and crazy exercises (breathing exercises, training exercises, etc.). Then you will be placed into groups and be given a variety of scenarios to perform. You will invent scenes of your own (which should come naturally to you, given your storytelling strengths). You will learn the rules of improv (such as accepting whatever piece of information, however ridiculous, your scene partner has introduced to the scenario). Why are these skills so vastly important? Because every business meeting I've ever attended literally feels like an imrov session. Meetings are a back-and-forth volley of ideas, opinions and corporate culture. How you speak and what you say will literally be part of the act. You will also learn how people communicate; you will learn the 'beats' people use when telling jokes or presenting ideas (which will also allow you to find those clutch points to jump into the conversation and get your ideas on the table effectively). You will learn how to more quickly consolidate your ideas and get your concept in front of the group as fast as possible. (Know what this sounds like to me? Pitching!) Improv classes are not only a lot of fun, you will also make friends who share an interest in the same business but with a completely different focus (which allows you the opportunity to learn the ins and outs of other professional avenues—aka Habit #3).

▶ **Acting Classes**—Joining an acting class accomplishes several objectives that improve your professional career objectives. First, you will be forced to read scripts from the point of view of a person using it as a tool, not as the bible to a film; and second, you will realize that many actors do not actually read their scripts; they simply scan the pages looking for how many speaking lines their character has (which they do to judge 'how important' their role is). This will force you, as a content creator, to understand that different people will evaluate different elements of your pitches (script, synopsis, cast lists etc.) in different ways. And while actors review a script with one mindset and a director another mindset, you must remember that distributors, acquisition executives and investors equally review such project elements with unique mindsets—business-oriented ones. In addition to acting classes helping you choose each word of your written materials carefully, they're also a great deal of fun and will also introduce you to completely new people (hoping to accomplish different goals while in the same industry). And as indicated in Habit #3, you will also learn aspects of the acting craft that allow you to better understand how actors approach their jobs.

▶ **Hollywood Pitch Fests**—These are very interesting events; as with most markets and conventions, there's a steep entry fee along with your standard bag of SWAG (which are mostly coupons and advertisements—aka more stuff for you to spend your money on). But during the actual 'pitch' event, for a small fee (between $15 and $30), you can schedule a ten- to 15-minute 'pitch' meeting with a staff member from a major studio. What will you find once you enter your meeting? A giant room full of small tables, each with a very young (22- to 25-year-old) intern. This is whom you're going to pitch to. Their job is to attend this event on the very off chance some brilliant material comes in. In reality, their job is to take detailed notes of the submission and any materials that might be handed off, just so it can be backlogged and cataloged at the studio in the very unlikely chance that their work takes off at some point in the future. Are these events worth it? If you expect to pitch your idea and see it optioned, then, no, these events are a total waste of money. But if you are looking to (i) improve your pitching skills and build confidence by pitching to a real person or (ii) make youthful connections who are opportunistic about making their own Hollywood dreams come to life, then a Pitch Fest might be a decent *one-time* investment.

▶ NETWORK, NETWORK, NETWORK

You're going to have to keep your social network growing if you ever want to get your projects into the industry hustle, and that means you're going to have to get out there and network. The problem is that most of entertainment's 'networking' scenarios force us into awkward situations and yield zilch in terms of results when all is said and done. No thanks!

Fortunately, there are very interesting ways you can approach networking that are absolutely one-way tickets to seeing huge returns for your efforts. The irony? You'll be heading to the exact same markets, industry events and festivals that everyone else will suggest you to approach, only you'll be experiencing them in a way where you'll glean more insight, contacts, and results than everyone else around you.

▶ **Film/TV and New Media Markets**—Now that I annually attend many of the world's most well-known media festivals and markets, I can give you the piece of advice I wished I had learned back when I first moved to LA: don't attend a film or TV market, *volunteer* for one.

Believe me, markets need people to handle all the grunt work. They might bring you in several weeks, possibly several months, early (maybe even for a paying job—minimum wage, of course). But you will be helping orchestrate the market itself and will be dealing directly with decision-makers. You will have access to buyers and exhibitor lists, catalogs, client/contact lists of production companies. You will witness all the screening schedules. You will get firsthand access to see which companies handle what genres of content. You can also volunteer as an intern for the companies exhibiting at the market. Sure, you'll be the 'door person' for the company, where you filter out people walking in, etc. But you will be on the inside. As a volunteer or employee, you will witness wannabe writers and producers entering the room and listen to them as they fumble through their pitches. Smile, nod and *learn* from their mistakes. But the best part is that there will be downtime. You will talk with this company about everything and nothing. Don't make the mistake of actually pitching your work to them during the market (unless they ask); keep your ideas to yourself for the moment. Instead, simply listen to them, and be accommodating whether they ask you to make coffee or fetch supplies. Listen to them talk about projects with others in the room, especially with their clients; listen to them discuss ideas. You will overhear meetings about collaborations and development, about money, even about content that works and content that doesn't. They will learn to trust you (three or four intense working days can reveal a great deal about a person's dependability and work ethic!). And when the market comes to a close, you will have several close contacts that have seen you perform under pressure and will know you are able to deliver what's needed. Attending a market costs a lot of money, whereas volunteering costs nothing but your time. And you'll probably get a few meals covered as well as more direct access to real working professionals than you could ever imagine.

▶ **Film Commissions**—Volunteer for your local film commission. Even if you're not in a major metropolitan area, you will be directly associated with professional individuals in and around your community that have a strong interest in films (and the business of bringing media productions to your region). Film commissions offer interesting opportunities on new productions, not generally found if only using Google or IMDb searches. Film commissions have entire databases of production companies (and development entities). Ask permission to copy email addresses; ask if you can be a point of contact for regional productions. Everyone you work with will have years of experience from which you can glean valuable insight; most of them will have legit contacts in the business, working professionally.

▶ **Be an Extra**—Contact a company that hires extras and tell them you want to become an on-set extra. You will get paid a minimum wage; however, you will gain access to the production office as well as to the crews and sets. Very politely, during a break, approach a member of the department you have interest in working for (e.g., production office, electrical lighting teams, grips, etc.). Simply state, "I'm working as an extra in order to meet professionals in the (fill in the blank) department. If you need any help on this production or on future projects, I'd be interested in helping out." You're not there to enter into a dialogue, just to announce you're available. It's not a crazy idea to print up some business cards (which you can get for free), with just your name, cell phone number and email address; you can even QR your info on the business card so they can quickly add you to their contact list. Keep it short and to the point, hand them your card and walk away (after saying 'thank you', of course). They are busy and cannot get into deep conversations about your love of cinema. Do not use this approach with the director, nor should you use this to become an actor/actress. This is more of an approach to use with production office personnel, production assistants and other (lower-ranking but well-connected) team members. The idea here is that if they get into a jam (a crew member is sick or they have a bigger-than-expected scene to shoot the next day), they might just give you a call since they're understaffed and you've put yourself in front of them. (I secured two major lighting gigs back in my production days using this technique.) One other note, *you must actually do the original job you were* *hired to do,* which is to be an extra in the film. Have fun watching the crews set up the shots—you're getting paid to network!

▶ BRAND YOURSELF

I mentioned earlier that a writer should focus on writing spec scripts from the same genre—or, at minimum, very similar ones—in order to be seen as being strong at delivering a certain type of script; directors should do the same as should producers, actors and future executives. Regardless of the role, ones 'arsenal' of available media or marketplace offerings should all essentially fall into the same content bucket so that they become associated with a specific type or style.

After giving this advice, I'm usually bombarded with several worries that individuals might become 'typecast' in such a situation (that they'll only be known for a specific genre type). This is true. And this is *exactly* the goal.

Speak to any actor about the value of being typecast; it's one of the most financially rewarding experiences they can achieve. When an actor is 'known' as something very specific, the work comes to them organically (because they are the person casting directors think of when they need that 'type' of role filled). The same is true for writers, directors and producers. If all of your content is aligned, you not only hone your skills to deliver that type of project more effectively, you become known as the best candidate to make it happen (and that's a great position to hold within the minds of distribution and production executives).

If you want to write spec scripts, then make them all the same genre (several consistent action film scripts coupled with several strong action ideas would prove that individual to be a 'go-to' action writer); for a director, they should focus on similar types of scenarios (maintaining a similar style and tone across the content); and for a producer, their projects should all be in alignment by content type (film or TV) and genre.

There is always a temptation to reject this notion, believing that showing a wide range of diversity is best (a director that can 'direct anything' would be more hirable over a director focused on one content style)—not true. (Consider Alfred Hitchcock being able to play the part of 'Master of Suspense' or Martin Scorsese's consistent return to the mean streets of New York.) In an industry whereby tens of thousands of people are all competing for those select directing roles, writing gigs or producing opportunities, the ones who have a proven track record—who are branded as the one most capable of reliably delivering the desired product—receive the jobs.

(And this is not isolated just to creatives; this concept stems from our principles of distribution. Distribution companies brand themselves by the content they sell, and investors brand themselves by the types of content they fund. You should follow the exact same approach branding yourself.)

▶ WHO YOU NEED TO KNOW

What follows are the three most likely 'direct-access' candidates whom you can reach out to when making first contact with a production or distribution company—including who they are, what role they serve and how they respond to new projects:

▶   **Acquisitions Assistants**—Executives serving in the acquisitions department are generally so pressured in finding new quality content in advance of their competitors, they're willing to go the extra mile and take phone calls (or accept unsolicited submissions) more freely than others. Again, this doesn't work in the studio world; this is more of a mini-major or indie-zone practice—but that's the zone you'll see the most results when starting out. Most executives have assistants who do the grunt work (logging data, compiling 'research' overviews of submissions, endless IMDb skimming, etc.) That's your target. The interesting thing about most acquisitions executives (and their assistants) is that they so often deal with producers—and have dealt with more troubling/annoying ones than easy ones—many of them have a mindset that they could easily stamp out their producer competition and take on a film project themselves; makes sense—they already know what works and have a powerful contact list. As a result, the acquisitions department in general is a great place to be connected both for the short term (for your immediate spec scripts or projects) as well as the long term (for more coproduction opportunities or collaborations if you really hit it off), but reaching out directly to an acquisitions agent's personal assistant is one of the most direct pathways you can take to getting your work into the right team member's hands.

▶   **Directors (or Coordinators) of Development**—Not development *executives*; go for the 'director' or the 'coordinator' of development (still a prominent connection, though not the top of the food chain). The development team is sort of a collection of 'in-house' producers; they're on the hunt for new projects but also are assigned productions based upon upper management decisions and corporate relations. Development executives are a major part of those decisions (and are directly involved in those major high-level relationships); the *directors* of development (who are one step below the executive level) and their respective coordinators and assistants are part of that executive's immediate team of 'go-to' people. That means directors are crucial (and well connected) inside an organization but still have quite a bit to prove before they can move up that next rung in the corporate ladder. As a result, they are eager to find new writers, new projects and new opportunities—not just for the company they're working for but also for *themselves* to grow professionally. Directors of development are at that beautifully hungry point in their professional careers where they're willing to put in the 18-hour days, all while still accepting the grunt work. They are not only open to taking your call, they're also looking for their own big-ticket opportunity to 'make it' on their own. If you're scrolling the development team's 'titles' and aren't seeing a director of development, then the 'coordinator' is your next best match. After that, just call the reception desk and inquire which assistant on the development team would be best to speak with (focus here on the assistant or lower-ranking individual filtering the new projects).

▶ **Sales Teams**—This one's a bit more out of the box, because the first instinct for a writer, producer or novice director is to approach those in a company that can actually make a film from their script. But think big picture for a moment; if you go directly for the sales team (the employees whose job it is to make money for the company by selling its media properties), they will be much better suited to either (i) give you practical advice on your project or (ii) push your project info through to the right person within the organization. And remember what we said about acquisitions and development teams relying on someone they trust to vouch for a project in order to take it more seriously? Then consider the impact of a sales executive—an individual with the strongest barometer of what content will sell in the marketplace—excitedly pitching their internal production, acquisitions and development teams about your project (you better believe they'd give it a fair review).

▶ THE MYTH OF GOING TO THE TOP

Bypassing the hierarchy of a production or distribution company and attempting to speak directly with the head honcho decision-maker (such as the president or CEO) certainly sounds like it'd be the most effective way of moving the ball, but in reality it can be counterproductive (and sometimes detrimental).

Don't forcibly reach out to whom you perceive to be a 'decision-maker'; go instead to the more approachable employees who are already on the inside and have direct access to the people you need (and who will actually hear you out). They're the junior executives, managing directors, interns and assistants. If you want your project to have a higher chance of being read (and have more favorable coverage written), then don't struggle going only to the top of the food chain in a given company; focus on those with whom you have actual access (that can spin opportunities in your favor from the inside).

Not only have writers broken this unwritten principle; filmmakers and producers make this mistake all the time. Many people have this false impression that they must 'fight' through the barriers of middle management, interns and assistants to get to the top executives at a company in order for action to take place—and more often than not, they treat these middle managers, assistants and interns with little respect in the process (a bad idea).

Befriend those in the middle (and even the interns and assistants). Empower them; don't think of them as low-rank (they are extremely useful and strategically placed individuals). After all, mid-level managers, interns and assistants are already on the inside of the very organization you're trying to get your material into. They know the company politics and how their particular supervisors like material to be presented to them (including at what time of day and in what temperament).

▶ NAVIGATING THE RECEPTIONIST'S DESK

All companies (big and small) have a person designated to answer calls—yes, people still use the phone—or manages all those blindly submitted 'info@company' emails. From the idealistic side, this person is designed for guiding all those messages and delivering them to the right persons within the organization. But in reality, the receptionist's desk is every company's first line of defense from allowing the unprofessional writers and producers from gaining entry. As a result, no matter who you wish to speak to in any organization, you will first have to navigate the receptionist's desk in order to be properly passed along (either to get directly connected by phone or to obtain key contact names and email addresses). And in a post-COVID 'work from home' world, the virtual desk is even more complex to navigate. Fortunately, the general human principles still allow for success:

1) Respect the reception desk—They work very hard and take shit from everyone (and are dealing with more virtual pileup than ever before). Don't continue that cycle! Treat them like people, not like a call center bot. They have all the leverage when they pick up the call or get your email as to whether your message actually goes through to the right person.

2) Get to the point—It's okay to admit you're a novice. It's okay to say the truth, that you have some scripts or project ideas that are in line with what the company produces and that you'd like to see if there's someone you can speak with to see if there's 'synergy' or 'opportunities'. The more forthright with them you are, the better able they will be to get you to the right person who can actually handle your requests.

3) Don't put them on the spot—It's okay to state, "if it's not appropriate to put me through, that's fine, I can always reach out to them (or their assistant) by email if that's easier". You'd be surprised how reluctant some people are to push you through to a direct line (especially today when so many are using their own cell phone numbers post-COVID), but how readily they'll hand you a direct name along with their email address.

▶ WORKS IN PROGRESS

Don't reach out unless you have something to offer. It's okay to reach out and inquire if a company has interest in what you're working on, but certainly don't get them excited about a project until it's complete and ready to deliver.

There is nothing worse to tarnish your image than building up your capabilities and not being able to follow through after you've cast the line (essentially, overpromising and under delivering). There is no worse missed opportunity than the one where you pitch what you're working on and having the other side say 'sounds great, send it over', only you're far from completion.

This happens in my world all the time. Filmmakers reach out with movies, only they're not completed; writers pitch scripts, but they're not ready to show, etc. Executives can't do anything with it, so the conversation goes to waste.

And never send a project that's a 'work in progress' or a script that's only at 'draft' phase. No matter how many times you preface that the project is in early stages (or that the script still needs a polish), everyone will judge it based upon its current shape. They will not know what tweaks you'll be making next. All they can use to evaluate your project is what's sitting before them. And if the project before them feels not quite ready, that first impression will be very hard to change later on.

▶ OBTAINING A PITCH MEETING

First, they're rarely called 'pitch meetings'; they're simply 'meetings'. And second, there is no formula for how to obtain one other than by simply asking someone from the acquisitions department, development department or the creative team.

After you've made 'first contact' by email or phone and after you've presented the goods (emailed a *requested* copy of your script and/or discussed a few project ideas that are in alignment with what that particular company is looking for), you simply need to ask for the meeting. Nothing overwhelming here, just a simple "would it be possible to meet in person to discuss some of these ideas?" Or the old "maybe we could meet up to see if there's any upcoming projects of yours that I could help out with?"

I find it's best to always be in the position of moving the ball forward—meaning being the one who's asking. And by following the advice from our positive habits (and by utilizing the skills you've developed from places like your improve classes) you can introduce the idea of a face-to-face meeting into the conversation. Assure them your schedule is flexible and that you understand they're busy.

You always need to be the one traveling to them. Meet at their offices (or at a coffee shop or other agreed location that they suggest). Their time is limited, and your objective is to show them you're a person who understands (and respects) the time they've carved out to hear your ideas.

In a post-COVID world, teleconferences (often shorthanded as virtual conferences (or 'VC')) have become quite common. Although nothing beats a face-to-face, in-person meeting, a quality virtual conference can be equally effective in pinning down your pitch. Always use a headset to reduce noise and have decent-looking lighting. And even though you might be at home, still dress like you're heading into an office (your appearance still matters).

▶ THE PITCH MEETING

You've finally secured the coveted pitch meeting, a half hour of legit face-to-face time with a Hollywood professional for the sole purpose of sitting down and discussing *your* projects, *your* ideas and how *you* can serve their needs. Has the panic set in?

Problem is that far too many novices treat the pitch meeting as a job interview, which adds unnecessary stress to the scenario and causes them to second-guess their talents and abilities. The truth is, you *are* talented and *do* possess the ability to create and deliver content (otherwise you wouldn't be there). So it's much more important to view the pitch meeting for what it really is: a first date.

Although it's quite true that the quality of your pitch (and ideas) are absolutely important during your meeting, this is only a small percentage of the overall purpose of the meeting. The 'pitch' meeting is really more about seeing how well you can interact with the team (e.g., how well can you take criticism and hear others' ideas). And if the development executives start tossing around curveball ideas on how the script could be 'improved', they're curious to see whether you go with the flow or get defensive.

Again, these are generally informal meetings. Just as a job interview begins with "So tell me about yourself" (which translates to "what have you done that proves you're worth hiring?"), and a first date generally begins with a "So what do you do for a living?" (which translates to 'tell me details about yourself that prove you're worth dating'), the first question during a pitch meeting is usually "So what do you have?" (which means, 'tell us about some of your projects so we can see where our ideas overlap').

Out of all three, I think the pitch meeting is probably the most informal and the most fun. Remember, you're only in the room because you've had the command of craft personally to secure confidence in the team, and you have been vetted already that your projects can be seen as quality. All you need to do now is enter the room and have fun.

Keep the room relaxed and the conversation flowing. It's inevitable that as you begin presenting your ideas, the team might interrupt you in the middle of your pitch and say "that doesn't work with us, we do more (fill-in-the-blank) content". . . .. Don't get distracted and focus only on the first part "that doesn't work with us", listen to what they're telling you ("we think your ideas are very good, but we need your ideas focused on the genres that work best with us".).

Don't think twice, just shift gears and keep your concepts focused on the genre style the team is looking for.

▶ PITCHING MATERIALS

In addition to a fully completed screenplay, you will need two additional pitch materials ready to go: a pitch deck and a synopsis/one-sheet:

▶ **Pitch Deck**—Take the time to create a simple (two- to ten-paged) pitch deck for your project. This slideshow presentation is essentially a visually focused sample of your script in action. It's usually broken down into a 'synopsis' slide, a few 'character' slides, a 'visual mood board' page or two, some imagery on 'locations' followed with an 'about the creator(s)' slide. Yes, text is used, but sparingly. This document is primarily heavy on your vision for the project—using existing images from online—to provide a quick 'snapshot' understanding of what your project aims to be.

▶   **Synopsis (One-Sheet)**—Executives are busy, and nothing is more eye-rolling than another screenplay to read (on top of the dozens of other scripts, plus contracts, emails and reports they're actively compiling). Make their job easier with a simple one-sheet overview that bullet points the story. More often than not, executives will take the time to review your pitch deck, then expand on this by evaluating the one-sheet. Many in the industry base their opinions on these two materials alone (and as long as the script is 'close enough', they can quickly gauge whether they can move forward or not). A synopsis is also known as a one-sheet because it should max out at one single-spaced 12-point-font typed page. Make sure to include the title, author *and* the project format (e.g., feature-length film, television series).

One point to note, it's quite common when pitching and presenting original projects for evaluation that you might have to sign a submission release form and/or nondisclosure agreement. This is all standard business practice, but do give each document a read prior to signing so that you understand the details.

Author's note: *Introduction to Media Distribution* is primarily focused on the business of film/TV and new media distribution workflows. If you are interested in learning more about the business of pitching, creative work or building a career as a writer, producer or director, then please check out my other books *Writing for the Green Light* (targeting which scripts to write) and *Mastering the Pitch* (focused on how to pitch/present all genres and formats of media content professionally).

▶   FOLLOWING UP (WITHOUT LOOKING DESPERATE)

Following up is a delicate art; it's really part of the same game as 'pitching' and accurately presenting all your points during a meeting. When you follow up appropriately, you are announcing that you understand business etiquette and Hollywood's social norms and procedures. However, if you follow up in an unprofessional way, you can unintentionally give off a very negative image.

The best way to really master this is to simply follow standard dating etiquette to time your follow-up moves. If you had a successful pitch meeting (similar to a first date), send a quick email note such as a "thanks for your time, looking forward to next steps". If during that meeting you discussed action items (such as sending material elements back and forth, like additional story ideas), go ahead and send them along. Otherwise, mention an approximate ETA so that the other party knows when to expect them. Also regarding dating etiquette, it's important to know when you might be coming off a little too strong. A simple pitch meeting (as with a first date) does not guarantee automatic forward momentum. And following up with emails and/or phone calls several times in the days thereafter can quickly put a sour taste into the other parties' mouth.

There's no rule book here (such as a 'wait three days before following up'). Personally, I try to send a very quick one- or two-sentence "thanks" email, then wait a full ten days before a formal follow-up (but there is no standard). If the other party is interested, they will respond and be receptive to your emails and phone calls. If they are not, it's okay to continue a soft push for a bit, but it's also important to understand that after a few attempts without any response, it's most likely just not going to happen (and that's okay; be professional and move on).

▶ DON'T SAY YES TO OPPORTUNITIES. . . . *INVENT THEM*

When opportunity knocks, my best advice is to simply open the door and say, Yes! The problem is, opportunity doesn't knock very often, and when it does, it rarely arrives in the way you imagined.

That's because *real* opportunities begin as broken leftovers or disjointed ideas—in other words, opportunities usually show themselves first as 'problems'. What transforms these problems into 'opportunities' is when *you* see a way to solve them by applying your skills or talents in order to 'fix' them. That 'knocking' that everyone talks about has nothing to do with an opportunity being presented to you; it's your own realization that you're able to see a way to apply your skills to 'fix' it.

Sending a blind email 'pitch' to a production company, trying to sell your screenplay or project to them, does not solve any of *their* problems—it only adds to their workload. But learning directly from the heads of development at that company what scripts they need written or what projects they're hoping to land in order to lighten their workload will help them tremendously. That's opportunistic thinking; it's more about approaching the situation in the way others are not that usually gets the job done.

You don't have to be some mind-reading genius to be an opportunistic thinker; you just have to be observant. Thinking 'outside the box' has very little to do with inventing the next great 'it' thing and is much more about simply stepping up to the plate when you see a reasonable chance where you can assist.

Success in media, as with any industry, is about *making* situations work in your favor.

You're going to have to be one promoting your talents, building your connections and securing your initial professional opportunities. Waiting around for others to swoop in and kick-start your career just isn't going to happen. Essentially, you're going to have to represent yourself.

No successful entrepreneurial CEO blindly opens a division to offer a product that the market doesn't need; they instead look for what the market *wants*, then makes themselves available as the best company to provide that service. But all too often, novice writers push scripts they think the marketplace wants and are deflated when no one bites (same with producers hawking projects no one has a need for, or directors pushing content that has little market value).

Just like any great entrepreneur, you are simply identifying a problem in the marketplace (producers and development executives are looking to get ahead) and bringing an answer to your demographics problems (helping them put together a project which allows them to advance).

Think a busy development executive with a great idea for a movie (and all the connections to make it a reality) has time to go home each night and pound away at a script or connect all the dots to make it a pitch-ready project? No, but *you do*. And, more importantly, *you can*.

Utilizing the habits we've discussed about schmoozing and pitch meetings, you can wedge your way into their professional lives with solutions; you're offering the 'answers' to their problems ("I could write that script for you, if you have the means to produce it"), rather than trying to add one more job task which is what most do ("you wanna read *my* script?"). One scenario *helps* professionals in the media industry, while the other one hinders them. Which do you think they'd be more receptive to? (And which do you think will help kick-start your professional career?)

▶ FINAL THOUGHT

There has never been a time when the opportunities for one to develop a career in the entertainment industry has been more available to anyone, anywhere, around the globe.

Today, user-generated YouTube videos have the level of computer-generated visual effects that were worthy of Academy Awards just a few years ago. Camera, lighting, editing and sound technologies have never been available to consumers with such professional quality standards at such affordable prices. And the explosive growth of digital platforms and social media sites have never made the notion of DIY releasing and self-marketing more possible for indie filmmakers regardless of where they live or what language they speak.

As technological advances continue to dramatically reshape our world—and make the production and reception of media content more readily available globally—the one constant variable that continues to govern everything are the principles that have (and always will) explain why certain projects get produced and others lose steam and fade away.

No matter how innovative technology might become—even with fascinating growth in AI and machine learning!—writers will still need to craft an idea into an emotionally driven story; producers will still need to juggle all the issues that arise during the course of a production; and distributors will need new content to keep their pipelines of media properties in full motion to satisfy audience and marketplace demands.

In a time when we feel like we've seen it all, I can safely assure you that there are profound and moving stories taking place right now all throughout the world, ones that merit being told. And I can assure you that there is a global audience out there excited to experience it. All that's needed is for someone to take the first step toward making those projects a reality.

Appendices

In this second edition of *Introduction to Media Distribution,* I've expanded the appendices to include the following:

1) A list of commonplace exploitable rights with definitions

2) A breakdown of a standard 'distribution agreement'

3) A breakdown of a 'format option agreement'

4) A standard 'materials delivery schedule'

5) Territory-by-territory financial projections

6) An overview of metadata documentation

Please note, I've written all of these 'samples' in my own words; these are not boilerplate agreements nor exhibits. The reason for this decision is due to the fact that each company has their own way of compiling these materials (with their own wording/ phrasing); I've opted instead to provide you with universally applicable breakdowns of the core concepts of each contract or schedule to make these more valuable learning tools (especially since readers of this book are based all over the world). For those who would rather see 'real-world' examples of contracts, I highly encourage you to seek them out from reputable online sources or within more in-depth media-related texts.

I am not a lawyer nor a legal professional; this section is for informational and educational purposes only. Although I do offer a fair bit of advice regarding each term or requirement throughout, I strongly recommend readers consult with a professional— or, at minimum, a knowledgeable friend—prior to entering into any legally binding distribution agreement.

Appendix I
List of Exploitable Rights With Definitions

What follows is a list of the most commonly licensed media rights with digestible definitions clarifying what these rights encompass and how they're commonly applied. Although most companies use the same language when referring to these generalized categories, a few will define these using their own language and might include alternative phrasing.

Ad-Supported Video on Demand (AVOD)—Ad-Supported Video-on-Demand (AVOD) rights refer to the exhibition of media content on any platform whereby the content is available to viewers at a time of their choosing—via electronic distribution—where each view is 'funded' by advertisers. In other words, the viewer is required to pay no money—or a 'reduced' subscription fee—in exchange for viewing the content; however, they must 'screen' or experience an advertisement before or during the transmission of the program. (See also "FAST" below).

Ancillary Rights—Ancillary means 'secondary', so this rights category can mean different things in different regions of the world. In North America, Ancillary rights (often shorthanded as 'Ancil' rights) refer to media exploitation on airlines, ships (e.g. cruise liners) and hotels but can even be expanding so as to include buses, trains, hospitals and even prisons. These rights can be exploited at differing points during a property's 'windowing' life span since (i) the audiences are isolated to a compartmentalized grouping of clients, and/or (ii) the content can be placed behind a transactional pay wall (working as a pay-per-view rental). In other regions of the world, Ancillary would refer to as 'derivatives' of a media property—therefore implying format rights, remakes and/or repurposing of the original content (including sequels or prequels).

Basic Cable—'Basic' cable is really just a simplified form of a Pay TV right. The concept of the right is that a consumer must pay for access to the channel but does so in that the channel is generally offered as part of a bundled package of channels (e.g. as part of a cable package). Since the revenues from subscribership alone will not cover the entire cost of running the network, Basic cable channels will often broadcast commercials despite the fact a consumer is paying for access. What separates Basic cable as a specific right—apart from other forms of Pay TV (including Satellite Rights)—is that the transmission of the media content arrives to consumers via a physical fiber optic cable.

Catch-Up Rights—Broadcasters (of both Pay TV and Free TV) will sometimes offer digital access of a program after its initial broadcast date. The exploitation is generally limited only to those individuals with a subscription to the channel or by means to the broadcaster's owned and operated website. The idea is to allow consumers, who may have missed the initial broadcast, an opportunity to 'catch up' on the latest episode. Catch-up rights are commonplace in almost every TV deal, but restrictions can be applied for how long a given program is available to consumers after its initial broadcast date (e.g., a catch-up window of only a few days but potentially up to a 30-day allowance) along with how many episodes the broadcaster is permitted to make available at a given time (e.g., no more than four episodes available at any given time).

Cinematic Rights—Sometimes referred to as 'Theatrical' rights, the blanket definition of Cinematic rights encompasses traditional theatrical exhibition (where tickets are sold to the general public to experience pre-scheduled screenings) but can also include 'Non-Theatrical' Rights and 'Public Video' or 'Public Exhibition' Rights. Non-Theatric and Public Video refer to screenings conducted for more specialty circumstances such as a private screening for a business, a screening for an educational setting or even exhibition for niche audiences (such as a screening within a prison for the inmates). This is why 'home entertainment' deals might include 'Non-Theatric' or 'Public Video' even though these rights are generally lumped into the 'Cinematic' bucket.

Closed-Net Rights—Not as common but still applied, the notion of a Closed-Net refers to a 'closed network' of exploitation (specifically focused on limiting the digital access of a program to only those individuals capable of accessing it through a limited (or closed) network. The best example would be those programs compiled as part of a promotional loop limited to playing in the background of a franchised restaurant, corporatized retail store or within hospitals, museums or any other branded retail/consumer chain.

DVD, Blu-ray or 'Physical Home Entertainment' Rights—The concept of any 'home entertainment' right is the granting of permission for a consumer-facing platform to manufacture and sell physical copies of a media property explicitly for purchase in retail stores, rentals in stores or kiosks or the right to manufacture physical copies on demand (a right sometimes called 'Manufacture on Demand' or MOD); these rights are often described as 'video' rights or more traditionally as 'videogram' rights within agreements, of which DVD/Blu-ray is simply the latest iteration. After a physical home entertainment window comes to a close, contracts generally include a 'sell-off' period (usually lasting six months) where the acquiring party has a window of six months after the expiration of the term to sell off (or liquidate) the physical copies it has in stock.

Electric Sell-Through (EST)—Electric Sell-Through (EST) rights offer the ability for a consumer to purchase and own a digital copy of a program via electronic distribution; this is in contrast to Transactional Video on Demand (TVOD) which is technically limited to a one-use rental of a media property. EST rights are often granted along with TVOD and DVD/Physical Home Entertainment rights (to bucket all of these direct-to-consumer rights together), but there can be instances where these are split apart or restricted. Oftentimes, there are preestablished windows determined where a product can be made available as a TVOD (rental) for several weeks before the EST (purchase) option is made available. Please note, some companies refer to EST as 'Download to Own' (DTO) rights.

FAST—FAST is an acronym for Free Ad-supported Streaming Television and is therefore a derivative of AVOD. Similar to Linear streaming (below), FAST streaming exists as stand-alone 'channels' of highly targeted/focused content. A distributor can launch any number of FAST channels covering any conceivable category. Some are genre based, while others exist to exploit a single—yet long-running—television series. A FAST channel is more often 'programmed' with an actual schedule or running time (e.g., episodes or a film will start at a preprogrammed time slot).

Format Rights—Format Rights generally refer to episodic television programs whereby a clearly established and replicable 'format' exists, one that can be adapted by acquiring companies into local languages while keeping the 'brand' of the original show intact. Most of the time, such series follow very formulaic productions (such as game shows or other heavily structured content); however, scripted series with story arcs and character development can also be adapted.

Free TV—Free-to-air television rights allow a media property to be received by consumers at no cost. However, to compensate for the expense of making this transmission possible, nearly all Free TV channels have scheduled blocks of advertisements placed before, during and after the broadcast of each media property. The means by which a Free TV signal is sent (e.g., terrestrial, cable or satellite) will often be identified within the definition of 'Free TV' rights within each agreement.

Free Video on Demand (FVOD)—Following the logic of AVOD, Free Video on Demand (FVOD) offers consumers the ability to screen a program at a time of their choosing—via electronic distribution—without having to pay a fee. However, what is different about FVOD is that no ads are embedded nor required. The purpose for FVOD rights are generally for promotional purposes (to give consumers free access to the first episode of a TV series in order to get them to acquire future episodes; or as a form of encouraging consumers to acquire a monthly subscription to a Subscription Video-on-Demand (SVOD) service (e.g., a 'free month' of Netflix before a consumer incurs charges)).

Home Entertainment Rights—See 'DVD or Physical Home Entertainment Rights' earlier.

Internet Rights (aka IPTV)—The definition of 'Internet' rights have changed substantially since the mid-2000s, but today they have evolved—and settled—on the notion of Internet Protocol Television rights (aka IPTV rights). IPTV functions like a normal television channel, but its signal is transmitted digitally and is received by consumers via Internet access. While the signal could be available only to paying consumers (similar to a Pay TV channel) or completely for free with embedded advertisements (as seen on a Free TV channel), IPTV rights technically don't conflict with traditional TV rights—unless there is a stipulation either including IPTV rights or restricting them. See also 'Closed-Net', of which IPTV would also classify.

Linear Streaming—An ad-supported derivative of IPTV rights (earlier), linear streaming mimics the look, style and feel of a traditional free-to-air or cable television channel by programming content into time slots. The ability to 'program' content into different time slots has a direct impact on the values associated with the embedded advertising. Linear streaming is classified as an AVOD right but sometimes conflicts with traditional television rights depending on the language of third-party agreements.

Merchandising Rights—Refers to the manufacturing and sale of products—other than the media property itself—that are associated with or inspired by the program.

Mobile Rights—Refers to a digital signal intended for media consumption via a mobile (or 'cell') phone. Although other rights categories have encroached on the concept of 'mobile' rights (e.g., many VOD services see smartphones as computers allowing their subscribers access by means of smart television, laptop or mobile phone), there are still entities interested only in transmitting signals to mobile devices. Also, in that media consumption is different on mobile devices, 'mobile' rights can be included to permit specific editing to programs (e.g., taking a half-hour TV episode and cutting it into several pieces, each only lasting a few minutes). Mobile rights can also be used when licensing content to media apps or other direct-to-consumer services available only by means of mobile access.

'Non-Standard' Television Rights—'Non-Standard' Television has become a simplified way of describing TV rights as a whole rather than dissecting or splitting each right by means of transmission. Many Pay TV operators now have the capability of reaching audiences via satellite, terrestrial, cable and digital signals; rather than defining their exact modes of transmission one at a time, they instead use 'Non-Standard' as a way to simplify the process. This also future-proofs companies against what new forms of media transmission might be the 'norm' years ahead of time.

Non-Theatric(al)—See 'Cinematic Rights' earlier.

Pay-Per-View (PPV)—Pay-Per-View (PPV) rights were the original form of an 'on-demand' right, whereby a consumer could transact upon a program of interest directly with their cable operator. Although Transaction Video-on-Demand (TVOD) and EST rights share a great deal in common with PPV, the real difference is that PPV content is made available via traditional Basic and Pay TV transmission (by means of physical fiber optic cable or satellite transmission), whereas VOD applies to digital access (made available by means of electronic distribution). Often, these rights are granted in unison since most media signals are now sent across both electronic and traditional feeds.

Pay TV Rights—'Pay TV' rights refers to a transmission of television content available only to those consumers paying for its access. Although many bundles of basic cable channels fall into the category of Pay TV (see 'Basic Cable' earlier), so do premium pay television channels like HBO, Starz, FX and Showtime (that require individual monthly subscriptions on top of a standard cable package for consumers to access their high-end titles). As with Free TV, Pay TV is also available by terrestrial signal and satellite in addition to fiber optic cable.

Satellite TV Rights—Applicable to both Free TV and Pay TV, the concept of 'Satellite' TV rights refer to a television signal that is transmitted via satellite and pulled down by designated parties (those that have a satellite dish capable of receiving the signal). As with Terrestrial TV rights, satellite rights are rarely licensed independently and are generally lumped together into a Free TV or Pay TV licensing agreement definition.

Subscription Video on Demand (SVOD)—Subscription Video-on-Demand (SVOD) rights permit the reception of a media property on a viewing device via electronic distribution. SVOD rights limit a program's streaming exposure to a select service provider's on-demand platform for streaming capability; end user access to the content is limited to the platform's subscriber base (customers who pay a fixed subscription fee in exchange for an unlimited viewing time—while the SVOD rights are granted—for a platform's library of media offerings).

Terrestrial TV Rights—Applicable to both Free TV and Pay TV, the concept of a 'terrestrial' television signal simply means one that is classically received by consumers via antenna; the true definition identifies these signals as Hertzian waves. Rarely are terrestrial TV rights acquired on their own, but they are often defined as one of the many means of transmission permitted in a TV deal.

Transactional Video on Demand (TVOD)—Transactional Video-on-Demand (TVOD) rights permit the reception of a media property on a viewing device via electronic distribution by any means of transmission. TVOD rights are to be limited to a select service provider's on-demand platform, allowing an end user the ability to stream or download a program in exchange for a one-time transactional fee. Service providers generally offer programs at different price points—that is, a slightly discounted price for standard-definition (SD) image quality versus high-definition (HD). TVOD has replaced the traditional 'video rental' concept; unlike EST rights, there is a limited viewing window granted to the end user, which is why TVOD is occasionally referenced in agreements as 'download to rent' (abbreviated as DTR).

Video on Demand (VOD)—The notion behind Video-on-Demand (VOD) rights is to allow a consumer the ability to screen a program by means of electronic distribution in a location and time of their choosing. VOD is often defined within agreements as either 'transactional', 'subscription', 'ad-supported' or 'free' (abbreviated as TVOD, SVOD, AVOD and FVOD), but given VOD's similarity to traditional PPV, it can also be prefaced with 'cable' or 'satellite' (e.g. 'Cable VOD', 'Satellite VOD'); a VOD offering on 'basic cable' (as a 'Cable VOD' offering) would refer to a transact-able program acquired in a traditional cable setting where the program is accessed and transmitted via fiber optic cable. For a better understanding, please review Ad-Supported Video on Demand (AVOD), Free Video on Demand (FVOD), Pay-Per-View (PPV), Subscription Video on Demand (SVOD) and Transactional Video on Demand (TVOD) earlier.

Appendix II
Sample Distribution Agreement

In Chapter 4 we outlined the commonly used terms found within a standard distribution agreement; this appendix will put those concepts into practice to provide you with a much deeper understanding of how these agreements function in the working world of media distribution.

Although the example herein may look like a simple copy/paste of a boilerplate agreement, it reads just like any chapter of this book. It's a complete breakdown of how to understand complete distribution agreements without all the confusing legal jargon or business terminology (written in a manner that allows you to understand each section of the contract as well as how they collectively relate to the entirety of the agreement).

Despite the fact that there are dozens of variations of this agreement—depending on the status of the project, what type of media it actually defines (film, TV series or new media property), etc.—what follows offers all the core nuts and bolts one needs to gain a solid understanding of the transfer of a media property's intangible rights in exchange for revenue.

However, just to give some level of context, let's assume the following hypothetical scenario: an independent producer named JESSICA FILMMAKER has just completed an action film called COOL ACTION FILM. Jessica Filmmaker is an American, but she produced this project through a Canadian-based partner named EXPRESS PRODUCTIONS INC. (which—on paper—currently manages all rights in the film). By shooting the film in Canada, major tax credits were secured that greatly reduced Jessica's net out-of-pocket expenses. On the Westside of Los Angeles, distribution company STUDIO RELEASES is seeking new action films for its upcoming slate of content and wants to acquire COOL ACTION FILM for its latest release window. After weeks of negotiation, STUDIO RELEASES has made an offer of $250,000 to acquire the US rights to COOL ACTION FILM, and JESSICA FILMMAKER has agreed to license it over to STUDIO RELEASES.

What follows is an example of what their agreement might look like.

* * *

DISTRIBUTION AGREEMENT
"COOL ACTION FILM"

This Agreement ("Agreement") is entered into as of <u>DD/MM/YYYY</u> ("Effective Date") by and between **EXPRESS PRODUCTIONS INC.** with offices at (4321 W Queen Street, Toronto M5V 2Z5, Canada) ("Licensor"), and **STUDIO RELEASES** with offices at 1234 Sunset Blvd., Suite ABC, Los Angeles CA 90028, USA ("Distributor" or "Licensee", or together with Licensor "The Parties"), in connection with Distributor's acquisition of certain exclusive rights in and to the picture produced by Licensor currently titled Cool Action Film ("Picture").

For good and valuable consideration, the receipt and sufficiency of which are hereby acknowledged, the Parties agree as follows (translation: here's what the parties agreed to):

1. <u>Picture</u>: The Picture will conform to the following Specifications ("Specifications"):

   1.1. <u>Title</u>: *Cool Action Film*

   1.2. <u>Budget</u>: USD $1,225,450 (this needs to be the actual gross amount paid to produce the film; soft monies or tax credits are not included; also, because this agreement crosses an international border, the currency will be specified since exchange rates vary.)

   1.3. <u>Country of Origin</u>: Canada (I'm saying Canada here because it is not uncommon for US films to be produced in other countries—for tax purposes—or for American distributors to acquire foreign-produced media properties; the country holding the copyright is the country of origin. Although Jessica Filmmaker is American, Express Productions Inc. holds the copyright).

   1.4. <u>Running Time</u>: Actual HH:MM:SS of the film (e.g., 01:37:22)

   1.5. <u>Writer(s)</u>: Writer's name.

   1.6. <u>Technical Specifications</u>: Think of this more as a 'status of the project' description. It's not uncommon to see a section that defines 'what a movie is' (basically explaining that a film is an 'original' story that features on-screen talent that's edited together into a completed production). Although this seems silly for a completed film, this section can be utilized for presales (when defining the status of a project that one party is acquiring or selling when the feature film itself doesn't yet exist). The more detailed delivery requirements (e.g., master file formats, etc.) are generally spelled out in later sections.

   1.7. <u>Director</u>: Director's name

   1.8. <u>Principle Cast</u>: Here the top two to three on-screen talent names are listed.

   1.9. <u>Principle Photography</u>: Principal photography occurred in CITY, COUNTRY and ended on DD/MM/YYYY.

1.10.   Genre: Action (in this case its action, but this could easily be Romance or Horror depending on the project; the real purpose for including genre is to further identify the property, but for a presell, this detail further assures that all Parties understand what end result is expected).

1.11.   Language: English (if more than one language is used, you can list each here).

2. Territory: The "Territory" is the United States of America and its possessions and territories. (However, for an 'all-rights' worldwide deal, it's not uncommon to see phrases such as "Worldwide" or even "the Universe").

3. Term: The "Term" defines the Effective Date upon which the contract formally starts (or commences) as well as when the terms of the agreement expire. Some deals simply have a clear start date listed, while others are directly attached to some type of verifiable 'action' or event; each agreement is unique. For example, the Effective Date might commence upon signature by both Parties, while for other deals the term won't start until the film is fully delivered. In circumstances of presales, the Term may be defined by periods of preproduction, start of principal photography and/or delivery of the fully edited master. The duration of the agreement is also specified with either a clear conclusion date or by defining the duration of the rights (e.g., the Term shall commence upon full delivery of the Picture (Effective Date) and shall continue for five years).

4. Rights: The "Rights" are the understanding between the parties for how the Licensee (in this case, Studio Releases) shall be permitted to exploit the Picture within the territory. While an 'all-rights' deal is extremely clear to understand, the nuanced definitions of rights play a critical role when brokering multiple deals with different clients all within the same territory or country. Rights can be 'exclusive' (meaning only one entity can exploit those particular rights) or 'non-exclusive' (meaning multiple parties can exploit the same rights within the same territory). Rights can also be restricted by means of 'holdbacks' (where a company has no interested in exploiting a certain set of rights but does require that no third parties are able to exploit those rights during the active term. We won't get to granular here; all that's important to note is that this section will spell out the details of who can do what with the film; for a much deeper understanding of rights, refer to Chapter 4 or Appendix I.

5. Grant of Rights: While the "Rights" block of text earlier (in Section 4) defines the rights, the 'grant' of rights is the formal acknowledgement of the handover (the understanding that one party is granting rights to the other).

6. Delivery: Although the actual deliverable elements (the stuff that's legally and materially required so that Studio Releases can actually exploit *Cool Action Film*) will be defined later as an attached Schedule "A" (the "Delivery Schedule"), this section is much more focused on the understanding of when certain elements must be delivered and in what specific form. Do email attachments of documents count as delivery, or are physical copies required? How many days after full execution of this agreement must all required deliverable materials be delivered? And once the entire Delivery Schedule is delivered, what proof or verifiable confirmation will Express Productions have that their

responsibilities have been fulfilled/complete? Those are the main ideas that this section focuses on. Not the 'what', but rather the 'how' and 'when'.

7. <u>Delivery Date</u>: The "Delivery Date" is usually a final drop dead date whereby Delivery must be fully completed (or complete enough so that Studio Releases can actually exploit *Cool Action Film*). If this date were to come and go (and Express Productions still had not yet delivered the core basics), then this could be considered breach of contract and therefore make the entire agreement moot. The reason for these 'no-later-than' dates is because it takes a great deal of time to actually release a project into the market. Most networks and VOD platforms require delivery months prior to the formal premiere date just to ensure adequate time to prep, quality-check and market the project. Since Studio Releases is acquiring *Cool Action Film* to fit a very specific slot in its lineup, a delayed delivery could cause Studio Releases to cancel this agreement and fill that available slot with a Picture from a different producer.

8. <u>Fee</u>: As the Licensee or Distributor of *Cool Action Film*, Studio Releases isn't buying into this project for their love of film. They see the opportunity for long-term repeat sales and intend to shave off a piece of every dollar generated. This section defines the percentage they intend to take from the Gross Receipts (as hereunder defined). The percentage applied can differ from one project to the next—spanning a wide gap from 10% up to 50%—but more often than not lands within the 20% to 30% range.

9. <u>Performance Guarantee</u>: Signing over one's rights can be scary, especially with that ever-present fear that the Licensing party could simply shelve the film or broker poor deals. As a way to ensure some minimal level of sales—or at least the ability to get the rights back if the Licensee has been underperforming in their distribution responsibilities—a guarantee of minimum performance can be defined (one that's reasonable for the Licensee in terms of monetary expectations as well as duration of time while also being reasonable so that if sales performance is weak, the Licensor can regain rights in their property, while the property still possesses further market value). Duration of time can easily span many years—for example, three years up to seven years—and generally has a minimum performance of at least half the out-of-pocket cost to produce the project (usually a bit more). Key understanding here is that this 'performance guarantee' is fair for both parties (that the Licensee gets a meaningful chance to exploit the film, while the Licensor has a reasonable window to request the rights back if they feel the project hasn't been distributed as promised).

10. <u>Advance or Minimum Guarantee</u>: Although there are slight differences between an 'Advance' versus 'Minimum Guarantee' (often referred to as a 'MG'), they both define a lump sum of cash payable by the Licensee to the Licensor either upon signature of the acquisition or paid out over a mutually agreed payment schedule. The amount of money listed in this section can vary widely depending upon the budget and/or market value of the project. In some instances, this section might be 'zero' (meaning it's an agreement where the revenues are simply split by percentage only starting at the first dollar generated and split according to the 'fee' defined earlier); in other instances this could be several hundred thousand dollars if the project commanded such a sum of cash (very few in

the independent space reach that level). The most critical note here is that up-front cash is always a great option for a Licensor; however, any monies paid up front will need to be recouped by the Licensee (and generally they're still applying fees on top of this lump sum). As an example, let's say the up-front advance is $100,000; the Licensee paying this cash will understandably want to 'recoup' this money from future business before having to pay out an additional dime to the Licensor. However, it's important to understand that they're also recouping their 'fee' on top of this recoupment off every sale. This distribution fee kicks in on gross sales from the first dollar generated, with the net amount after the fee is deducted applicable to the recoupment. For more information on this concept, check out 'waterfall' in Chapter 8 as well as in the glossary of terms.

11. Expenses: Distributing a movie isn't free; it costs a lot of money to make a film 'market ready' in relation to marketing expenses, business overhead and even placement of the film onto company websites or logging the project with a lab. Think of this section as 'the cost of doing business'; however, that doesn't mean that 'expenses' should be ongoing or that there shouldn't be some ceiling as to what can be written off. I always try to place a fixed cap (an actual dollar amount the distributor is allowed to bill as expenses), so that it never exceeds a predetermined amount. It's perfectly fine to have additional language that some other expenses can be permitted, but only if they're agreed to in advance by written acceptance. Also, it's critical to define that this 'capped' dollar amount is all-encompassing (meaning it applies to all expenses, not only selected expenses as the distributor defines them). Bottom line, pay critical attention to how expenses are defined. Although expenses are addressed within this section, do be vigilant about where/how expenses might be woven into other areas of the agreement (in other words, hidden in plain sight elsewhere). This is a good time to remind you that you can always consult an expert or lawyer to help with such matters; they're trained to look for such hidden language.

12. Gross Receipts: 'Gross' simply refers to any and all monies received. By contrast, 'net' refers to whatever is left after all the taxes, fees and other expenses are deducted. It's important to commit the difference to memory, especially in that the Licensee or Distributor will be taking on their fees and recoupments of cash from all 'gross' sales, whereas you (the Licensor) will be entitled to a cut of the 'net' proceeds. In other words, they get to eat first, and you get a 'piece' of what's left over (even if it's only a plate of crumbs). You will often hear stories of producers or other talents shouting angrily that they aren't getting the royalties they're owed; however, in almost all cases their agreements were written in a way that greatly pushes down the 'net' total, resulting in a sliver of a very small remaining portion of cash. Check out 'gross' versus 'net' in the glossary, but also check out the definition of 'waterfall' in Chapter 8 to get a solid sense of how this all plays in relation to one another.

13. Statements: Statements refer to a Picture's financial statements (commonly referred to as "Participation Statements"). Statements are generally sent via email on a recurring basis to provide the Licensor visibility to the financial performance of the Picture (specifically to relay the Picture's total Gross Receipts or Revenues and whether a share of money is payable or not). This clause is generally quite lengthy, primarily because it must relay

a wide range of detailed information including (i) how the statements are to be sent, (ii) at what point the Licensee is obligated to initiate generating/sending such statements and (iii) how long after the term of the contract statements are required to be released. There are also details about any minimum sums of monies that must first be generated before payments can be issued as well as how a potential audit must be handled if there is a discrepancy in payment totals. If you have any inquiries regarding visibility to financial performance, this is the section where everything will be detailed. This is a great section to spend time truly thinking through and negotiating.

14. Copyright Revenues: Without going into too deep a rabbit hole, it's important to understand that anything owned by a third party that exists within a media property—especially music—essentially gains a tiny revenue share for every dollar the project generates. The idea is that the third-party-owned content—like a song or musical composition—aided in the success of the finished product and therefore deserves a small cut of the proceeds. There are organizations throughout the world called "performance societies" that monitor the broadcasts and transactions of media properties with a keen eye toward utilized music or other copyrighted elements managed by third parties. Each time a property is broadcast or made visible to the public on a traditional outlet, that broadcaster or outlet is required to send a pre-allocated sum of cash to one of these performing rights societies (who then in turn send a pre-allocated amount back to the artist or entity that manages those rights). The reason this clause is usually placed into an agreement is so that the licensing party deflects financial obligations to the producer as well as to any third-party outlet. The distributor will certainly relay any music cue sheets or other information to clients with whom they license the rights, but they are essentially providing the best information made aware to them (delegating any related financial responsibilities to the appropriate third parties). For your purposes, what's most important is (i) to provide clear and accurate information relating to any licensed copyrighted elements like musical compositions (via a music cue sheet) and (ii) to note that any revenues generated from copyrighted IP—including from music publishing funds—are counted as Gross Receipts.

15. Credits: Distributors love to see their company name and logo on the properties they release. So somewhere within an agreement like this, there will be a clause that obligates a producer to insert the distributor's company name and company logo within the media property as well as on all marketing materials. When you're watching a film, generally, the first logo you see will be that of the distributor (and usually the first credit that appears will be "Such-and-Such Company Presents", which again is almost always the distributor's title card). In this scenario, it would be language specifying that the Studio Releases' logo be added to the front of the film and that the title card "Studio Releases Presents" be listed prior to any other entity. This section can be expanded to detailed individual credits as well, such as Executive Producer credits (including their chronology).

16. Distribution Rights: Although a bit redundant, there is usually a clause that specifies that the distributor shall have all normal and customary rights that 'distributors' get in the territory and media granted, including without limitation control of the distribution and

exploitation in its sole discretion. The reason for this is to ensure that the distributor—in this case Studio Releases—is able to make sound business decisions without a third party questioning its decisions or claiming it doesn't have rights that may not have existed when the parties entered into this agreement. Such a clause also limits any objections or intrusions a frustrated producer may have if they feel the distributor isn't managing the rights in the manner they'd ideally like to see. Although it feels repetitive, such clauses aren't random and usually are placed to add layers of protection for the licensing party.

17. <u>Censorship of Force Majeure</u>: There are occasions when monies are paid out which subsequently become refundable for any number of reasonable scenarios. For instance, the film could have an actor on screen that suddenly becomes a controversial figure (and deals are scrapped or cancelled); those monies may have initially been paid out but later retracted. Since the money was rightfully paid, no one would expect an immediate repayment so as a reasonable way to remedy. Generally, these 'refundable' sums are added as a deduction on a future royalty statement. You will find other similar examples of this in action within the physical space (e.g., DVDs or other transactional forms of exploitation); items can be returned for reimbursement, which means the monies are deducted from the Gross Receipts. Consequently, funds can be payable during one financial statement yet become a negative on a future financial statement due to such scenarios.

18. <u>Residuals</u>: This is an important clause. Labor unions—especially SAG-AFTRA—require the rights holder of a media property which utilized talent from their union to hold on to a minimum percentage of cash from all future revenues received that will be payable to that talent. The details and percentage splits differ by union, but the concept is critical to understand; having union talent in a film will require the rights holder to always retain a portion of the Gross Profits (even if they're only being paid net profits) so that they can pay the union all calculable residuals. All of this is generally managed via a pre-approved payroll company, one that specializes in handling such matters. However, more often than not, the distribution company (or a licensing party) isn't technically the rights holder; they're simply borrowing the rights (therefore they are not obligated to hold onto any excess cash owed to a union). Therefore, unless otherwise clarified, this burden is placed upon the shoulders of the copyright owner or producer. If the media property is a non-union production or is produced outside the jurisdiction of the union (e.g., if a US film were to be shot in Canada or Australia), then the union would have zero claim. Again, one could write endlessly about hypothetical scenarios; for your purposes, keep an eye out whenever you see clauses that indicate how future payments to third parties are to be managed/handled to ensure you don't end up holding the bag for everyone else.

19. <u>Third-Party Obligations</u>: The rights holder, in this case Jessica's company Express Productions, Inc., is responsible for all third-party payments and obligations in relation to the Picture. Similar to Residuals clause earlier, the promises and agreements entered into by the production team are of no responsibility to the distributor; their job is only to borrow and exploit the Picture's rights. All of the steps necessary to get the film into

its final form fall back on Jessica's team. This clause is primarily placed as a liability matter for the distributor; as long as all documentation and protocols are followed relating to union residuals, music rights or any other conceivable third-party agreement—which is standard operating procedure during a film production—then this clause is essentially commonplace fine print.

20. <u>Security Interest</u>: Although not every distribution agreement will have this clause, most will include it (even if under a slightly different name). The main reason for its existence is to ensure the licensing party (Studio Releases) is undeniably first in line in terms of revenue. In fact, they're so undeniably first in line that they will likely include a 'Short Form Assignment of Rights' that clearly transfers any ounce of ownership away from Express Productions, Inc. and places it squarely into the hand of Studio Releases. If some new rights category trends or some alternative unforeseeable revenue-generating trend that COOL ACTION FILM can benefit from pops up, those funds must first be routed through Studio Releases coffers and can only be dished out according to the agreed upon waterfall. This is also critical should Studio Releases ever sell itself to another company, at which point all its assets (including COOL ACTION FILM) become the asset of another firm; this clause would guarantee that future third-party bankable financial projections on this title would be clear of any outside claims. Even though this sounds intimidating, it's really just further clarifying the rights you're already signing over. However, a critical thing to understand with this clause is that should Studio Releases actually change hands in the future, you may be obligated to file and/or reapprove the terms herein (as is, without additional negotiations) in some future agreement or term sheet. This can even sometimes mean that a distributor has the right to enter into agreements with certain guilds or unions (if verifiably necessary) in the Licensor's name (meaning in Express Productions, Inc.'s name) and require Jessica to sign as if she were the one filing.

21. <u>Right of First Negotiation and Last Refusal</u>: Successful projects occasionally lead to sequels, spin-offs, remakes, reboots or even adaptations into unexpected media formats that may not even yet exist. However, rather than attempting to define the potentially undefinable, many agreements will include a generic clause such as this one. Eventually this distribution agreement will come to a close. And when it does, the parties will go their separate ways. However, in the event that a third party steps in with the desire to reinvent COOL ACTION FILM into some future version, then this clause will always require Jessica and/or Express Productions to first reach out to Studio Releases to make a first bid on the newly created media property (hence the 'right of first negotiation'); however, it's possible Studio Releases makes a low offer, and Jessica or Express Productions feel they could get better terms elsewhere; they're absolutely allowed to seek out other opportunities; they're only obligated to start the process with Studio Releases. Down the line, if Jessica or Express Productions manage to get a *better* offer from another company, they must go back to Studio Releases to see if they'd match the new commercial terms (hence the 'right to last refusal'). The logic here is that Studio Releases' efforts in distributing the original version of COOL ACTION FILM helped lead to a sequel, prequel or other alternative recreated version (and therefore should have the

first option to bid on the new property as well as the final opportunity to match the market's best terms).

22. <u>Representations and Warranties</u>: Every contract will have this clause buried within. It's generally a massive block of mish-mashed legalese that really boils down to the notion that both parties are in good legal standing, that they have the right to enter into this agreement, that they're not misrepresenting who/what they are and that the media property itself does not have any legal baggage (e.g., claims, liens, infringements, defamations, stolen/uncleared copyright or IP violations, etc.). We could do a deep dive, but these clauses really speak for themselves (and are considered commonplace, which is why they're found universally in agreements).

23. <u>Product Placement Warranty</u>: Pay attention to the inclusion of such clauses. While product placement in the recent past only referred to the use of commercial products appearing on screen—whereby they were actually filmed on set—in today's world, Virtual Product Placement (VPP), or the integration of ads/products after the media property is filmed via computer engineered visual effects, is fast becoming a monetizing opportunity for broadcasters, platforms as well as distributors. Note that this is a fast-changing subject and that commonplace trends have not yet become standard. That said, at present, one should, at minimum, have the right to add integrated ads prior to presenting it to third parties. Keep your eyes open for such language; it could yield you an opportunity (or block you from one).

24. <u>Indemnity</u>: Another overly wordy yet universally understood paragraph within an agreement. In short, should this deal fall apart (and both parties go after each other on valid legal claims), OR if some unforeseen event takes place resulting in verifiable damages that leads to legal action against one of the parties, then the claims and/or assertions can only apply toward the applicable party. In other words, if a lawsuit were to take place between Express Productions and Studio Releases, then they can only go after each other; they cannot in any way go after individuals, entities or other 'connected' parties or properties outside of the scope of this agreement (even if they are connected or partnered with the parties). Hypothetically, if Express Productions has a valid legal claim against Studio Releases and wishes to pursue the matter in court, the extent of their case can only involve Studio Releases and its owned/managed financials; Express Productions cannot go after board members, employees or vendors doing business with Studio Releases.

25. <u>Default</u>: To default basically means to fail in one's contractual obligations, which would cause the overall deal to fall apart. There is usually a window of time for the defaulting party to remedy the situation. If there is no action to remedy—or no specific way to solve the issue—then the contract will essentially be dismantled (but not without damages being rewarded to the party in good standing). You might also see the word 'breach' herein, which basically implies that one of the parties have taken action that steps beyond the scope of the agreement (it's not a failure of action, but rather too much action). To be in breach of contract can also be remedied but could also cause the party

in breach to default. The course of action is the same: a window of time to remedy or termination of the agreement (with damages).

26. Termination: This is essentially the 'exit clause' or the block of text that explains how both parties agree to end the relationship early should some unforeseen matter require it to conclude prior to the expiration date. Termination could be obligatory if one party is in breach or defaults (and no remedy is agreed upon), but could also be requested by a party for any reasonable purpose. Generally, there is a financial payment required for the party requesting—or causing—the termination to take place. One should always read this clause carefully to understand how an early exit might actually play out (and how much it might cost).

27. Notices: Contracts will commonly have a specific section that details how information will be presented to each party. This section will list out who, where, how for each party (generally a specific person representing each party, their contact address, phone number and email address). This section will also list methods of acceptable 'notice' (for instance, that email is an approved method for communicating critical contract-related information). Always make sure this section is up to date. If a party changes contact information while the contract is valid, they are required to notify or update the other party.

28. E&O Insurance Certificate: Errors and Omissions insurance (E&O) will always be a requirement. Don't put this off thinking you can save the cash, assuming a distributor will 'add' you to their policy down the line. Get the required insurance, and always secure the rights to IP you do not own. The idea with an E&O policy is that it protects the distributing party against any claims for production/producing oversights related to third-party IP. For example, if a clip from an existing TV show or excerpt from a third-party musical composition were used in *Cool Action Film*—both of which were copyrighted and managed by a separate entity—and the 'rights' to exploit these within *Cool Action Film* were not secured by Jessica nor Express Productions, then the owners of the IP could sue Studio Releases since it is now on the front line profiting from the media property. Since a lawsuit opens the door to risk, Studio Releases will require a reduction to that risk (which in this case would be an existing E&O policy).

29. Assignment: The concept of assignment is the right to transfer this agreement—along with all of its responsibilities, terms and understandings—to a third party. Generally this clause is a bit lopsided in favor of the distributor, but there is a reason for that. Jessica will always be the producer of *Cool Action Film*, but Studio Releases may not always be the distributor (even during the agreed duration of term of the agreement). The reason is that Studio Releases may be acquired or 'bought' by a third party down the line—and that new owner would want to acquire all assets in Studio Releases portfolio (including Jessica's movie). Therefore, Studio Releases would require the right to actually transfer or 'assign' its rights to that new third party, whereas Jessica will remain the producer (she cannot 'transfer' her responsibilities to a third party). However, there is something to

be cautious of here; you want to make sure companies aren't simply 'flipping' rights to another entity—forever taking a cut/fee as a middle person.

30. <u>Confidentiality</u>: It will always be required that both parties stay quiet about the terms to which they've agreed. Let's be realistic; people certainly talk. However, there's a major difference between casual chit chat with a friend over lunch about what terms were secured when they licensed their film to a company versus stating it for all eyes to see on social media. The latter would put a party in breach of their contract (and therefore void them of any damage claims). Distributors do dish out different terms to different producers for a variety of reasons. In some instances, they'll offer steeper terms that are more advantageous to their internal bottom line; in others the prospect of managing a specific property is so valuable they might bend/fold on terms they'd never consider doing for another other media property. As a result, releasing such information would simply be a headache of explanation to third-party producers that are separate from this agreement. There are also matters of liability and protection of third-party information at play with such clauses. (You wouldn't want information shared without your permission, would you?) There will always be a confidentiality clause, and it's good business practice to keep mum about the details; it's your business with the distributor and no one else's (except a lawyer or accredited professional with whom you may be working, but they would also be bound by client confidentiality provisions).

31. <u>Force Majeure</u>: A French phrase found in nearly all contracts, describing things that are out of our control, like a flood, war, political protest, or any other unforeseen and unstoppable event. Basically, in the event of something that would fall into this category, one cannot be held in breach or default (with damages applied against them) for actions for contractual requirements they are unable to deliver upon.

32. <u>Choice of Law and Jurisdiction</u>: The location of jurisdiction is always specified within an agreement so that if a dispute were to arise, both parties would know the exact state, county and city (and potentially country) where the terms and conditions would be evaluated (which would affect the legal lens through which a third party would be interpreting the fine print). Ninety-nine times out of 100, the governing law and jurisdiction will be those where the distributor (in this case, Studio Releases) was organized.

33. <u>Miscellaneous</u>: There will always be a large amount of words crammed into this 'Miscellaneous' section. The reason is that it covers a random collection of points or concepts that don't easily fit elsewhere herein. Examples include the following:

33.1 – Stating that this distribution deal doesn't represent a 'partnership' between the parties (clarifying that rights and damages can only be applicable to those linked to *Cool Action Film*);

33.2 – The Agreement constitutes the 'Entire Agreement', meaning if a word or phrase is in dispute about how it should be interpreted, then its understanding must be filtered through the spirit of the entire agreement.

33.3 – That this Agreement is only valid if fully executed (signed by both parties) and that proof of the distribution of fully executed versions must be guaranteed (reference 'Notices' earlier).

33.4 – That this Agreement can be amended by the parties via written approval; also that the terms of this Agreement can change if the laws in the jurisdiction governing this Agreement were to change. Any such adjustment would be discussed by both parties and confirmed in writing as per the section on 'Notices' earlier).

33.5 – Any other conceivable point or idea that, on one hand, seems abundantly obvious yet will still be clarified in writing for absolute certainly that it was, at minimum, mentioned should some unforeseen scenario arise.

And then the parties sign blow—either with an actual pen, then printed, scanned and emailed to the other party—or via electronic signature and emailed.

AGREED AND ACCEPTED:

Express Productions, Inc.   Studio Releases
"Licensor"   "Distributor"

By: _____   By:_____

Its: _____   Its: _____

EXHIBIT 1

SHORT ASSIGNMENT OF RIGHTS

Thought the agreement covered the 'assignment' of *Cool Action Film*'s rights from Express Productions, Inc. over to Studio Releases? On one hand it does, but nothing cements the deal like a receipt (and that's what a Short Form Assignment of Rights essentially is).

This document will summarize the high-level terms of the agreement (title, duration of term and the parties involved), only here Express Productions, Inc. will be referred to as the "Assignor", whereas Studio Releases will be the "Assignee".

This document also formally spells out certain legal understandings—for instance that Studio Releases will have the right to sign on behalf of the film, may collect or receive damages for the film and hold privileges that any rights holder would have. The Assignor would also be obligated to assist and participate with Assignor should any lawsuit or legal action be required.

There is usually a simple sentence that this Assignment is subject to the terms and conditions of the Agreement.

Occasionally this document will need to be notarized, but not always.

IN WITNESS WHEREOF, the Assignor applies their signature here—formally transferring the rights to the Assignee; the Assignee does not need to execute or affix their signature to this Assignment since they're in possession of the rights:

Express Productions, Inc.
"Licensor"

By: _____

Its: _____

Date: _____

(Note: Additional 'Schedules' or 'Exhibits' will follow, generally related to Delivery requirements (the elements and items Express Productions, Inc. is required to delivery to Studio Releases). These are split into two categories: (i) physical delivery requirements (the files and artwork related to the film itself) and (ii) the legal delivery requirements (the forms, agreements and documents supporting all paperwork has been properly files and/or organized). Since these are comprehensive—and differ depending on company—we've provided detailed examples of both in Appendix IV.)

Appendix III
Sample Television Format Option Agreement

Most US television hits are actually imported from other countries via format option agreements. Megahit *America's Funniest Home Videos* was a format adapted from Japan's *Fun TV with Kato-chan and Ken-chan*; *Big Brother* was a format adapted from the Netherlands (utilizing the same title); *The Masked Singer* was adapted from Korea's *King of Masked Singer*; and both *Master Chef* and *Dancing with the Stars* both originated in the UK. On the scripted side, *Homeland* originated in Israel; *The Mighty Morphin Power Rangers* from Japan; and *The Office* and *Shameless* both from the UK. There are countless examples.

A 'format' is essentially the recipe or framework of a television project; it works very much like a franchise model where an individual entrepreneur (a franchisee) can establish their own fast-food restaurant by simply signing a franchise agreement with a McDonald's or other major franchise (with the franchisee fronting the cash to make it possible). The franchisee gets the benefit of managing a major known brand, whereas the corporation scoops up fees from the entrepreneur's efforts. It's a win-win model. And it works seamlessly in the media business.

In the realm of TV and new media, established networks and streamers in major countries like green-lighting formats because they have far more visibility to how the program is likely to perform. (Preexisting TV series have completed episodes to screen and ratings to digest.) But generally, its independent producers that actually do the heavy lifting during this process—quite similar to our franchisee analogy earlier.

Indie producers will scan the global market, seeking out high-quality existing content and then work to acquire the right to replicate the show's format in a foreign country. Some producers focus on scripted content, others on alternative TV (aka 'non-scripted'). But the workflow is essentially the same. They'll first need to acquire the 'format' rights, then they'll need to invest a great deal of time/effort in setting up pitches to showcase the strength of the foreign series for a local audience. Some are green-lit and become TV shows, others don't (but can be reacquired by other producers and reworked into a new fresh format pitch).

As far as workflows, after a producer has identified an overseas television program of interest, the first step they'll need to take is to secure its rights via a **format option agreement**. This agreement allows a local producer to hold or manage the rights exclusively for their territory for a limited window of time with the intention of 'setting it up' (aka securing a broadcast, platform or distribution deal). If the project is well received and the format option agreement is elevated into a distribution deal, then normal protocols take hold (see Appendix II for a standard distribution sample which would be the next phase during a format's life). But until that point, the format option agreement is the paperwork traded to transfer the rights.

Hypothetical Example

To give you some context as you read/review this agreement, imagine the following scenario: an Internationally Renowned Distributor from London has produced and manages the rights in a very successful six-episode scripted comedy series call *Hilarious TV Series!* Across the pond in Los Angeles, the successful Known LA Producer came across *Hilarious TV Series!* during a convention and thought it'd be perfect if it could be adapted into a US version (with local US actors and changing a few bits to make them feel more 'Americanized'). Known LA Producer reached out to Internationally Renowned Distributor to see if the rights were available; they were. After a few rounds of negotiation, the parties finalized their commercial terms (mapping out their needs and wants to make the deal workable). Internationally Renowned Distributor formally entered into a Format Option Agreement with Known LA Producer. What follows is a sample agreement showcasing what their deal would likely look like. And please note, I've avoided using legalese and have instead written this agreement in a way that essentially explains how each section works; although agreements come in different formats, they all have these same core ingredients. (And if you seek a real-world boilerplate, you can find them via online search engines; what follows is purely informational.)

Format Option Agreement

Date: January 14, 2024

Between: Internationally Renowned Distributor
           987 Quaint Sounding Street
           London, WC2H 9HB
           United Kingdom
           ("Licensor")
           Known LA Producer
           789 Santa Monica Blvd., Suite ABC
           Los Angeles, CA 90025
           USA
           ("Licensee")

WHEREAS the Licensor owns or exclusively controls certain distribution rights in, to and in connection with the Format listed below;

AND WHEREAS the Licensee wishes to license select or certain exploitation rights in the Format in the Territory, subject to an on the Terms and Conditions set out below;

NOW THEREFORE the parties agree as follows:

Commercial Terms

Format: "Hilarious TV Series!" (Format Only)

Licensed Rights: Exclusive Format Rights—Option

The exclusive format rights are generally defined as the exclusive right to arrange for the development and/or financing of the Format within the Territory during the Option Period, but NOT the right to produce the program (except for a single pilot episode or sample version to aid in the development and/or financing process).

Territory: United States of America (including possessions and territories)

Option Period: The term of format option agreements are generally kept quite short, averaging around six months. Some can be extremely short (one month), while others can extend to one full year or beyond, but the majority land in the six-month zone. This is ample time to put together basic marketing elements or pitch materials (and to gather market interest from networks or platforms).

Option Fee: The option fee is the amount of money required by the licensor from the licensee in order to initiate the exchange of rights. What's interesting with format option agreements is that, generally speaking, this sum is quite low (perhaps only a few thousand or even just a few hundred dollars). However, there are many occasions where this sum can be as low as one single dollar ($1.00) or even for free.

The reason for such low sums within option agreements is that these are longer-term relationships with a high rate of failure. The vast majority of optioned formats never gain traction, but when they do (in those rare circumstances), the rewards can be very strong in terms of large recurring revenues. A distributor of formats (like Internationally Renowned Distributor) would rather have its format rights actively being pitched/developed for the market (even at small to no option fees) with the hope of a big win rather than holding out for larger up-front option fees.

However, it does take a great deal of time and internal resources for distributors to negotiate, facilitate and execute these recurring/repetitive deals (resources that could be applied toward other projects), so any monies here are primarily used to cover the distributor's internal overhead costs. And with that, any up-front monies paid are 'recoupable' (meaning that the licensor receiving the option fee would get this small amount up front upon signature, BUT that amount would later be deducted from any future payment by the licensee (in this case, Known LA Producer).

Exercise of Option: The exercise of an option is essentially the point at which the option agreement transitions into a more elevated type of deal structure (a formal distribution agreement, acquisition agreement or series order agreement). It's basically the point when a studio, network or platform agrees to move forward with the series, and a new agreement structure is therefore required to outline the next relationship phase.

Option Overhead Fee: Upon licensee's written notice (Known LA Producer's notice to Internationally Renowned Distributor that a network has been secured for the series), this agreement will officially be 'exercised'. At this moment, the deal needs to transition into a more formalized deal structure; since this requires a larger drain on the distributor's internal resources (its overhead), a fee must be payable by Known LA Producer to secure these more formalized rights. Of course, generally, to get to this point, Known LA Producer would have secured a solid license fee from the network and is therefore simply paying out a portion of their share to the rights holder (Internationally Renowned Distributor).

Materials: The materials used during a format option vary depending on the status of the original project. If the format option is of an existing program, then materials usually include access to existing production budgets, marketing materials, full episodes of the program for screening purposes, trailers, any scripts or production notes as well as the production bible itself (which breaks down all of the granular details regarding 'how' to produce the program).

Many distributors hold onto the bible until an actual exercise of option takes place; the bible contains all of the trade secrets, so to speak; therefore, distributors want to ensure no theft or repurposing of the program takes place prior to a formalized agreement whereby the rights are secured.

For this example, it would be considered normal for Internationally Renowned Distributor to grant all materials (with the exception of the bible) to Known LA Producer at the option stage with additional language explaining the bible will be shared only after a formalized exercise of this option takes place.

Delivery Date: An agreed date by which Internationally Renowned Distributor must deliver all of the earlier-mentioned materials. And since most of these materials can be sent electronically via email or FTP, a business week is generally considered more than enough time.

Notices: Contact information for Known LA Producer will be specified here (if not done so elsewhere within this agreement). These contact details are where a copy of the fully executed contract, materials, invoices and/or future notifications about the agreement will be sent.

Terms and Conditions of License If Option Exercised

If Known LA Producer secured a deal with a US company, he/she will notify Internationally Renowned Distributor of the deal points, and together they will elevate this deal toward a formalized distribution agreement. This process is known as 'exercising' this option agreement.

However, many different variables can exist at the point of exercising a format option agreement, most of which are unknowable at the option stage—for example, the needs/ expectations of a US broadcaster would be very different from the needs/wants of a US VOD streamer in terms of casting and episode counts. But neither party wants to hand over the format without some understanding of how the format will be managed in the event of an exercised option, so they'll do their best to iron out some basic terms within the option agreement. Think of these as guardrails so that its understood Known LA Producer must, at minimum, meet these expectations in the event of an exercise of format rights:

Title of the Program: Some formats require a 'branded' title (e.g., *The Voice*); however, others can be adapted or localized (e.g., how UK's *Pop Idol* was re-titled *American Idol* when it was adapted for the US); generally, there is some language defining how the title 'approvals' process will be handled.

Number of Episodes: There is usually a block of text defining how many individual 'episodes' constitute a single 'season' of a TV or web series. The reason is that format values increase season by season. (If the format is a big success in another country, the producer of that adapted series should compensate the format rights holder—the initial distributor—for the continued growth of the IP). Therefore, language will be placed here defining the minimum and maximum number of episodes. Important to note that one cannot simply write "a minimum of 1 episode and a maximum of 1,000 episodes"; such a definition would be nonsense. One single episode would be a 'one-off' and would be treated very differently elsewhere in this agreement, and no territory on Earth—even those regions with very high episodic output—ever go above 60 or 70 episodes during one television season. The numbers need to align with the generally understood expectations defining a television season in the region of territory of acquisition.

Broadcaster: The 'broadcaster' can also be defined as a VOD platform (such as Netflix). Usually, in a blanket format deal this area will be left with language akin to 'to be agreed between the parties' since the eventual broadcaster would be unknown at the time of Internationally Renowned Distributor licensing these format rights to Known LA Producer. However, in some circumstances, a licensing party is actually acquiring the rights only to pitch/present them to a single channel or platform (which would be explained here,); or certain platforms or channels may actually be excluded or embargoed here (meaning, for one reason or another, the licensing party is not permitted to pitch/present the project to them).

Rights: Format rights are understood to be a grant of the right to produce one series for broadcast within the Territory during the License Period only by means of the Licensed Media and for the number of transmissions allowable. Therefore, all other rights are expressly withheld and retained by the licensing party (Internationally Renowned Distributor).

Licensed Media: This is where the allowable rights are spelled out, defining which rights Known LA Producer is permitted to grant or make available to a potential broadcaster. While in most cases this can be a blanket 'all-rights' block of text, there are occasions when a single right is excluded on a global or multi-territorial basis.

License Period: Again, this is information that cannot be known until Known LA Producer is able to land an offer and/or deal from a broadcaster or platform. But language is usually included here that the license period will be defined later on.

Language(s):   This example focuses on Known LA Producer acquiring the rights and attempting to set up the series in the USA. Therefore, the permitted languages would likely be English and neutral Spanish (for the US Hispanic population). However, in more interwoven territories—such as European territories where multiple languages are used—a specific language would likely need to be defined since that's how rights are divvied up (E.g., 'Flemish' versus 'French' in Belgium).

Format Fee: This is essentially the License Fee or Minimum Guarantee for the series. Like all TV deals, these are calculated on a 'per-episode' basis (usually ranging anywhere between 4% up to 10% of the 'per-episode' budget but generally average at 6.5% to 7%). Added to this, there is usually a separate minimum price point—which is important for smaller third world territories where 'per-episode' budgets can be shockingly small; this 'minimum per episode' allows for a reasonably scalable format fee for the distributor. To verify this, Known LA Producer would be required to provide Internationally Renowned Distributor with a broadcaster authenticated copy of the budget. None of this is payable until this format is executed and the series actually goes into production. Also, there is usually added language explaining that this fee shall increase (by 5% up to 15%) on a 'per-season' basis; therefore, if a series is a big hit, then all parties benefit by the increase in business.

Script Fee: Although this does not apply to factual or non-scripted TV content (e.g., game shows, etc.), for a narrative/scripted TV series, there is a 'script fee' applied on a per-episode basis. This fee is payable by Known LA Producer even if they—or the broadcaster—adapt, alter or revise the scripts for the local territory. If the program is natively in a different language, an additional 'marked-up' fee is applicable for the script translation.

Payment Terms: To be negotiated in good faith once this option is exercised and the broadcaster/platform—as well as the TV schedule itself—is finalized. All payments will be based on the minimum number of episodes; any adjustments necessary for including additional episode payments shall be made in pro-rata payments based upon the total verified number.

Deliverables: At the point of exercise, Internationally Known Distributor will be required to provide Known LA Producer with the following materials:

1) The Production Bible

2) Access to ALL produced episodes (including a minimum of one full season made available with English subtitles)

3) 1x HD Master of all promotional materials

4) Subtitle files

5) Scripts (with time-codes)

6) Logos, graphics and layered key art

7) A minimum of 30 production stills

8) All music files and audio cues

Consultation: This is another critical 'fee' built into a format deal. In the event the format option is exercised—and the show is green-lit for production—the format owner (which is usually its original producer or creator) is often required to oversee a period of preproduction or production in order to consult or advise the team on best practices. Of course, this all comes at a cost (paid by Known LA Producer). The fees can vary and are scalable by territory, but minimums of USD $150 to $500 per day, plus meals, plus hotel, plus car/travel and plus airfare (usually as business class or higher) are common. The idea here is that the original producer/creator can provide insight and expertise; another important factor is to ensure the adaptation is in alignment with the original product (and is not being misrepresented). The on-set consultation is done in person. However, additional consultations are generally woven in here as well (such as introductory phone calls, teleconferences, etc.) so that the original producer/creator can walk through high-level logistics.

Credit: The original production company, the new production company (Known LA Producer), the format distributor (Internationally Renowned Distributor) will all want credits, both on screen as well as company logos. This section spells out the sequencing of those credits as well as duration of on-screen logos if applicable.

Distribution Rights: If this format option is exercised—and *Hilarious TV Series!* becomes an actual produced program—then Known LA Producer's domain of rights would be limited only to the territory granted herein (the US only). The format owner—Internationally Renowned Distributor—would therefore be able to sell the finished American version to the rest of the world. There would, of course, be a distribution fee sharable to all parties (a percentage going back to Known LA Producer as well as the original format producer/creator—that way everyone shares. Also, these percentages would be split after the subtitling and/or dubbing take place.

Future Seasons: These agreements will always spell out that the parties are on a first right to negotiate and last right to refuse on opportunities for future seasons. However, these generally have a time stamp built in (e.g., the first/last rights apply only within a 12-month window after first broadcast of last episode, etc.).

Additional Terms

There will always be additional text here—what we would refer to as 'standard terms and conditions' (or ST&Cs)—that simply iterate that this agreement doesn't constitute any formalized partnership between the parties and that both entities have the legal right to enter into this agreement. Also, these agreements are never 'assignable' to third parties—meaning Known LA Producer cannot simply flip this agreement to another producer. In general, the idea with ST&Cs is to protect both sides and keep the nature of the relationship clearly defined. Also, since this is an international agreement, the 'jurisdiction' of the agreement would need to be stated (so that if any legal issues or conflicts arise in the future, it has been established the laws of which country will be used to review/interpret this agreement (these are generally the laws of the distributor's home country; in this example, the UK)).

And then both parties sign:

BY: BY:

———————————————————   ———————————————————

Known LA Producer   Internationally Renowned Distributor

———————————————————   ———————————————————

Print name and title   Print name and title

Appendix IV
Materials Delivery List With Definitions

Any distribution agreement granting a party the right to sell, license or exploit a media property will inevitably include a list of required 'materials' the producer or rights holder is expected to deliver.

The purpose of a Materials Delivery List is to ensure the distributor has direct access to all available materials related to a media property in order to appropriately—and legally—distribute it. Although a Materials Delivery List can go by a variety of names (e.g., 'Delivery Schedule' or 'Technical Delivery Requirements'), it is very often attached to the acquisition agreement as an additional 'section', 'exhibit' or 'schedule'.

It's important to note that nearly every company has a different standardized list of required materials and a different format in which it's presented. Therefore, I've opted to extrapolate the most commonly requested materials and define them below.

One piece of advice: a Materials Delivery List is just as negotiable as any other portion of a distribution contract. Prior to agreeing to deliver all that's listed, a rights holder should consult with an individual familiar with the technical specs required for a media property and focus on delivering only the core essentials.

The most common way for producers or rights holders to deliver the following material elements is via FTP (e.g. utilizing Aspera, Signiant Media Shuttle or WeTransfer). However, file transfer options can be perfectly acceptable as can physical deliveries of tangible materials or via hard drives.

Physical Deliverables

Master Digital Files—A 'master digital file' is a fully completed digital version of the program, sent in its native format at the highest available quality with all required audio files. This is the *final* version of the property and will include bars and tone, slate, along with a full audio mix. The idea with this file is that it can be used to create every conceivable technical layout a buyer might request: a digital print for theaters (DCP), television broadcast versions or altered to play on digital platforms. Master files also include full ten-channel audio layouts (including stereo tracks, 7.1 or 5.1 sound and music and effects tracks (see below)). Often, Materials Delivery Lists will require 'textless' elements included on the master file; a textless element is a duplicate of any shot which appears in the film with burnt-in text placed at the end of the program free of any text. In other words, if a shot at the opening of a feature film has the 'title' appearing as text on screen on top of an actual image, this exact image will be placed at the end of the program with the title removed—that way a foreign version of this same title (e.g., the title translated into Chinese or Arabic) can be placed.

Physical Tapes—Although a master digital file of the completed project can easily be recorded to tape, it's still fairly common for distributors to request a tape copy as well. There are a wide variety of tape formats (e.g., HDCams and digi-beta tapes), but the specs for each can also vary greatly (e.g., PAL versus NTSC or 4:3 image ratio versus 16:9). This means you could have 4 HDCam flavors in addition to 4 DigiBeta flavors. There is real value for having tape formats readily available; even in such a digitized world, many countries still require a tape delivery (and most of these countries are the ones who lack the additional funds to cover the conversion or encoding costs). For a rights holder, producing and performing quality-control (QC) checks on each of these tape formats can be a frustrating process (especially since the physical masters will need to be stored in a professional lab or vault). Although major distributors will ask for these elements, physical tapes are usually a material asset that can be made to order (rather than producing multiple versions up front).

Special Features Files—All supplemental materials (special features, featurettes, behind-the-scenes, bloopers, etc.) need to be treated as a separate video files, meaning each requires a 'master' just like the principle piece of media content. Supplemental materials still require QC checks, audio mixing, music and effects tracks as well as bars and tone and slates. In short, even though these feel like 'add-ons' when screened, they must be delivered with as much precision and care as other master elements. (For ease, especially if physical tapes are required, multiple outtakes, featurettes or additional supplemental content can be combined onto one tape.) These elements are not required but serve as a major assist in marketing a media property.

Trailers—Trailers, sizzle reels and other 'sneak peek' overviews (which are used to promote, market or advertise a media property) must also be delivered at the same technical level as other master elements. Therefore, while audiences might only see a 'trailer' made available on YouTube or television, the native version delivered includes bars and tone, slates, full audio layouts and has passed a full quality-control check. Even if an independent producer delivers a self-cut trailer, distribution companies will generally create their own—one that better speaks to the global marketplace as well as matches other trailers in their library. It is not uncommon for multiple trailer variations to be delivered within the same file or tape (e.g., a two-minute version, 90-second version, multiple 30-second versions or even a short ten-second version, etc.). Textless elements are required for trailers for international versioning.

B-Roll—When licensing content to foreign countries, it's not uncommon for censors to take issue with select scenes or sequences deemed inappropriate for their territory. Because excising a single scene or shot can greatly impact the plot of a film or media program—a great example would be *The Crying Game* (1992), wherein the entire plot depends on a reveal within a single shot—distributors potentially risk having their film banned or dramatically altered if they do not have innovative 'fixes' available. Therefore, 'B-roll' elements are often required for films potentially seen as controversial. If censors take issue with a scene, select shots can be replaced with B-roll to allow the same plot information to be revealed, but in a way that censors approved (i.e., Stanley Kubrick had to replace two shots in *A Clockwork Orange* (1971) to bring its 'X' rating down to an 'R' rating for its original US video release). There are occasions when the theme or idea within a scene is what causes censorship issues, at which point no shot replacements will alter the outcome. Less controversial programs (family or TV-safe content) generally require no 'B-roll' requests.

M&E Tracks (aka Split Audio Files)—Music and effects (M&E) tracks refer to the stereo audio tracks living on channels 3 and 4 of a properly formatted delivery master. Every sound from the media project exists on those tracks, except for spoken dialogue. This is because foreign-speaking territories can use these tracks to add in the voices of their foreign-speaking actors portraying the leading roles (without the expensive remixing process). You might occasionally see these referred to as 'fully filled M&E tracks'—that's in reference to there not being any 'gaps' or 'dropouts' in these audio tracks. Although there is almost always ambience of some kind present in audio tracks, on rare occasion, audio mixers will allow these tracks to go completely silent since there is an English speaker's voice filling the void. This can be problematic overseas where some languages require fewer spoken words to reach the same translation (all the audio would drop to zero, and a red flag would be raised, causing the title to fail a quality-control check).

Audio Stems—When a master file is delivered, its ten-channel audio tracks contain fully mixed audio. But there are thousands—if not tens of thousands—of individual audio files included within those mixes (ranging from actors' voices to music or even to Foley effects). If there is a minor audio dropout or clip that has made its way into the final mix, there's nothing that can be done to correct it; therefore, the audio stems (or all of the individual audio files as unmixed elements) are provided so that a distributor can make any required alterations later down the line. Such access is vital with regards to music clearances, foreign language dubbing or simply adjusting or replacing certain sounds of voices. Audio stems can also be used to edit trailers—where reworkings of complex scenes or replaced audio is required. And since audio files are quite small in digital size, these can easily be placed onto an audio CD, within a single folder (sent via FTP) or via hard drive delivery.

QC Reports—QC stands for 'quality control'. Once a lab completes work on a master element, they will include a technical report which indicates whether or not the file meets all minimum technical standards. The ranking is generally given as a simple 'pass' or 'fail'. For any 'failed' QC reports, there are clear notes as to why the file or tape was rejected. Although distribution companies will generally conduct their own QC inquiry on every material element issued to them, they will still require QC reports from producers or rights holders as a way to verify the overall workflow—primarily to ensure there are no conflicts or contradictions in their findings.

Audio CD of Music Tracks—In addition to 'audio stems', which are just the snippets and bits of audio actually used within the project (e.g., the three seconds of 'squeaky door' sounds or twelve seconds of ambient 'airplane noise'), a full version of each song is generally required on a separate disc or within a transferable separate file. Therefore, even if only ten seconds of the song were used in the final mix of the media project, here the entire song would be placed. The purpose is to ensure the distributor has the exact version of the song used in the project—and therefore the exact version the rights holder cleared for use. Depending on the specific scope of clearances, distributors can utilize such recordings and use them within sizzle reels or alternative cuts of the media property—including variations that will be for business-to-business promotional purposes only.

Reference Copy With Time Code—A 'Reference Copy' is a full version of the media property with a running time code clearly present on top of the image. The time code (listed in an HH:MM:SS;FF format) starts at the 'one-hour' mark (01:00:00;00) and begins counting as soon as the media property formally starts. The purpose of this 'reference' copy is to have an actual version of the property whereby technicians can sync foreign language audio tracks, subtitles, closed-caption files along with any other audio or visual element required to be manipulated or matched. These are generally supplied as low-resolution video files (ones that are easily opened or sent via shared link or FTP).

Digital Stills—Stills are one of the best tools utilized for promotional and marketing needs. These are images pulled from the actual media property (of the actors performing real scenes in the project); stills are not behind-the-scenes shots of cast, crew or locations. Many material delivery lists will require a minimum number of stills (20 to 30) and will specify the minimum technical specs (e.g., minimum 300dpi). The use of these stills will be to create key art, to be used as images on digital platforms and to supply to buying clients to consumer-facing promotions.

Key Art (as Layered files)—Key Art refers to a media property's poster art. However, the material delivery required is that this artwork file is 'layered' so that each visual element (cast faces, backdrop, billing block, title, etc.) can all be moved, removed, reversed or replaced. Distributors must often repurpose or recreate artwork for differing clients' needs; what makes a media property appealing in Europe might be completely different than what sells it in Southeast Asia. Layered key art allows distributors to make minor or major alterations without having to recreate artwork from scratch. There are also numerous occasions where images of talent or the alignment of cast members names follow heavily regulated contractual obligations (see 'Paid Ads' below); if an alteration is required, layered key art allows a distributor to adjust select elements while maintaining the legal paid ad requirements.

Legal or Publicity Materials

Press Kit—A press kit has morphed into the 'electronic' press kit (or EPK) in the sense that it is primarily delivered via hard drive, email or FTP. But the concept remains the same: this is a package of available promotional elements provided to distributors for purposes of exploitation and marketing. Although EPKs can be extraordinarily massive, a minimal one includes cast lists (including bios and previous credits), director(s)' statements, producer(s)' statements, along with art work, stills, press clippings and or social media tools (accounts, subscribership, etc.).

Metadata—In reference to media properties, metadata is a consolidation of technical and promotional information. Usually delivered as a single Excel or Word document, a metadata file will list out a wide range of details from production company credits, cast names, key creative roles (director, writer, etc.) as well as synopsis, rating, keywords for promotions and links to microsites. The purpose of metadata is to provide distributors a single reference copy providing all basic details of a production, but also to give the producer or rights holder a means of providing cast names and/or synopsis information in a legally binding manner (whereby talent names must be listed in a certain order or that a synopsis has been carefully worded to include talent names in a way that their agents and lawyers have approved).

Billing Block—A 'billing block' is that block of text seen traditionally in the lower pane of a theatrical poster (the one that lists production company information, cast, composer, director of photography, editor, writers, producers and director). Although it seems quite cookie-cutter, a great deal of attention is paid to the exact ordering of names, spacing between names and manner in which names are titled (e.g., 'Cinematographer' rather than 'Director of Photography' or 'A Martin Scorsese *Picture*' versus '*A Film by* Quentin Tarantino' or the application of guilds and unions associated with key roles). Since theatrical companies and home entertainment companies tend to be operated by different teams, a firmly vetted billing block ensures consistency. Usually, billing block details are organized within cast, crew and distribution agreements; copies of these are often required as well.

Closed-Caption Files—Closed-caption (or 'CC' files) are transcribed text blocks that describe what words are being spoken and what music is playing—their purpose is not for subtitling foreign language content, but rather to assist those who are hard of hearing. Although CC files are 'optional' in many international countries (including Canada), the Federal Communications Commission (FCC) of the United States requires all media broadcast on television to include a closed-caption option. Many VOD platforms have taken it upon themselves to require CC files in their delivery requirements—realizing they're slowly replacing traditional TV and will soon be bound by traditional TV rules.

Final Shooting Scripts—A copy of the script is required primarily for legalities (not for reference). It is understood that titles can change or that arrangement of scenes and exact spoken dialogue versus written text can be different. The requirement of a final shooting script is used to have verification that the property delivered was adapted from a particular shooting script for purposes of linkage. A final shooting script is also required so that a 'script clearance' can be performed (see later).

Dialogue Continuity Script (aka Transcript)—A transcription is an exact record of every spoken word, verbal cue or music cue existing within a media property. Unlike a final shooting script which can undergo changes, the transcription is created after a media property has been fully completed. In addition to the dialogue or music cue, there is a column identifying which character is speaking as well as the exact timecode (in a HH:MM:SS format) that the cue is taking place. For application of transcript and how these cues are placed within a property for delivery purposes, a reference copy of the media property with a burned-in running time code is used for syncing (see 'Reference Copy with Time Code' earlier).

Main & End Credits—Every word appearing in the film as a 'credit' will usually be required in a word document or other word processing format. Some will be very specific (e.g., if a title appears by itself, it must be listed on a single page, etc.). The idea here is so that distributors can copy/paste credits for purposes of creating artwork, billing blocks (see 'billing block'), run clearance reports and/or translate text into foreign languages. Main and end credits within a document also ensure a distributor arranges the sequencing of names appropriately so that all names match their contractually obligated placements.

Cast and Crew Agreements—A photocopy or digital copy of a fully executed agreement for each cast member is required to assure distributors the performer has agreed to appear on screen (and in what capacity) via a performer release form as well as how their name and likeness can be used in promotional materials. Crew agreements, primarily those serving major roles (such as director, producer, writer, etc.), are also used for purposes of how individual names are to be credited and in what ways their name should be handled for promotional or marketing purposes. Union and guild affiliations, if any, are also gleaned from such agreements.

Music Cue Sheet—Music cue sheets (often abbreviated as 'MCS') are documents sequentially detailing every recorded piece of music heard within the media property. MCS detail the exact timecode at which point the music is heard along with the recordings title, composer and legal owner. Also listed are any affiliations to which the composer or the rights owner belongs. Media outlets—such as broadcast television networks—are required to pay music royalties for every music recording transmitted; the details of a MCS allow accounting teams to appropriately disperse residual payments and legal teams to verify all music usage has been properly cleared.

Music License Agreements—Music rights must be cleared prior to exploitation. Unlike 'appearance' releases (which are pretty straightforward), music rights can be sliced and diced in numerous ways; there are different fees and royalties paid out for music appearing in trailers versus as background in a scene or songs playing where lyrics have been removed (such as a character playing a well-known song on a piano without vocalizing lyrics). Distributors require fully executed music license agreements clearly stating the producer or rights holder not only has permission to use the music composition within the program but in exactly what capacity. A hired 'composer' for any music would fall within Cast and Crew Agreements (earlier).

Acquired Footage or Stills License—All third-party clips, stock footage or still images used prominently on screen must be properly 'acquired' for their use. Distribution companies will screen media properties—or have vetted services specializing in clearance matters screen on their behalf—specifically looking for potential conflicts. A producer or rights holder must be able to showcase they are legally permitted to use such third-party imagery; otherwise they must excise such content from the property.

Script Clearance Report—A Script Clearance Report is an evaluation of a screenplay with the sole purpose of noting any potential legal red flags (e.g., infringement of pre-existing copyrights or trademarked materials, plagiarism, etc.). The clearance report will also skim through actual lines of dialogue and description blocks to see if trademarked phrases are used, as well as seek out anything that could be deemed as defamatory to any person, organization or entity.

Chain of Title—This phrase describes the compilation of all relevant documentation associated with a single media property verifying it is completely cleared from any potential third-party claim. The associated documents include cast and crew agreements, copyrights, certificates of authorship or origin, footage and music licenses, title and script clearances, location releases, E&O insurance, along with any partnership agreements of production companies taking ownership in the media property. Essentially, anything that would require permission or clearance for it to exist within the media property needs a form of documentation proving such permission was granted.

Title Clearance Report—A title clearance report is a document verifying that the use of a particular title does not conflict with or raise issue with any preexisting trademark. In essence, since titles themselves are not copyrightable, the report evaluates similar titles across all forms of media (film, television, publication, etc.) to confirm that no marketplace confusion or trademark infringement will take place. A vetted title clearance report will always be required to obtain an Errors and Omissions policy (see "Errors and Omissions" below).

Copyright Search Report—A copyright search report details the history of a media property's assigned rights. The purpose is to ensure that no third party can claim they hold any assignment over the media property (e.g., that they have an existing option on a script or preexisting agreement granting them rights to a novel, etc.).

Certificate of Origin—A 'certificate of origin' is a notarized document used for trading purposes that essentially states from which country a media property originated. These are generally required when brokering international deals with countries that have quota regulations in place (such as the European Union, China, Brazil or Canada, among other regions that require broadcasters and/or theaters exhibit a minimum number of locally or regionally produced content).

Paid Ad and Credit Obligations—Performance agreements—especially ones related to more established actors—will generally have detailed language regarding how that name, image, likeness and voice of a specific individual can be used within marketing, promotional and press materials. The purpose is to protect the name and image of an actor from any outlandish marketing stunts distributors might pull in order to increase sales. As distributors create artwork and marketing materials, they will regularly check these requirements to ensure they're in compliance; any deviation could result in an expensive recall of materials or potential defamation lawsuit.

Lab Access Letter—A lab access letter is a legally binding authorization (usually formatted as a letter, hence the name) whereby the producer or rights holder grants a distributor permission to access master materials related to a specific project. The idea here is that a distributor can directly request a specific file or element to be created by the lab rather than coordinating the work through the producer. The letter usually states the distributor will be financially responsible for all requests, leaving the producer held harmless should the distributor default on their payments.

MPAA Rating Certificate—Higher-end feature films (especially those with wide theatrical releases) are usually required to obtain a rating certificate from the Motion Picture Association of America (MPAA). Smaller features—ones with more limited releases—are generally not required to obtain a rating.

Residuals Setup Agreement—Members of unions or guilds (e.g., SAG/AFTRA) are generally entitled to residual payments for their performances within a media property. In the case of SAG/AFTRA, a producer must accurately assemble a residuals cast list during production; any failure or omission can cause a series of headaches which can lead to payroll issues, audits or misallocations. To avoid any unnecessary claims or inquiries from such affiliations, distribution companies require proof all residual obligations have been properly filed and accounted for.

E&O Insurance Certificate—An Errors and Omissions policy is a specialized type of insurance used to protect a producer or rights holder from third-party claims made against the media property. Specifically, E&O Insurance protects against scenarios such as infringement, defamation, plagiarism, unjust competition due to preexisting trademarks, copyrights or slogans and any breach of contract whereby use within the media property extended beyond agreed parameters (such as using music cleared for use as background only for the opening credits).

Appendix V
Projections Form and Schedule of Minimums

Prior to acquiring or green-lighting a media property, distribution companies will first evaluate its revenue potential. The most common way to compile this data is by having sales executives project realistic financial values—on a territory-by-territory basis—sourced from their experience and knowledge in those regions. The sum total allows acquisitions executives and financial teams to evaluate a given media property's likely margin of profit versus its potential for risk.

When acquiring media content, acquisitions executives must occasionally agree to 'minimum' values for major territories (meaning if the media property were to be formally acquired, distribution agreements below the 'minimum' would require special approvals from the producers or rights holders).

On paper, the document outlining a media property's projections versus a document listing its minimums look quite similar. As with other agreements, forms and documents, the look of these can vary from one distribution company to the next.

What follows are three samples: (i) a projections form for long-form media properties (e.g., feature films or one-off documentaries), (ii) a projections form for serialized content (e.g., television series) and (iii) a generalized schedule of minimums.

For simplicity—and to gain a better understanding for how this information is evaluated—we'll use the same format for all three examples (and will keep the values for each territory similar).

One note is that pricing is based on the duration of a single program, meaning a price associated with a feature film will define the value associated with the entire film, whereas the price associated with a television or new media series will be on a 'per-episode' basis and will need to be multiplied across the total number of episodes.

It's also important to understand that these numbers are generalizations and that prices vary greatly from one project to the next; my hope here is to allow readers to understand how such documents work (and how prices vary by percentage from one territory to the next). So don't get fixated that all movies or every TV series is priced at these levels; use this to see how different values range.

* * *

Exhibit I: Projects of Long-Form Media Properties

Projections of longer-form media properties (e.g., feature films) are generally used for internal evaluations only. Unlike documents that will be seen by a producer or rights holders—where a number is usually applied to every territory (even ones unlikely to sell)—a projections form offers one realistic value for each *sellable* territory which provides an overall real-world snapshot of a property's likely revenue potential. If a territory is considered non-sellable (or very unlikely to sell), no value is placed, effectively signifying zero revenue is anticipated.

One thing that can be complicated during the 'projecting' process is that it uses total numbers—meaning that if a sales executive anticipates a sale of 'TV rights' for USD $25,000 and an SVOD deal for USD $15,000, the figure might be listed as a 'total' of USD $40,000. This can occasionally cause contention in scenarios where producers insist on certain threshold minimums before a deal can close or question why a distributor is 'under-selling' a title (when the reality is the sales team is closing at fair market value for the select rights associated).

The subsequent example of a 'feature film' projection would therefore showcase an expectation of receiving a grand total of USD $25,000 from Belgium while highlighting that the territories of Spain and Greece would be unlikely to garner meaningful deals (doesn't mean they won't sell, just not at a level that a distributor should expect with any meaningful level of likelihood).

EUROPE	Value
Belgium (Benelux)	$25,000.00
France	$100,000.00
Germany	$150,000.00
Greece	—
Italy	$100,000.00
Portugal	—
Spain	—
United Kingdom	$100,000.00
Total Europe	**$475,000.00**

EASTERN EUROPE	Value
Bosnia/Herzegovina/Macedonia	—
Croatia	—
Czech Republic/Slovakia	$25,000.00
Estonia	—
Hungary	$15,000.00
Latvia	$10,000.00
Lithuania	—
Poland	$35,000.00
Serbia/Montenegro	—
Romania	—
Slovenia	—
Total Eastern Europe	**$85,000.00**

FAR EAST	*Value*
China	—
Hong Kong	$10,000.00
India	—
Indonesia	—
Japan	$45,000.00
Malaysia	—
Pakistan	—
Philippines	—
Singapore	—
South Korea	$25,000.00
Taiwan, Province of China	—
Thailand	—
Total Far East	**$80,000.00**

LATIN AMERICA	Value
Argentina	—
Bolivia	—
Brazil	$25,000.00
Chile	$10,000.00
Columbia	—
Costa Rica	—
Dominican Republic	—
Ecuador	—
El Salvador	—
Honduras	—
Mexico	$25,000.00
Peru	—
Venezuela	—
Total Latin America	**$60,000.00**

AUSTRALASIA	Value
Australia	$25,000.00
New Zealand	$15,000.00
Total Australasia	**$40,000.00**

SCANDINAVIA	Value
Denmark	$15,000.00
Finland	$20,000.00
Iceland	$10,000.00
Norway	$15,000.00
Sweden	$15,000.00
Total Scandinavia	**$75,000.00**

MIDDLE EAST	Value
Middle East (incl. North Africa)	$15,000.00
Israel	$15,000.00
Turkey	—
United Arab Emirates	$10,000.00
Total Middle East	**$40,000.00**

RUSSIA	Value
Russian Federation	—
Total Russia	**—**

AFRICA	Value
Africa	$5,000.00
South Africa	$5,000.00
Total Africa	*$10,000.00*

NORTH AMERICA	Value
U.S. and Canada	$225,000.00
Total North America	*$225,000.00*
GRAND TOTAL	*$1,090,000*

* * *

Exhibit II: Projections of Short-Form Content

Television or other serialized content is often projected across multiple rights windows (e.g., TV rights versus VOD rights) and will usually include a first-cycle-versus-renewal period. Unlike longer-form content, where the first window represents its strongest level of value, serialized content can hold a strong shelf life, meaning it can retain financial value over a longer duration of time. Also note that each value represents one single episode of a series (which will need to be multiplied by the total number of episodes on a 'per-season' or 'per-series' basis).

The below would likely reflect a TV series whereby its initial TV broadcast would hold the most value. With a 'TV First' model, a VOD release can still take place, but a traditional broadcast network would be the ideal. As an example, a major scripted Norwegian series might transmit on Norway's NRK1 channel first (as a traditional broadcast) but might be a Hulu premiere in the US with no broadcast network taking on rights; some territories are likely to see traction in both TV and VOD, whereas others only apply anticipated value in one category. The 'renewals' values apply after the first TV and/or VOD window is exploited in full.

EUROPE	First-Run TV	First-Run VOD	Renewals
Belgium (Benelux)	$ 5,000.00	$—	$—
France	$—	$ 30,000.00	$ 15,000.00
Germany	$ 45,000.00	$ 15,000.00	$ 20,000.00
Greece	$—	$—	$—
Italy	$ 15,000.00	$—	$—
Portugal	$—	$—	$—
Spain	$—	$ 15,000.00	$—
United Kingdom	$ 35,000.00	$ 10,000.00	$ 20,000.00
Total Europe	*$ 100,000.00*	*$ 70,000.00*	*$ 55,000.00*

EASTERN EUROPE	First Run TV	First Run VOD	Renewals
Bosnia/Herzegovina/ Macedonia	$—	$—	$—
Croatia	$—	$—	$—
Czech Republic/ Slovakia	$—	$—	$—
Estonia	$—	$—	$—

EASTERN EUROPE	First Run TV	First Run VOD	Renewals
Hungary	$ 3,000.00	$—	$—
Latvia	$ 1,500.00	$—	$—
Lithuania	$ 1,000.00	$—	$—
Poland	$ 5,000.00	$—	$ 2,500.00
Serbia/Montenegro	$—	$—	$—
Romania	$—	$—	$—
Slovenia	$—	$—	$—
Total Eastern Europe	**$ 10,500.00**	**$ -**	**$ 2,500.00**

FAR EAST	First Run TV	First Run VOD	Renewals
China	$—	$ 500.00	$—
Hong Kong	$ 2,500.00	$—	$ 1,000.00
India	$—	$—	$—
Indonesia	$—	$—	$—
Japan	$—	$—	$—
Malaysia	$—	$—	$—
Pakistan	$—	$—	$—
Philippines	$—	$—	$—
Singapore	$ 2,000.00	$ 500.00	$—
South Korea	$ 5,000.00	$ 2,500.00	$—
Taiwan, Province of China	$—	$—	$—
Thailand	$—	$ 500.00	$ 250.00
Total Far East	**$ 9,500.00**	**$ 4,000.00**	**$ 1,250.00**

LATIN AMERICA	First Run TV	First Run VOD	Renewals
Argentina	$ 3,000.00	$—	$—
Bolivia	$—	$—	$—
Brazil	$ 3,000.00	$ 1,000.00	$ 2,000.00
Chile	$—	$—	$—
Columbia	$ 2,500.00	$—	$ 1,500.00
Costa Rica	$—	$—	$—
Dominican Republic	$—	$—	$—
Ecuador	$—	$—	$—
El Salvador	$ 500.00	$—	$—
Honduras	$ 500.00	$—	$—
Mexico	$ 25,000.00	$ 5,000.00	$ 10,000.00
Peru	$ 500.00	$—	$ 250.00
Venezuela	$—	$—	$—
Total Latin America	**$ 35,000.00**	**$ 6,000.00**	**$ 13,750.00**

AUSTRALASIA	First Run TV	First Run VOD	Renewals
Australia	$ 10,000.00	$ 5,000.00	$ 5,000.00
New Zealand	$ 5,000.00	$—	$ 2,500.00
Total Australasia	**$ 15,000.00**	**$ 5,000.00**	**$ 7,500.00**

SCANDINAVIA	First Run TV	First Run VOD	Renewals
Denmark	$ 2,000.00	$ 5,000.00	$—
Finland	$ 2,000.00	$ 5,000.00	$—
Iceland	$—	$ 1,000.00	$—
Norway	$ 2,000.00	$ 5,000.00	$—
Sweden	$ 2,000.00	$ 5,000.00	$—
Total Scandinavia	**$ 8,000.00**	**$ 21,000.00**	**$ -**

MIDDLE EAST	First Run TV	First Run VOD	Renewals
Middle East (incl. North Africa)	$ 4,000.00	$—	$ 800.00

MIDDLE EAST	First Run TV	First Run VOD	Renewals
Israel	$—	$ 4,000.00	$ 1,000.00
Turkey	$—	$—	$—
United Arab Emirates	$—	$—	$—
Total Middle East	**$ 4,000.00**	**$ 4,000.00**	**$ 1,800.00**

RUSSIA	First Run TV	First Run VOD	Renewals
Russian Federation	$—	$—	$—
Total Russia	**$ —**	**$ —**	**$ —**

AFRICA	First Run TV	First Run VOD	Renewals
Africa	$—	$—	$—
South Africa	$—	$—	$—
Total Africa	**$ —**	**$ —**	**$ —**

NORTH AMERICA	First Run TV	First Run VOD	Renewals
U.S. and Canada	$ 75,000.00	$ 75,000.00	$ 35,000.00
Total North America	**$ 75,000.00**	**$ 75,000.00**	**$ 35,000.00**
GRAND TOTAL	**$257,000**	**$185,000**	**$116,800**

* * *

Exhibit III: Schedule of Minimums

Unlike internal 'projection' forms—which are primarily used for internal financial evaluation of media properties—a 'Schedule of Minimums' is meant for the eyes of third parties (namely the film's producer or rights holder). Occasionally, these are sent to producers or rights holders during the negotiation process but then can also be included in the media property's acquisition agreement.

The prices below could indicate either a lower budget feature film or the value of a single episode of a non-premium level (lower-budgeted) television series. The important note here is that a number is generally applied to every territory—even the ones distributors know are very unlikely to sell. Also note that there is usually an 'asking' price and a minimum number a distributor can 'accept' (sometimes referred to as a 'high/low'); this is tricky because the minimum acceptance is really the value a distributor can accept without special permissions (meaning the prices could actually come in lower). The real takeaway is that these are best-guess estimates for the value a title might hold in each territory and should never be taken as a guarantee for real-world revenue expectation.

EUROPE	Minimum Accept	Asking Price
Belgium (Benelux)	$ 10,000.00	$ 25,000.00
France	$ 45,000.00	$ 125,000.00
Germany	$ 45,000.00	$ 150,000.00

EUROPE	Minimum Accept	Asking Price
Greece	$ 10,000.00	$ 25,000.00
Italy	$ 25,000.00	$ 100,000.00
Portugal	$ 10,000.00	$ 25,000.00
Spain	$ 30,000.00	$ 100,000.00
United Kingdom	$ 45,000.00	$ 100,000.00
Total Europe	**$ 220,000.00**	**$ 650,000.00**

EASTERN EUROPE	Minimum Accept	Asking Price
Bosnia/Herzegovina/Macedonia	$ 5,000.00	$ 15,000.00
Croatia	$ 5,000.00	$ 15,000.00
Czech Republic/Slovakia	$ 10,000.00	$ 25,000.00
Estonia	$ 3,500.00	$ 10,000.00
Hungary	$ 5,000.00	$ 15,000.00
Latvia	$ 3,500.00	$ 10,000.00
Lithuania	$ 3,500.00	$ 10,000.00
Poland	$ 15,000.00	$ 35,000.00
Serbia/Montenegro	$ 3,500.00	$ 10,000.00
Romania	$ 5,000.00	$ 15,000.00
Slovenia	$ 3,500.00	$ 10,000.00
Total Eastern Europe	**$ 62,500.00**	**$ 170,000.00**

FAR EAST	Minimum Accept	Asking Price
China	$ 5,000.00	$ 25,000.00
Hong Kong	$ 2,500.00	$ 10,000.00
India	$ 4,000.00	$ 15,000.00
Indonesia	$ 3,000.00	$ 10,000.00
Japan	$ 15,000.00	$ 45,000.00
Malaysia	$ 2,500.00	$ 10,000.00
Pakistan	$ 1,000.00	$ 5,000.00
Philippines	$ 1,000.00	$ 5,000.00
Singapore	$ 2,500.00	$ 10,000.00
South Korea	$ 5,000.00	$ 25,000.00
Taiwan, Province of China	$ 1,000.00	$ 5,000.00
Thailand	$ 2,000.00	$ 7,500.00
Total Far East	**$ 44,500.00**	**$ 172,500.00**

LATIN AMERICA	Minimum Accept	Asking Price
Argentina	$ 5,000.00	$ 15,000.00
Bolivia	$ 500.00	$ 5,000.00
Brazil	$ 5,000.00	$ 25,000.00
Chile	$ 5,000.00	$ 25,000.00
Columbia	$ 4,000.00	$ 20,000.00
Costa Rica	$ 500.00	$ 5,000.00
Dominican Republic	$ 500.00	$ 5,000.00
Ecuador	$ 500.00	$ 5,000.00
El Salvador	$ 500.00	$ 5,000.00
Honduras	$ 500.00	$ 5,000.00
Mexico	$ 20,000.00	$ 65,000.00
Peru	$ 1,000.00	$ 7,500.00
Venezuela	$ 1,000.00	$ 7,500.00
Total Latin America	**$ 44,000.00**	**$ 195,000.00**

AUSTRALASIA	Minimum Accept	Asking Price
Australia	$ 10,000.00	$ 25,000.00
New Zealand	$ 5,000.00	$ 15,000.00
Total Australasia	**$ 15,000.00**	**$ 40,000.00**

SCANDINAVIA	Minimum Accept	Asking Price
Denmark	$ 5,000.00	$ 15,000.00
Finland	$ 7,500.00	$ 20,000.00
Iceland	$ 1,000.00	$ 10,000.00
Norway	$ 5,000.00	$ 15,000.00
Sweden	$ 5,000.00	$ 15,000.00
Total Scandinavia	**$ 23,500.00**	**$ 75,000.00**
MIDDLE EAST	*Minimum Accept*	*Asking Price*
Middle East (incl. North Africa)	$ 4,000.00	$ 15,000.00
Israel	$ 4,000.00	$ 15,000.00
Turkey	$ 4,000.00	$ 15,000.00
United Arab Emirates	$ 2,000.00	$ 10,000.00
Total Middle East	**$ 14,000.00**	**$ 55,000.00**
RUSSIA	*Minimum Accept*	*Asking Price*
Russian Federation	$ 5,000.00	$ 25,000.00
Total Russia	**$ 5,000.00**	**$ 25,000.00**
AFRICA	*Minimum Accept*	*Asking Price*
Africa	$ 1,000.00	$ 5,000.00
South Africa	$ 1,000.00	$ 5,000.00
Total Africa	**$ 2,000.00**	**$ 10,000.00**
NORTH AMERICA	*Minimum Accept*	*Asking Price*
U.S. and Canada	$ 75,000.00	$ 225,000.00
Total North America	**$ 75,000.00**	**$ 225,000.00**
GRAND TOTAL	**$505,500**	**$1,617,500**

Appendix VI
Sample Metadata Forms

A metadata file in relation to media distribution is a document providing all of the key points required by a distributor to actively sell a project. Generally delivered in the form of Excel or a Word document, metadata provides vetted language and billing details which can be later copy/pasted by distributors for purposes of marketing, promotion, title clearance or other legal requirements.

At a high level, a metadata document would list the official title of a film or media property—including international titles or 'also-known-as' titles—followed by key crew and cast names (e.g., director, writer, producers, top-bill actors, etc.). A point here is that cast names can occasionally require special handling—that the top three cast members must be listed together in a specific order. The metadata would provide that stipulation.

On the more technical side, a metadata document will include an official synopsis (usually broken into 'short' and 'long' synopsis—with language drafted and approved by the producers), rating information, taglines, key words, or other 'sales' points.

The reason distributors require this documentation is to (i) have crucial identifying components of a media property (titles, names, technical specs, etc.) all grouped together in one location and (ii) to have the easy ability of simply referencing a single document rather than going back to the producer to confirm key details or legal obligations.

The benefit to the producer is that providing metadata ensures all legally binding wording, phrasing and terminology will be accurately reflected to all companies with whom the distributor does business. It's important to note that the exact look and style of metadata request forms can vary from one company to the next, but in general, they're all seeking the same basic information.

What follows are examples of commonplace metadata templates for feature films and television series. Please note that the programs listed are completely fictitious; any similarities to other media properties (already produced or currently in development) is purely coincidental:

Feature Films and 'One-Off' Titles

A feature film is a single program (one-off) with a finite running time, plot and crew. Therefore, all relevant details pertaining to cast, production credits and synopsis information rarely change after a film is completed. Even if sequels, remakes or 'follow-up' episodes are created, they are treated as additional single-run projects.

Although the structure and look of the metadata might adjust from one company to the next, the basic information requested is quite similar across the board. The metadata requirements of a feature film are also the same for any one-off title—meaning the metadata used for movies is essentially the same for one-off TV docs or single-program new media projects.

* * *

Title (including domestic, international and AKAs if applicable)	*The Wretched* (domestic); *Evil Eyes* (international).
Production Company	Industrial Images, LLC
Cast (in billing order)	Megan Willardson; Steven Harting; Kelly McKenzie
Director	Tom Benton
Writer(s)	Jill Davenport
Producers	Produced by: Stacey Miller. Executive Producers: Bob Jacobs, James Coolidge and Stephanie Sampson
Short Synopsis (275 characters maximum including spaces)	Emily's (Megan Willardson) life takes a turn for the worst when she hires a new live-in nanny (Kelly McKenzie) to care for her infant son. Her world soon crumbles when her nanny enters into an affair with her husband and slowly begins to replace Emily as the new woman of the house.
Tagline	It's hard to find good help these days.
Key Words	affair, murder, nanny, houseguest, seduce, havoc, killer, babysitter, revenge, woman in peril
Genre	Thriller
Run time (TRT)	88 min
MPAA Rating	R
TV Rating	TV-MA
Year	2024
Copyright (year and owner)	2024 by Industrial Images, LLC
Country of Origin	United States of America
Original Language	English
CC Files	Yes
Descriptive Audio	Yes
Audio	5.1
Specs	1920x1080
Production Company Contact Information	Rich Levinson, 11400 Olympic Park Drive, Suite 204, Beverly Hills, CA 90210. Phone: 310-609-4257

* * *

One difference not noted in the earlier example is that some companies request several different 'synopsis' variations—that's to say, they might request a 'long', 'medium' and 'short' (ranging from 1,000 characters for the 'long' synopsis down to less than 250 characters for the 'short'). The reason for this is that some consumer-facing platforms require longer synopsis while others want it short; a distributor would rather be ready with pre-vetted text than go through the hassle of coordinating language approvals.

Another unique point is that one-off titles now generally require a TV rating in the US. Traditionally, an MPAA rating was more than enough for a feature film, but as VOD platforms become a more commonplace home for media entertainment (and fewer indie titles are required to obtain an official MPAA rating due to a lack in theatrical release neccesisty), the TV rating—or the assumed TV rating even if the title has not been formally rated—has become a wider used barameter for content suitability.

Television and New Media Series

In contrast to a feature film or one-off program, television or new media series contain multiple episodes—each with a different episodic title and running time—while carrying an overarching 'series' title. Additionally, TV and new media series can also have separate seasons which must be appropriatly identified. And while the overarching series synopsis stays the same, the metadata associated with TV or new media series content must offer a short synopsis for each season and individual episode.

The other component with a series is that the cast might retain the same billing from one season to the next, yet each episode can have a different director and writer (while each season can include or remove producing talent). Although it might seem trivial, the exact running time is required (even if the difference between one episode to the next is only a few seconds); to digital platforms and TV stations, each second is critical. And unlike a film or 'one-off' that carries a single premiere date, each episode of a series has a its own broadcast date.

* * *

	1	2	4	5
Series Title	Night Owls	Night Owls	Night Owls	Night Owls
Episode Title	"Nobody's Perfect"	"Late Again"	"Back to the Beginning"	"Call Back"
Run Time	24:19	23:57	24:08	24:02
Genre	Comedy	Comedy	Comedy	Comedy
Production Company	Caterpiller Prods.	Caterpiller Prods.	Caterpiller Prods.	Caterpiller Prods.
Season	1	1	2	2

	1	*2*	*4*	*5*
Series Synopsis	Three 20-somethings develop an odd friendship while working the night shift at a local grocery store.	Three 20-somethings develop an odd friendship while working the night shift at a local grocery store.	Three 20-somethings develop an odd friendship while working the night shift at a local grocery store.	Three 20-somethings develop an odd friendship while working the night shift at a local grocery store.
Episode Synopsis	Tom decides to be vegan, while Jane and Susan get cleaning detail.	When Jane arrives late, Susan and Tom take revenge for the excess workload.	Jane suffers a massive hangover after Tom Proposes to his girlfriend.	Susan gets caught shoplifting, and Jane tries to cover for her.
Cast	Carol Sandusky, Brent Baum, Tanner O'Shance	Carol Sandusky, Brent Baum, Tanner O'Shance	Carol Sandusky, Brent Baum, Tanner O'Shance	Carol Sandusky, Brent Baum, Tanner O'Shance
Director	Jason Wentworth	Andrew Powels	Andrew Powels	Ellie Sinclaire
Writer(s)	Kristin Berg	Yasmin Morgallis	Kristin Berg	Kristin Berg
Producer(s)	Daniel Scheffield, Liz McGowski	Daniel Scheffield, Liz McGowski	Nathan Worthington, Daniel Scheffield, Liz McGowski	Nathan Worthington, Daniel Scheffield, Liz McGowski
Tagline	Your mid-20s never made less sense	Your mid-20s never made less sense	Your mid-20s never made less sense	Your mid-20s never made less sense
Key Words	stoner, postgraduate, millenial, love triangle, quarterlife crisis, crap job	stoner, postgraduate, millenial, love triangle, quarterlife crisis, crap job	stoner, postgraduate, millenial, love triangle, quarterlife crisis, crap job	stoner, postgraduate, millenial, love triangle, quarterlife crisis, crap job
TV Rating	TV-14	TV-14	TV-14	TV-14
Broadcaster	DTV	DTV	DTV	DTV
Broadcast Date	10/10/23	10/17/23	3/13/24	3/20/24
Copyright (year and owner)	Caterpiller Prods. 2023	Caterpiller Prods. 2023	Caterpiller Prods. 2024	Caterpiller Prods. 2024
Country of Origin	USA	USA	USA	USA
Original Language	English	English	English	English
Audio	5.1	5.1	5.1	5.1
CC Files	Yes	Yes	Yes	Yes
Descriptive Audio	No	No	Yes	Yes
Specs	2K	2K	4K	4K

* * *

Across the board, even though many aspects of a series remain consistent through-out its life, each season—and new episode—requires a few alterations regarding legal documentation and consumer-facing presentation (e.g., copyright notices, key cast and crew, as well as episodic titles and synopses). Therefore, although it might seem tedious to duplicate a vast majority of the information, metadata related to any form of series must treat each individual *episode* as if it were a signle one-off feature. To see how series related metadata is used in the real world, check out a long-running series on a digital platform—for example, Roku, Tubi, Pluto, Freevee. By clicking through all the episodes of each season, you'll quickly see how much organized detail is required and why a well-crafted metadata can make one program pop while leaving another to blur in with the competition.

Glossary

Advance   Monies paid in advance of profits generated from revenue share or royalty distributions. See also 'Minimum Guarantee'.

Agent   Offers a service of talent or intellectual property (IP) representation in exchange for a percentage based fee. Agents broker deals between the talent and producers or production companies for either commissioning their services to contribute to the project or negotiating the acquisition of their intellectual property. See also "Manager".

Arbitration   A much more muted type of legal proceeding, arbitration is the process where two parties with a disagreement formally seek out a pre-vetted (and licensed) arbitrator to hear out both sides of their argument, granting them the authority to make a formal (and final) decision siding with one party over the other.

Attachments   Actors, director(s), or other 'elements' (i.e., composers, political organizations, etc.) who legally commit themselves to work on a project prior to, or during the process of, funding. This process is called "packaging" and is used to increase the value of a script (or property) in order to presell and/or raise funds for productions, therefore increasing the potential for a 'green light'.

Back-Door Pilot   A gimmick used to introduce a new series or concept by making the 'series premiere' or 'pilot' feature-length, therefore making it capable of existing as a stand-alone TV movie if that pilot never transitions into a full-fledged series.

Bible (or Series Bible)   A massive document, similar to a business plan or proposal, used to present the complete breakdown of a scripted serialized program; these generally flesh out all details regarding character, location, theme, concept, and tone. Most include at least the first season's full episode slate (with a detailed synopsis for each episode); many offer clear direction where the series will lead in future seasons. The Bible is the 'filter' which keeps all associated parties (i.e., showrunners, writers and producers) on target.

Blackout Period   A temporary period whereby a distributor must restrict or block third parties from exploiting specific rights to satisfy an acquiring company's licensing agreement. A 'blackout period' generally only applies to content already exploited within the marketplace (not to first-exhibition windows).

Bonus   Describes the monies payable to an individual or entity for achieving a specific goal or target in relation to a media property (e.g., raising a certain threshold of the budget, achieving a minimum level of sales or owning the rights to a series commissioned for a second season).

Box Office   Refers to the volume of revenue generated from ticket sales during a theatrical exhibition.

Broadcast Date   The date of first transmission or 'broadcast' of a media property in a select territory by means of television signal (regardless whether signal is via Internet Protocol (IPTV), terrestrial, digital or analog). This term encompasses all forms of television rights   for example, premium, basic cable or Free TV.

Budget   The 'cost' of a media production; the budget can be heavily inflated (or deflated) depending on who's asking (and who's telling).

Cap   Describes the ceiling or maximum amount of money a party is allowed to spend and later recoup against. Generally applies to marketing or material-related costs.

Catalog   Describes a distribution company's entire library of sellable media properties. Can be presented in the form of a physical (or printed) catalog or an online or digital catalog. Older titles are often described as 'back catalog'.

Churn   See 'Subscription Fall-Off'.

Closed Captions   Unlike subtitles   which are used to translate a media property for a foreign-speaking audience   closed captions are text files that match the verbal text being spoken; their purpose is to assist audiences that are hard of hearing. The United States requires closed-caption files for all televised exploitation; most territories do not require these.

Closed-Ended Series   Describes television or new media content whereby no further seasons or episodes will be created (e.g., a mini-series where the story concludes after a specific number of episodes). For contrast, see 'Open-Ended Series'.

Commissions   Describes fees payable to individuals or entities for brokering, orchestrating or aiding in the finalization of a media deal. Also describes the action of a network or entity pre-buying the rights to a media property (agreeing to fund a major portion of the budget).

Completion Bond   A financial instrument whereby a bank or financial institution agrees to cover unforeseen overages   should they occur   so a media property can reach completion (therefore guaranteeing it to become exploitable).

Cross-Collateralization   A financial designation applied to a collection of titles, allowing for the sum total of all revenues from the package of titles to trigger specific financial benchmarks. Primarily, this is used to protect a buying party from having to pay heavy revenue shares or royalties against a single title that's performing when the other titles in a package deal are still struggling.

Crossover Film   A feature film that 'crosses' from its anticipated audience to gain appeal   and revenue   from an unexpected audience.

Day-and-Date   Describes the distribution strategy of simultaneously releasing a media property across multiple rights categories (e.g., theatrical, TVOD/EST, television) on the same date.

Delivery Schedule   A list of material elements required by an acquiring company for formal exploitation of a media property; includes both video assets as well as legal documentation. (See 'Appendix II' for more information.)

Development Hell   A joking expression used to describe the (sometimes endless) process of getting a script or property of interest from initial acquisition to green light. Sometimes these projects are constantly re-revised during their 'development' periods in order to satisfy different investors; other times the company keeps the script 'as is' but must take a long period of time in order to secure proper funding for the film's eventual production. Some projects never get out of development hell; others seemingly float through very easily.

Direct to (blank)   A phrase used to describe an independent film or production specifically designed *not* to exhibit in theaters. Films or productions can be produced as 'Direct to Video', 'Direct to TV' and now 'Direct to VOD'. These are targeted, middle-zone productions, generally with limited budgets and heavy on genre appeal.

Distribution Fee   The percentage of monies taken from a media property's sales revenue that serve as the distribution company's fee   or commission   for brokering or orchestrating a deal.

Driver   A high-level film or project (either completed or in development) that gives a seller or distributor leverage to place additional titles (usually of lesser quality) into the package.

Domestic– The word used to describe the 'territory' (or geographic marketplace) of the United States of America and *English-speaking* Canada (also called 'North America'). In the film industry, anything outside of this definition would refer to the 'international' marketplace (even French-Speaking Canada or Mexico). However, 'domestic rights' can just as easily refer to the home territory of a given programs country of origin (e.g., Norway for a Norwegian-produced series or Japan for a Japanese-produced film); this term is often tossed around and should be clarified to its meaning on a given property before any assumptions are made. For more information, see also "International" and "Territory" below.

Dubbing   The process of replacing an actor's voice speaking a native language with that of a foreign actor's voice speaking a foreign language for the purpose of adapting a media property to a foreign-speaking market.

Elements   See 'Attachments'.

Episodic   The word used in contracts to classify a program as multiple 'episodes' in total duration, as opposed to a single one-off feature film. The exact running time of each 'episode' differs on genre and platform (from 90-minute episodes in a long-running 'episodic' mini-series, 42-minute episodes for a dramatic series with ad breaks, down to five- to ten-minute episodes for an online web series). The total number of episodes will also depend on genre, platform and longevity. (Compare to 'Feature'.)

Expiration Date (aka Sunset Date)   Describes the last calendar date a licensee may exploit a media property's rights before they revert back to the distributor (or transfer to a third party).

Feature   The word used in contracts to classify the length of a film or program as a one-off production that is traditional 'movie length'. The exact running time of a 'feature' differs on genre (and on whom you ask), so the word 'feature' is often used to simply indicate what is perceived to be 'movie length'. For decades, a feature was described as a film comprised of seven reels or more (or an approximate minimum of 61 minutes); today, a running time under 80 minutes is generally deemed too short. (Compare to 'Episodic'.)

First-Look Deal   An arrangement whereby a distributor agrees to pitch or present all new media properties exclusively to a single acquiring company prior to presenting them to any competing third party.

Flat Fee   A payment made whereby no future revenues are required; even if a film or media property becomes extraordinarily successful, a 'flat' payment concludes the required payments an acquiring company owes a distributing company.

Force Majeure   A phrase found in agreements describing scenarios out of the control of individuals (e.g., acts of war, natural disasters, etc.) that indemnify either party if such events directly cause a breach or break of any contractual obligation.

Format   A rights category describing the distribution or acquisition of a media property's structure. Allows a branded and replicable series to be created for local markets (e.g., adapting *The Voice of Holland* into the US series *The Voice* as well as *The Voice France* and *The Voice Arabia*).

Four-Walling   Describes self-booking theatrical exhibitions of a media property; often associated with DIY media distribution.

Green-light   The coined phrase signifying the official moment when the party controlling necessary financial resources agrees to produce (invest in) a project guaranteeing its move toward production. 'When' a project receives a green light can vary wildly   projects can be green-lit with or without a completed script, a locked cast, or even an attached production crew.

Gross Points (or 'Gross Royalties')   A 'point' is equal to 1%; gross refers to all monies (in total) earned *before* expenses or outside costs are incurred against that figure. Therefore, a single gross point is 1% of all monies earned, which is a far contrast from the commonly distributed 'Net Point' (see later).

High-Concept   An overly thrown-around phrase that essentially describes a film or TV concept that is extremely straightforward and easy to describe (does not mean 'big budget'; it means within a few words of pitching, your audience can grasp a very clear understanding of your project).

Holdback   A period of time whereby specific rights are restricted from exploitation to allow a licensing company an unimpeded exhibition window.

Hook   The unique   and often simple   aspect of a story that makes it stand apart from its competition.

Independent   Refers to any company or film production that exists outside of the major studios. Can range from tiny micro-budget operations to major Hollywood entities.

International– The word used to describe any country or region outside a media property's native country of origin. Divisions between 'domestic' markets and 'international' markets are vital in the presales process, which has major influence on which projects receive a green light. For more information, see also "Domestic" and "Territory".

Letter of Intent (LOI)– A formal means for one entity to express a (generally) legally binding 'interest' in working with another party. An LOI essentially functions as a 'proof of commitment' in moving forward with a formal agreement *if* all the elements required to enforce a functional deal come together. Example: to presell a movie, a distributor might 'secure' a name actor with a letter of intent; if the distributor moves forward with the production, that actor will be required to take on their agreed to role; however, if the pieces don't come together and no film is green-lit, the actor is not required to perform (and the distributor is not required to pay them).

License Fee   A fixed financial value paid to obtain the rights of intellectual property.

Licensee   Describes an entity acquiring the rights to a media property from its rights holder (aka its 'licensor'). (See 'Licensor'.)

Licensor   Describes an entity owning the rights to a media property. The licensor will license or assign the rights of a media property to an acquiring party (see 'Licensee').

Logline   A short descriptive sentence (less than 100 words); it quickly summarizes a story's concept while clearly defining its genre type and overall 'hook'.

Minimum Guarantee (MG)   An agreed minimum amount of money paid by a licensing party to acquire the exhibition rights in a media property. MGs can be paid in a variety of ways, either as one payment upon signature or over several payments spanning a pre-agreed duration of time. MGs are considered a recoupable sum, meaning the licensing party owes no further monies or financial statements until they have recouped their financial investment. See also 'Advance'.

Music and Effects Tracks (M&E)   Two audio tracks designated to house all of a projects fully mixed music and fully mixed sound effects; if listening only to these two tracks, one would experience a film normally yet hear no words from the actors   only seeing moving lips. This allows international buyers to only have to record foreign-speaking actors' voices rather than completely remix the film.

Net Points (or Net Royalties)   A 'point' is equal to 1%; net refers to the monies left over after all other parties owed money (and after all expenses incurred) have been paid out or recouped   essentially all the 'leftover' cash. Therefore, a single net point is 1% of all the left over money, which is a fraction of a 'gross point'.

Non-Union   Refers to a production or a potential project that is being produced independent of any unions. Some unions, such as the Writers Guild of America (WGA), do not permit their members from working on non-union projects; other unions are more flexible.

One-off   A term used to describe a television program or new media property that is shorter than feature-length running time and has no additional episodes.

One-Sheet   A small 'sales' sheet, generally an 8 1/2" × 11" or A4-sized mini poster, that is handed to clients to provide insight to the cast, genre and budget level of a film. It would appear almost as DVD cover art (front and back), only on a sheet of paper for easy filing and reference.

Open-Ended Series   Describes a television or new media series that allows for additional episodes or seasons to be created. For contrast, see 'Closed-Ended Series'.

Option (or Option Purchase)   An 'option' is when all rights to a script or piece of intellectual property (IP) are leased by a producer, generally for an up-front fee and for a period between six to 18 months. During this 'option period' the producer will pitch the film to investors or attempt to package the script in order to get a green light from a production company. If the project is green-lit and the film is produced, the rights owner will generally receive a production bonus   pre-negotiated in the initial option agreement. If the script is not green-lit, upon expiration of the option period, all rights will revert back to the rights owner.

Output Deal   An agreement between two parties whereby one entity agrees to take on all (or a confirmed minimum number) of produced media content for a pre-negotiated price.

Packaging   The process of making a script a more attractive property by "attaching" actors, directors or other elements who contractually commit themselves to work on the project if it were to be funded or receives a green light. (See 'Attachments'.) Can also refer to the process of adding more titles to a distribution agreement in order to increase its overall license fee.

Pitch   The presentation of a script or media property's story; can be verbalized or written (as in a 'pitch' email), but it's generally a short, concise explanation identifying genre type and concept.

Pilot   A fully produced 'sample' episode of a proposed TV or new media series, generally made as a 'one-off' example to present to studio executives or international clients to gauge interest. If the series receives a green light, the pilot generally broadcasts as the first episode. See also, "Back-Door Pilot".

Preempting   Refers to the ability of a select client or territory to preemptively release, broadcast or otherwise 'make available' a property ahead of another party (i.e., transactional platforms like iTunes or Amazon can occasionally offer titles *before* they broadcast on television, effectively 'preempting' the premiere).

Presale   A sale of a media property's distribution rights *before* it is completed.

Premiere   Describes the first commercial exhibition of a media property within a territory regardless of the rights category.

Procedural   Describes a television or new media series where each episode 'stands alone' and requires no previous information from earlier episodes or seasons to follow along.

Purchase (or a Preemptive Purchase)   When a producer or production company purchases all rights to a script in advance of packaging or financing. Though rarely done, the purchase is generally a one-time lump-sum payment, and the writer revokes all right to the script into perpetuity. Studios and large media companies sometimes employ this technique to weed out potential competition.

Quality Control (QC)   The process of reviewing material video assets in accordance to minimum marketplace standards of technical specifications.

Ready-mades   Describes the original media content that has been adapted into a regional version (generally by means of a 'format' deal). In example, the Showtime series *Shameless* is an adaptation of the UK Channel 4 series of the same name; the original UK version would be considered the 'ready-made' *Shameless*.

Renewal   The re-licensing of a media property by a company that had previously acquired the rights (e.g., a company acquires TV rights to a feature film for a two-year window; at the expiration of the two years, they 'renew' the feature for a second two-year term because it was successful.)

Revenue Share   A deal structure whereby monies are split between the licensor and licensee (often in lieu of a minimum guarantee or advance). The rights holder will often receive a majority share (anything above 50%).

Rollout Release   Describes the process of releasing a media property in small waves across a single-rights category (e.g., focusing on a small portion of theaters before expanding to add more screens, or targeting a handful of TVOD platforms before including additional ones).

Running Time or Total Running Time (TRT)   The total duration of time required to screen a media property in full, inclusive of all company logos and credits. TRTs are generally listed in metadata forms as a simple number (e.g., "95 minutes") but are occasionally specified as hours and minutes (HH:MM); hours, minutes and seconds (HH:MM:SS); and, occasionally, hours, minutes, seconds and frames (HH:MM:SS;FF). Distribution contracts and/or production services agreements will specify exact TRT requirements (or provide a 'no-shorter-than' or 'no-longer-than' framework).

Schlock   Extremely low-quality product, generally ultra-low-budget films with very poor image and sound quality (sometimes purposefully, other times due to a filmmaker's lack of resources).

Screener   A noncommercial copy of a completed (or near-finished) media property, intended only for the purposes of a professional to evaluate. Screeners can be handed out as physical DVDs (with a 'burn-in' on screen to prevent piracy) or as online screening links (with password protection).

Screening(s)   Scheduled premiere or private exhibition of a finished (or near-finished) media property, primarily for business-to-business purposes.

Season Pass   An option available on most transactional digital platforms, where a consumer can opt to purchase a full season of a select series' episodes   at a reduced rate   in lieu of purchasing higher-priced episodes individually.

Showrunner   The true king of the serialized content or television world, a showrunner outranks even the director! Part executive producer, story doctor, and visionary, the showrunner is a jack-of-all-trades that is generally waist-deep in a series' writing process, its scheduling and its overall conceptual flow.

Sleeper Hit   A media property, expected to be small and forgettable, surpassing all expectations by ballooning into an unexpected hit.

Spec Script   A screenplay   either for feature-length content or episodic content   which is voluntarily written without any up-front payment, client request or contractual obligation. A writer conceives of an original idea and writes a script from scratch with the hope of selling it later, upon completion. (A writer may also voluntarily acquire the rights to a story or book and write an Adapted Screenplay on Spec based upon that material.)

Street Date   The date a media property is released in its 'home entertainment' window (refers to the date physical versions   such as DVDs   were available on store shelves but today includes TVOD/EST releases).

Subtitling   The process of adding synced text on screen to translate the verbal foreign language spoken within a media property.

Subscription Falloff   The phenomenon of SVOD customers signing up for a service, keeping their subscription active for a period of a few months (generally to watch only one or two popular programs) and then cancelling their subscription, shifting to a competing service. Referred to as 'churn', this process makes it difficult for SVOD services   like Netflix and HBO   to predict future subscriber numbers, which can affect stock prices.

Talent   A generalized industry term describing creative performers (includes on-screen actors and performers, but also behind-the-scenes talents such as writers or directors).

Territory   "Territory" is a distribution term, used to describe a country (or often a group of countries) that are commonly accepted to represent a geographical region where the rights to a film can be licensed. On one hand, the individual nations of Poland or Japan represent a 'territory', but so does the Middle East, which is made up of over 20 individual countries. For more information, see also 'Domestic' and 'International'.

Through line   Describes the overarching storyline or plot carried across several episodes of serialized content; generally focuses on how a series will reach a resolution.

Trades   A slang word used to describe various publications and websites focused on relaying media news (e.g., *Variety*, *Hollywood Reporter*, Deadline, C21, Worldscreen, Prensario, etc.)

Treatment   An outline of a story concept (ranging from a few pages to dozens, lacking any dialogue) that is used by a writer to present his/her ideas to a production team.

Turnaround   The process after a script is purchased, where the writer attempts to reacquire (purchase back) the rights previously signed away. Also a production term whereby the crew has exhausted all potential shots aimed at one side of the set and must relocate all lighting, camera and sound equipment to begin filming shots aimed at the other side of the set.

Wide Release   Describes the distribution strategy of exhibiting a media property in multiple theaters across all major markets   potentially across multiple countries   on the same date. (For contrast see 'Rollout Release'.)

Windowing   The strategy used by distributors to maximize the profit margin of a media property by carefully orchestrating the time allowance a title must be exploited within a specific rights category before it can transition to a lower price point. In example, a major SVOD entity will pay a larger license fee than a niche AVOD company; the distributor would enter into deals for both rights but would strategically 'window' the agreements to first allow the SVOD a meaningful window of time before exploiting it with the AVOD company.

References and Sources

The information within this book is based primarily on my years of personal observation and experience working within the film, television, and new media distribution industry—including the bulk of explanatory definitions, factoids and anecdotes.

That said, I have utilized the following resources to further verify, reference or more accurately explain various sections throughout this book:

▶ CHAPTER 1

Biskind, Peter. *Down and Dirty Pictures*. Simon & Schuster: New York, 2004.
Cook, David. *A History of Narrative Film*. 3rd ed. W. W. Norton & Company: New York, 1996.

▶ CHAPTER 2

Epstein, Edward Jay. *The Hollywood Economist 2.0: The Hidden Financial Reality Behind the Movies*. Melville House: New York, 2012.
Evens, Robert. *The Kid Stays in the Picture: A Notorious Life*. Hyperion: New York, 1994.
Hamsher, Jane. *Killer Instinct: How Two Young Producers Took on Hollywood and Made the Most Controversial Film of the Decade*. Broadway Books: New York, 1997.
Hollan, Mike. "6 Differences Between Reboots and Remakes". July, 2016. Website: www.smosh.com
Lewis, Hilary. "'Midnight Rider' Director Randall Miller, Producers Charged with Involuntary Manslaughter, Criminal Trespass". Retrieved July 3, 2014. Website: www.hollywoodreporter.com
Valby, Karen. "Diablo Cody: Juno Makes Ex-Stripper a Hollywood A-Lister". November 5, 2007. Entertainment Weekly. Website: www.ew.com

▶ CHAPTER 4

Litwak, Mark. *Dealmaking in the Film & Television Industry: From Negotiations to Final Contracts*. 2nd ed. Silman-James Press: Los Angeles, 2002.
Parks, Stacey. *The Insider's Guide to Independent Film Distribution*. 2nd ed. Focal Press: New York, 2012.

▶ CHAPTER 6

Anderson, Bill with Cady, Eric. "IFTA International Schedule of Territory Definitions". Update January, 2014. Website: www.ifta-online.org
Canaves, Sky. "Ten Things to Know About Working in Film in China". August 26, 2016. Website: www.chinafilminsider.com

Carême, Florent. "One TV Year in the World". Issue: 2016. Eurodata TV Worldwide.

Diez, Dr. Ethel Pis with Ferrara, Fabricio, Maria Iregui, Lucila Sarquis and Nicolas Smirnoff. "Understanding Latin America: Current Trends in the TV Market". Issue: Spring, 2016. Website: www.frapa.org

La Combe, Claire. "European Distribution: Focus on France". April 6, 2016. Website: www.europa-distribution.org

Tartaglione, Nancy. "Cannes: Netflix CEO Responds to Fest Decree That Competition Films Must Commit to French Theatrical Release". May 10, 2017. Website: www.deadline.com

▶ CHAPTER 7

Blumenthal, Howard J. and Oliver Goodenough. *This Business of Television: The Standard Guide to the Television Industry*. 3rd ed. Billboard Books: New York, 2006.

Brzoznowski, Kristin. "Nielsen TV Ratings Now Include Hulu, YouTube TV". July 25, 2017. Website: www.worldscreen.com

Hype! Dir. Doug Pray. Lions Gate Entertainment, 1996. Film.

Levison, Louise. *Filmmakers and Financing: Business Plans for Independents (American Film Market Presents)*. 7th ed. Focal Press: New York, 2013.

▶ CHAPTER 8

Litwak, Mark. *Risky Business: Financing & Distributing Independent Films*. Silman-James Press: Los Angeles, 2004.

Moore, Schuyler M. *The Biz: The Basic Business, Legal and Financial Aspects of the Film Industry*. 4th ed. Silman-James Press: Los Angeles, 2011.

Ulin, Jeffrey C. *The Business of Media Distribution: Monetizing Film, TV, and Video Content in an Online World (American Film Market Presents)*. 2nd ed. Focal Press: New York, 2013.

▶ CHAPTER 9

Press, Skip. *The Ultimate Writer's Guide to Hollywood*. Barnes & Nobel Books: New York, 2004.

▶ APPENDIX IV

The Clearance Lab. Website: www.theclearancelab.com

LoBrutto, Vincent. *Stanley Kubrick: A Biography*. Donald I. Fine Books: New York, 1997.

About the Author

Scott Kirkpatrick is Executive Vice President of Co-Productions and Distribution for Nicely Entertainment—a Los Angeles-based production and distribution company that produces original TV movies and scripted TV series—where he brokers major content deals and has executive produced a variety of TV movies including *The Art of Christmas*, *The Abby Brooks Mysteries*, *Sappy Holiday* and *The Snowball Effect*. Previously, Kirkpatrick served as Senior Vice President of North American Sales & Business Development for the London-based NENT Studios UK where he oversaw international television distribution deals on a variety of programs including BBC1's *The Cry*, Channel 4's *Shameless* as well as ITV's *Manhunt* and *Doc Martin*. Prior to this, Kirkpatrick served as Executive Director of Distribution for MarVista Entertainment, a Los Angeles–based production and distribution company that produces original TV movies and has managed international TV deals on major franchises, including *Mighty Morphin Power Rangers*. Before shifting to the distribution side of the industry, Kirkpatrick worked behind the scenes on major studio productions, including *Talladega Nights: The Ballad of Ricky Bobby*, and has produced and directed TV series and feature films including *Eye for an Eye* and *Roadside Massacre*. He is the author of the books *Writing for the Green Light: How to Make Your Script the One Hollywood Notices* and *Mastering the Pitch: How to Effectively Pitch Your Ideas to Hollywood*. Kirkpatrick lives in Los Angeles with his wife and two children.

Index

For Product Safety Concerns and Information please contact our EU
representative GPSR@taylorandfrancis.com
Taylor & Francis Verlag GmbH, Kaufingerstraße 24, 80331 München, Germany

www.ingramcontent.com/pod-product-compliance
Ingram Content Group UK Ltd.
Pitfield, Milton Keynes, MK11 3LW, UK
UKHW011457240425
457818UK00022B/884